COMPARATIVE PHILOLOGY AND THE TEXT OF JOB: A STUDY IN METHODOLOGY

SOCIETY OF BIBLICAL LITERATURE
DISSERTATION SERIES

edited by
Howard C. Kee
and
Douglas A. Knight

Number 34

COMPARATIVE PHILOLOGY AND THE TEXT OF JOB: A STUDY IN METHODOLOGY

by
Lester L. Grabbe

SCHOLARS PRESS
Missoula, Montana

COMPARATIVE PHILOLOGY AND THE TEXT OF JOB: A STUDY IN METHODOLOGY

by

Lester L. Grabbe

Published by
SCHOLARS PRESS
for
The Society of Biblical Literature

Distributed by

SCHOLARS PRESS
University of Montana
Missoula, Montana 59812

COMPARATIVE PHILOLOGY AND THE TEXT OF JOB: A STUDY IN METHODOLOGY

by

Lester L. Grabbe
Ambassador College
Pasadena, California 91123

Ph.D., 1975
Claremont Graduate School

Adviser:
William H. Brownlee

Library of Congress Cataloging in Publication Data
Grabbe, Lester L
Comparative philology and the text of Job.

(Dissertation series ; 34)
Originally presented as the author's thesis,
Claremont Graduate School, 1975.
Bibliography: p.
1. Bible. O. T. Job—Criticism, Textual.
2. Philology, Comparative. I. Title. II. Series: Society of Biblical literature. Dissertation series ; 34.
BS1415.2.G66 223'.1'06 77-23489
ISBN 0-89130-139-9

Printed in the United States of America
1 2 3 4 5

Printing Department
University of Montana
Missoula, Montana 59812

TABLE OF CONTENTS

To Elizabeth

PREFACE

The present study was originally completed in July, 1975. In accordance with the guidelines of the SBL Dissertation Series, no changes of substance have been made. I have, however, tried to take brief account of relevant literature which has appeared in the intervening year and a half, as well as of a few items which had escaped my notice when the thesis was first written.

For those readers--perhaps the majority--who do not plan to grapple with the study in all its technical details, I suggest the following approach: Chapter I provides general background and can be skimmed or skipped according to the needs of the reader. Chapter III is a detailed summary of the implications of the study and the most important section to peruse. The reader can then follow the references back to Chapter II for examples as the urge takes him. Chapter IV does not add significant new information to Chapter III but rearranges the material in the form of a positive program for doing comparative philology.

One of the points emphasized in this study is the necessity of scholarly cooperation. That any merit within it is greatly due to the help received from hundreds of scholars via their publications is at least partially indicated by the length of bibliography. In addition to these multitudes of learned persons upon whose knowledge and work I have been able to draw, there are several to whom I would like to express my appreciation individually:

Members of my doctoral study supervisory committee who directed the study and read the original drafts of it were Professor Ronald Macaulay, who gave help in the area of linguistics; Professor William Whedbee, who helped crystallize the subject of the thesis; and my adviser, Professor William Brownlee, who constantly assisted in all aspects of my program.

Professor James Barr kindly gave a number of hours of his time on two separate occasions in the autumn of 1973 to discuss my projected study. He also made available an unpublished article which was of considerable help. (Since Professor Barr was in no way involved in the actual research and writing of the dissertation, it should not necessarily be assumed that he is in agreement with the whole or any part of it.) Professor Walter Michel graciously sent me a copy of his dissertation, which unfortunately came too late to use in more than a superficial way. Professor Ziony Zevit made available an unpublished article and allowed me to cite it.

My friend, Professor Gunar Freibergs, cast an eye over my translations from German. Mr. Scott Rockhold, student in Assyriology at the University of California, helped in proofreading and made a number of valuable suggestions. My wife, Elizabeth, whose knowledge of Latin and French far exceeds mine, gave help with these languages as well as contributing to the proofreading. (In view of the recent form-critical study of the "acknowledgment to the wife"--C. Christ and J. Goldenberg, *CSR Bulletin*, June 1972--I will refrain from any excess expression of gratitude to my wife; nonetheless, this has not prevented me from dedicating this study to her.) Miss Wendy Shew, even though having typed a couple of drafts of the original thesis, cheerfully undertook the task of preparing the camera-ready copy for the SBL series.

It is customary at this point to add a note disclaiming from responsibility for errors those who helped and advised in the work. Naturally, one would like to share the blame for any short-comings. But considering that I did not always take good advice when it was offered, I can only be grateful for their help and assume the reader will be aware that mistakes ultimately fall on my shoulders.

L. L. G.

Pasadena, California
31 December 1976

ABBREVIATIONS

AHW	W. von Soden, *Akkadisches Handwörterbuch*
AJSL	*American Journal of Semitic Languages and Literatures*
Akk	Akkadian
ANET	J. Pritchard, *Ancient Near Eastern Texts Relating to the Old Testament*
AOAT	*Alter Orient und Altes Testament*
Aq	Aquila
Ar	Arabic
Aram	Aramaic
ASTI	*Annual of the Swedish Theological Institute*
BA	*Biblical Archaeologist*
BASOR	*Bulletin of the American Schools of Oriental Research*
BDB	Brown-Driver-Briggs, *A Hebrew and English Lexicon of the Old Testament*
BHeb	Biblical Hebrew
BJRL	*Bulletin of the John Rylands Library*
BL	Bauer-Leander, *Historische Grammatik der hebräischen Sprache*
Blommerde	A. Blommerde, *Northwest Semitic Grammar and Job*
BO	*Bibliotheca Orientalis*
Brockelmann	C. Brockelmann, *Lexicon syriacum*
BT	*Bible Translator*
BZAW	*Beiheft* to ZAW
CAD	*Assyrian Dictionary of the Oriental Institute of Chicago*
CBQ	*Catholic Biblical Quarterly*
CPTOT	J. Barr, *Comparative Philology and the Text of the Old Testament*
CTA	A. Herdner, *Corpus des tablettes en cunéiformes alphabetiques*
CW	J. Levy, *Chaldäisches Wörterbuch über die Targumim . . .*
DAFA	R. Blachère, *Dictionnaire arabe-français-anglais*
Delitzsch	Franz Delitzsch, *Job*
Dhorme	E. Dhorme, *A Commentary on the Book of Job*
Dillmann	A. Dillmann, *Hiob*
DISO	Jean-Hoftijzer, *Dictionnaire des inscriptions sémitiques l'Ouest*
DJD	*Discoveries in the Judaean Desert*
Driver	S. Driver (and G. Gray), *The Book of Job*
DSS	Dead Sea Scrolls
Ehrilich	A. Ehrlich, *Randglossen zur hebräischen Bibel*
ESA	Epigraphic South Arabian
ET	*Expository Times*
Eth	Ethiopic
Fohrer	G. Fohrer, *Das Buch Hiob*
GAG	W. von Soden, *Grundriss der akkadischen Grammatik*

GB	Gesenius-Buhl, *Hebräisches und aramäisches Handwörterbuch*
Gibson	J. Gibson, *Textbook of Syrian Semitic Inscriptions*
GKC	Gesenius-Kautsch-Cowley, *Hebrew Grammar*
Gray	see Driver
HAL	Koehler-Baumgartner, *Hebräisches und aramäisches Wörterbuch* (3rd edition)
HDB	J. Hastings, *Dictionary of the Bible*
Horst	F. Horst, *Hiob*
HTR	*Harvard Theological Review*
HUCA	*Hebrew Union College Annual*
IDB	*Interpreter's Dictionary of the Bible*
IEJ	*Israel Exploration Journal*
IOS	*Israel Oriental Studies*
JANESCU	*Journal of the Ancient Near Eastern Society of Columbia University*
JAOS	*Journal of the American Oriental Society*
JAram	Jewish Aramaic
Jastrow	M. Jastrow, *Dictionary of the Targumim . . .*
JBR	*Journal of the Bible and Religion*
JJS	*Journal of Jewish Studies*
JNES	*Journal of Near Eastern Studies*
JNSL	*Journal of Northwest Semitic Languages*
JQR	*Jewish Quarterly Review*
JSJ	*Journal for the Study of Judaism*
JSS	*Journal of Semitic Studies*
JTS	*Journal of Theological Studies*
KAI	Donner-Röllig, *Kanaanäische und aramäische Inschriften*
Kazimirsky	A. Kazimirsky, *Dictionnaire arabe-français*
KB	Koehler-Baumgartner, *Lexicon in Veteris Testamenti libros* (2nd edition)
Lane	E. W. Lane, *An Arabic-English Lexicon*
Leslau	
Contributions	W. Leslau, *Ethiopic and South Arabic Contributions to the Hebrew Lexicon*
Amharic	W. Leslau, *Hebrew Cognates in Amharic*
LXX	*Septuagint*
Margoliouth	J. Margoliouth, *Compendious Syriac Dictionary*
MD	Drower-Macuch, *Mandaic Dictionary*
MGWJ	*Monatsschrift für Geschichte und Wissenschaft des Judenthums*
MHeb	Mishnaic Hebrew
MT	Masoretic text, Masoretic tradition
MS(S)	Manuscript(s)
Muss-Arnold	W. Muss-Arnold, *Assyrisch-englisch-deutsches Handwörterbuch*
MV	Minor Versions
NAB	New American Bible
NEB	New English Bible
NT	New Testament
NTS	*New Testament Studies*
NW	J. Levy, *Neuhebräisches und chaldäisches Wörterbuch . . .*
Or	*Orientalia*

OT	Old Testament
OTS	*Oudtestamentische Studiën*
PAAJR	*Proceedings of the American Academy for Jewish Research*
PEQ	*Palestine Exploration Quarterly*
Phoen	Phoenician
Pope	M. Pope, *Job*
PS	Proto-Semitic
Rahlfs	A. Rahlfs, *Septuaginta* (manual edition of the LXX)
Rowley	H. Rowley, *Job*
RQ	*Revue de Qumran*
RSP	L. Fisher, *Ras Shamra Parallels*
RSV	Revised Standard Version
Schleusner	J. Schleusner, *Novus thesaurus . . . in LXX*
Syr	Syriac translation (Peshitta)
Syr-Hex	Syro-Hexapla
Sym	Symmachus
Tg	Rabbinic targum to Job
Th	Theodotion
Tur-Sinai	N. Tur-Sinai, *Book of Job*
UF	*Ugarit-Forschungen*
Ug	Ugaritic
UT	C. Gordon, *Ugaritic Textbook*
Vogt	E. Vogt, *Lexicon linguae aramaicae Veteris Testamenti*
VT	*Vetus Testamentum*
VTS	*Supplement* to VT
Wehr	H. Wehr, *Dictionary of Modern Written Arabic*
Whitaker	R. Whitaker, *Concordance of the Ugaritic Literature*
WKAS	J. Kraemer, *Wörterbuch der klassischen arabischen Sprache*
WO	*Welt des Orients*
WUS	J. Aistleitner, *Wörterbuch der ugartischen Sprache*
ZAW	*Zeitschrift für die alttestamentliche Wissenschaft*
ZDMG	*Zeitschrift der deutschen morgenländischen Gesellschaft*
Zorell	F. Zorell, *Lexicon hebraicum et aramaicum Veteris Testamenti*

CHAPTER I

INTRODUCTION

CHAPTER I

INTRODUCTION

In the year 1968 James Barr's epoch-making book, *Comparative Philology and the Text of the Old Testament*, appeared. The adjective "epoch-making" seems appropriate since hardly an Old Testament textual critic or philologist has been able to avoid dealing with the implications of the book in some form or another. Reactions have varied widely, but even the negative responses attest to the fact that Barr's treatise cannot be ignored.

The most persistent criticism of CPTOT has been that it is "excessively negative." An often-negative and critical approach was understandably necessary for the author to make his point and give it the impact needed to put it across. Because of this, the positive side is more implied than explicit at times. On the other hand, Barr has shown his position on the legitimate use of comparative philology in other writings (such as the article, "Seeing the Wood for the Trees?"). Yet even as Barr himself observed in the last few sentences of his book, his was "the first to be wholly devoted to this purpose," namely, "the exploration of the method in itself." The task of exploring the method is thus far from exhausted.

As the title indicates, the purpose of the present thesis is to take Barr's suggestions, both explicit and implicit, and apply them to a selected corpus of literature in an attempt to test them as systematically as possible. The selected section of literature is the book of Job, chosen because of the many philological riddles which still taunt each new exegete who thinks he can mark trails where others have failed. This study is not devoted to adding new suggestions to those already proposed. Its central concern is the methodology of comparative philology and how it can be used objectively and scientifically without the arbitrary and questionable results so often arrived at in the past.

Naturally, in any research of this nature one must take account of the prolific publications and observations of Professor Mitchell Dahood. Since a large proportion of his writings and those of his students has been devoted to the wisdom sections of the Old Testament, many parts of the book of Job have been treated by the "Dahood school." Thus, a large number of the passages dealt with in Chapter II will take into account Dahood's suggestions in the discussion. Professor S. P. Brock in a recent review stated, "One might suggest that the next subject for such a study might well be the work of Professor Dahood and his pupils" (JSS 17 [1972], 260). I have made no special attempt to fulfill Brock's suggestion. On the other hand, it is the inevitable state of affairs that any monograph devoted to comparative philology and Job must to some extent undertake that task.

Another major figure who must not be overlooked is Professor Marvin Pope. His important commentary makes full use of the work of older commentators but adds the dimension of Northwest Semitic philology. He often interacts with the suggestions of Dahood. Probably more space is devoted to the proposals of Pope and Dahood than those of anyone else.

As Dahood correctly pointed out in his review of CPTOT, "comparative philology" is a much broader field than just that of lexicography. Therefore it is important to note that my major concern is with the lexicon of the Old Testament rather than with the grammar. No treatment can deal with one in complete isolation from the other, but my concentration will definitely be on lexicography.

The number of passages selected had to be severely limited to keep the length of the study within reason. My primary criteria were that the passages contain a recognized difficulty and/or be one for which a comparative philological consideration has already been proposed. After these it was a matter of selecting passages which seem suited for the purpose of investigating the method of comparative philology. Let me emphasize that I am in no way attempting to write a commentary on all or any part of Job. If anyone is reading these pages solely for the purpose of finding some tantalizing new solution to a particular troublesome passage, he is very likely to be disappointed.

The rest of this chapter will be devoted to introductory comments relating to the different areas needing consideration, along with pertinent bibliographical material, especially as it relates to the different texts, lexica, and editions used for the study comprising Chapter II. Some material already listed in the table of abbreviations is here repeated in the bibliographies for the sake of completeness. All bibliographical references with full information on publisher, date, etc., are also included in the alphabetical bibliography at the end of the thesis.

General Considerations

Hebrew Text. The various editions of "the" Masoretic text are all so similar that for most purposes a choice of any particular one makes no difference. However, as the final court of appeal the *Biblia Hebraica* (edited by Paul Kahle from the Leningrad codex B 19^{A}) has been used. The new *Biblia Hebraica Stuttgartensia* does not yet cover the entire OT, though the text seems to differ only minutely from the one in the older edition.

Method of Citation. Throughout the rest of this chapter, the various editions of the versions and the lexica for the different languages are discussed. In Chapter II wherever I have used the standard reference works already described in this introductory chapter, I do not generally cite them. For example, for classical Arabic I have used WKAS where it exists (*K* and part of *L*), DAFA where it is available (*ʼ* through *Ḥ*), and Lane for the rest of the alphabet. Wherever Ar is mentioned with no reference to a source, one of these three is used, depending on where the word occurs in the alphabet. Any other sources for Ar will be cited each time. Thus, there should never be any doubt about the source of any definition given. Since each unit in Chapter II is self-contained, the major sources not already listed in the table of abbreviations are given at the beginning of each § and referred to only by author in the discussion. Any other incidental sources are cited both by author and short title in the discussion. Further information for these can be found in the general bibliography. Standard footnotes are used in Chapters III and IV and the Appendix.

<u>Translations</u>. With some exceptions I have tried to give translations of all non-English material. They are simply for the convenience of the reader and are not intended to represent polished or definitive renderings. Unless some notation to the contrary is given, they are my own.

<u>Proto-Semitic</u>. In the following study a proto-Semitic (PS) form will occasionally be mentioned (preceded by an asterisk as is customary with hypothetical forms). This is done only for the convenience of the discussion and is not to be taken as evidence of adherence to some particular theory of one proto-language from which the various Semitic languages derive. The concept of a proto-language is useful for explaining many relationships between the various dialects, but there are also many complicating factors which may call into question its actual historical existence. (Cf. J. Blau, BZAW 103 [1968], 29-43.)

<u>Versions</u>

The purpose of including the versions in this study is to investigate their usefulness for comparative philology only. I do not intend to rehash questions of their use in normal textual criticism for correcting textual corruption, a purpose accepted as legitimate but irrelevant for the present investigation. The question is always this: assuming the text is essentially correct, how can the versions be of help in doing comparative philological work? Several major problems are involved in using the different versions:

1. The translator of the version may not have understood the particular passage in question any better than we do.

2. The version may be based on a Hebrew *Vorlage* different from our present MT.

3. The two foregoing questions may be made even more difficult by free renderings and even completely paraphrastic translation.

4. The version may present as many problems of understanding as the preserved MT.

5. The translation technique of the version may involve a one-to-one rendering of key words in the Hebrew text. That is, the same Hebrew word may generally be rendered by the same

word in the target language even when the result is a greater or lesser distortion of meaning. Aquila is a good example of this.

These and other points all contribute to a number of obstacles in using versional evidence in understanding the MT. A further problem has been too great a dependence on the unreliable *Biblia Hebraica* apparatus. As Orlinsky and others have demonstrated time and again, the versional evidence presented there cannot be trusted. A further requirement is the need to evaluate the translation technique used in a particular translation for a particular book. Perhaps no other version has been more abused than the LXX, especially considering the bedeviling problems of the origins and transmission of the LXX text.

6. The lack of proper critical editions and careful study of the versions in their own right is often a major problem. New discoveries sometimes only seem to complicate the questions rather than solve them.

Further general and bibliographical information on the versions can be found in several sources which have not been noted in the following lists: Dhorme's *Commentary on the Book of Job*; Eissfeldt's *The Old Testament: An Introduction* (1965); Roberts' *Old Testament Texts and Versions* (1951); despite its age, the treatment of the versions in HDB is quite helpful and often more thorough than the more recent IDB. However, the new supplement volume of the IDB (1976) has good articles on the LXX and some of the other versions.

Greek Versions

Abrahams, M. *Aquila's Greek Version of the Hebrew Bible* (1919).

Barthélemy, D. *Les devanciers d'Aquila* (VTS 10; 1963).

Bickermann, "The Septuagint as a Translation," PAAJR 28 (1959), 1-39.

Brock, S. "The Phenomenon of the Septuagint," OTS 17 (1972), 11-36.

______, et al. *A Classified Bibliography of the Septuagint* (1973).

Field, F. *Origenis Hexaplorum quae supersunt* (vols. 1-2, reprinted 1964).

Gard, D. *The Exegetical Method of the Greek Translator of the Book of Job* (1952).

Gerleman, G. *Studies in the LXX I. The Book of Job* (1946).

Goshen-Gottstein, M. "Theory and Practice of Textual Criticism," *Textus* 3 (1963), 130-58.

Hatch, E., and H. Redpath. *A Concordance to the Septuagint...* (vols. 1-3; 1897-1906).

Jellicoe, S. *The Septuagint and Modern Study* (1968).

Katz, P. "The Recovery of the Original Septuagint, A Study in the History of Transmission and Textual Criticism," *Actes du premier congrès de la Fédération Internationale des Etudes Classiques* (1951), 165-82.

______. "Septuagintal Studies in the Mid-Century," *The Background of the New Testament and its Eschatology* (1956), 176-208.

Liebreich, Leon J. "Notes on the Greek Version of Symmachus," JBL 63 (1944), 397-403.

Orlinsky, H. "Current Progress and Problems in Septuagint Research," *The Study of the Bible Today and Tomorrow* (1947), 144-61.

______. "On the Present State of Proto-Septuagint Studies," JAOS 61 (1941), 81-91.

______. "The Septuagint--Its Use in Textual Criticism," BA 9 (1946), 21-42.

______. "Studies in the Septuagint Text of Job," HUCA 28-30, 32-3, 35-6 (1957-9, 1961-2, 1964-5).

Rabin, C. "The Translation Process and the Character of the Septuagint," *Textus* 6 (1968), 1-26.

Reider, J. *Prolegomena to a Greek-Hebrew and Hebrew-Greek Index to Aquila* (1916).

______. *An Index to Aquila* (completed and revised by N. Turner, VTS 12; 1966).

Schleusner, J. *Novus thesaurus philologico-criticus: sive lexicon in LXX* (vols. 1-2; 1829).

Tov, E. "Some Corrections to Reider-Turner's *Index to Aquila*," *Textus* 8 (1963), 164-74.

We have already discussed briefly some of the problems with using the LXX. Further discussion is found in the literature just cited (especially Orlinsky, Brock, Rabin, Goshen-

Gottstein), but the major obstacle in trying to use the LXX for the book of Job is its brevity in comparison with the MT. The LXX text of Job is approximately one-sixth shorter. The debate over whether the LXX depends on a shorter Hebrew *Vorlage* or whether the translator simply shortened a Hebrew original about the same as our MT still continues. We have the detailed studies on Job by Gard, Gerlemann, and Orlinsky (the last gives a thorough critique of the first two). The bibliography edited by Brock and others gives all the help one could ask for in this area. Despite its age Schleusner is still a valuable tool, as is the Hatch-Redpath concordance.

The Greek Minor Versions would appear to have much in their favor as far as versions go. Aquila evidently knew both Hebrew and Greek quite well. He worked in the same circles that carried on the mechanical preservation of the Hebrew text. He apparently carried on and perfected a type of recensional activity already begun before his time on the Greek text, if Barthélemy's analysis is correct. The major difficulty with using Aquila is his regular translation technique of using word-for-word correspondences between the two languages. This means the Greek rendering may have sacrificed semantic subtlety for literalness in representing the underlying Hebrew text.

Theodotion was identical with the *kaige* recension according to Barthélemy (with whom Jellicoe, p. 93, agrees). If so, Theodotion carries considerable weight, especially since his is a somewhat freer and more readable rendering than that of Aquila. Symmachus was a master of Greek and makes his translation idiomatic and flowing. Yet he also seems to have a reasonable grasp of his underlying text. He would also have come from a Semitic speaking background and environment if tradition is correct about his being an Ebionite. Unfortunately, Aquila and Symmachus are both preserved only in fragments. Origen used mainly Theodotion to fill out the minuses in the LXX text of Job, but even this version is still rather fragmentary.

The most readily available edition of the Minor Versions for the book of Job at the present is Field. For the retroversions from the Syro-Hexapla, however, Field had to depend on Middeldorp's hasty and error-filled copy. All of my citations from the MV are from Field. For the LXX I have used Rahlfs' edition. It is unfortunate that the Göttingen edition of the book of Job, which will presumably include a new assembly of MV material, was not yet available at the time of writing.

Targums and Peshitta

Ancient Syriac Old Testament (Urmia edition, 1913).

Bacher, W. "Targums," *The Jewish Encyclopaedia* (1906).

______. "Das Targum zu Hiob," MGWJ 20 (1871), 208-23, 283-4.

Baumann, E. "Die Verwendbarkeit der Pešita zum Buche Ijob für die Textkritik," ZAW 18 (1898), 305-38; 19 (1899), 15-95, 288-309; 20 (1900), 177-201, 264-307.

Déaut, R. le. *Introduction à la littérature targumique* (1966).

______. "Les études targumiques," *De Mari à Qumran* (1969), 302-31.

______. "The Current State of Targumic Studies," *Biblical Theology Bulletin* 4 (1974), 3-32.

Fitzmyer, J. "Some Observations on the Targum of Job from Qumran Cave 11," CBQ 36 (1974), 503-24.

Gray, J. "Massoretic Text of the Book of Job, the Targum and the Septuagint Version in the Light of the Qumran Targum," ZAW 86 (1974), 331-50.

Grossfeld, B. *Bibliography of Targumic Literature* (1972).

Haefeli, L. *Die Peschitta des Alten Testamentes* (1927).

Kaufmann, S. "The Job Targum from Qumran," JAOS 93 (1973), 317-27.

Lagarde, Paul de. *Hagiographa chaldaice* (1873).

Ploeg, J. P. M. van der, and A. S. van der Woude. *Le targum de Job de la grotte XI de Qumran* (1971).

Rignell, L. "Notes on the Peshitta of the Book of Job," ASTI 9 (1973), 98-106.

Sokoloff, M. *The Targum to Job from Qumran Cave XI* (1974).

Sperber, A. *The Bible in Aramaic* (vols. 1-4; 1959-73).

Walton, B. (ed.). *Biblia Sacra polyglotta* (1663).

York, A. "The Dating of Targumic Literature," JSJ 5 (1974-5), 49-62.

The standard rabbinic targum for Job presumably reached its final form quite late. Le Déaut has concluded that the targums of the Hagiograph "carry very ancient traditions, of

Palestinian origin" (*Introduction*, 132). (However, York has shown that no objective criteria have yet been devised for determining what is early and what is late.) The targum includes haggadic material, approaching midrash at times. It sometimes gives readings from two or even three different targums (for a total of about 50 verses). Qumran has produced a targum MS of Job ante-dating the destruction of Jerusalem in 70 A.D. Only about 15 percent of the book of Job survives, but what remains is certainly quite valuable. There seems to be no direct relationship between the 11QtgJob and the rabbinic Job targum.

An estimation of the value of the targums has been put quite succinctly in CPTOT: "If there were rare words in biblical Hebrew, the knowledge of which was already dying out in ancient times, is it not much more likely that this knowledge survived among Aramaic-speaking Jews than among Greek-speaking? Yet I have found philological treatments to appeal relatively seldom to the Targums, in comparison with the number of appeals to the LXX" (271-2). This argument will itself be evaluated in the following study.

The Peshitta is generally a fairly literal rendering of the MT. At times it is paraphrastic to the extent of shortening or lengthening a verse or verses by a considerable amount. This could be the result of not fully understanding the original, though it is possible it had a slightly different Hebrew text at times. The translation seems occasionally to have been influenced by the LXX and MV. Rignell, who is responsible for the Job text of the Peshitta project of Leiden, concludes as follows (105):

> Summarizing it may be said that P[eshitta] of the Book of Job in some degree can give guidance to the interpretation of cruces interpretationes in the Book, albeit mostly on account of the fact that the Syriac language is so close to Hebrew. . . . However, it is certainly justified to warn against using the current Syriac text in the Book of Job with a view to elucidating a dim passage in the Hebrew text without first making a closer examination. The Syrian translators have, no doubt, worked too independently of the Hebrew text to be entirely relied upon.

Rignell does not give an expected date of publication for the new critical edition on Job. In any event it was not available for this study. The text of the Walton Polyglot was used instead and compared with that of the Urmia edition. Generally, the two have the same readings though a few differences were found in the passages dealt with here. (Ceriani's facsimile edition of Codex Ambrosianus was not available except indirectly as it is quoted in Dhorme's commentary.) The Lagarde edition of the rabbinic targum and the edition of the Qumran targum by van der Ploeg and van der Woude were utilized. Sokoloff's edition of 11QtgJob was compared with the *editio princeps*. The recent Hebrew University thesis by Raphael Weiss on the rabbinic targum was unavailable to me at the time of writing (see a description and review of the thesis in JBL 95 [1976], 158-60).

Vulgate

Barr, James. "St. Jerome's Appreciation of Hebrew," BJRL 49 (1966-7), 281-302.

Biblia Sacra iuxta Latinam Vulgatam Versionem (1925-).

Fischer, B., et al. *Biblia Sacra* (vols. 1-2; 1969).

Plater, W., and H. White. *A Grammar of the Vulgate* (1926).

Semple, W. H. "St. Jerome as a Biblical Translator," BJRL 48 (1965-6), 227-43.

Stummer, Fr. *Einführung in die lateinische Bibel* (1928).

______. "Beiträge zur Exegese der Vulgata," ZAW 62 (1949-50), 152-67.

______. "Einige Beobachtungen über die Arbeitsweise des Hieronymus bei der Übersetzung des Alten Testaments aus der Hebraica Veritas," *Biblica* 10 (1929), 3-30.

______. "Hauptprobleme der Erforschung der alttestamentlichen Vulgate," BZAW 66 (1936), 233-9.

Sutcliffe, Edmund F. "Notes on St. Jerome's Hebrew Text," CBQ 11 (1949), 139-43.

It is difficult to ascertain the extent of Jerome's knowledge of Hebrew. Considering the difficulties he worked under, he did a commendable job. We also know that he employed Jewish instructors and even hired one "Hebraeus" specifically for help on the book of Job (apparently without learning much--see his prologue to the book). He tells us he made considerable use of the MV, especially Symmachus, and may thus occasionally be a witness to a MV reading which is no longer extant in identifiable form. He was also influenced by the LXX at times. He is of course a much later witness to the text than a number of other sources but represents a link in the history of the understanding of the text in the area of Palestine.

All quotes from Job come from the excellent critical edition in the multi-volume *Biblia Sacra*. The manual edition edited by Fischer generally has the same text as the larger edition; although its critical apparatus has been reduced, it includes all the major variants. The manual edition has been used for any references outside of Job.

<u>Medieval and Modern Commentators</u>

Blommerde, A. *Northwest Semitic Grammar and Job* (1969).

Delitzsch, F. *Job* (reprinted 1973).

Dhorme, E. *A Commentary on the Book of Job* (Eng. tr., 1967).

Dillmann, A. *Hiob* (3rd edition, 1869).

Driver, S. R., and G. Gray. *The Book of Job* (1921).

Ecker, R. *Die arabische Job-Übersetzung des Gaon Saadja ben Josef al-Fajjûmî* (1962).

Ehrlich, A. *Randglossen zur hebräischen Bibel* (1908-14).

Fohrer, G. *Das Buch Hiob* (1963).

Horst, F. *Hiob* (1968).

Kimchi, David. *Radicum liber sive hebraeum Bibliorum lexicon* (ed. J. Biesenthal and F. Lebrecht, 1847).

Krauss, S. "Saadya's Tafsir of the Seventy *Hapax Legomena* Explained and Continued," *Saadya Studies* (1943), 47-77.

Michel, W. *The Ugaritic Texts and the Mythological Expressions in the Book of Job (including a New Translation . . .)*, (1970).

Miqra'ot Gedolot (rabbinic Bible with targums and commentaries, reprinted many times).

Pope, M. *Job* (3rd edition, 1973).

Rosenthal, E. "Saadya's Exegesis of the Book of Job," *Saadya Studies* (1943), 177-205.

Rowley, H. H. *Job* (1970).

Tur-Sinai, N. *The Book of Job* (1957).

Version arabe du Livre de Job (1899).

I have not made thorough or consistent use of the works of the medieval commentators, lexicographers, and grammarians. This is an area which deserves dedicated research and may pay worthwhile dividends. But it is a specialization in its own right and certainly an area of study outside the limits of this thesis. Wherever I do cite medieval writers, it is from the editions above: Rashi and Ibn Ezra--*Miqra'ot Gedolot* (the accuracy of whose text is anyone's guess); Kimchi-- his *Book of Roots*; Saadia--Derenbourg's *Version Arabe* and Ecker's study.

I have tried consistently to check a number of modern commentaries even though their information was passed over without comment if it seemed irrelevant for my purpose. Pope's value has already been mentioned earlier. Dhorme has produced a classic commentary with a good number of comparative suggestions. He also provides some of the best help on evaluating the versions. Dillmann sometimes gives a comparison with Eth or a unique explanation of the MT. Ehrlich gave information of interest in only a few instances, but he is the source of a few classic comparative suggestions taken up by almost all later commentators. Delitzsch is useful for two reasons: he almost always attempts to understand the MT rather than impatiently emending, and he provides a great many comparisons with Ar. Driver/Gray generally operate according to the normal canons of textual criticism, yet in his unfinished notes Driver often mentions and discusses comparative suggestions even if he does not accept them. Tur-Sinai occasionally brings up comparative suggestions worth investigating. Rowley's commentary was unfortunately left unfinished at his death. Even in this unpolished state it usefully summarizes much that is of value from his predecessors even when it offers nothing strikingly new. Blommerde concentrates on grammar rather than lexicography. However, in lieu of a full commentary on Job from Dahood, Blommerde often summarizes proposals which are otherwise scattered throughout the periodical literature. For the form criticism of Job, Fohrer and Horst (only chs. 1-19) have been consulted. Unfortunately, I obtained a copy of Michel's dissertation too late to make any but the most superficial use of it.

Semitic Languages Used for Comparison

Every Semitic language is a possible source of comparative information. Naturally, the closer the language to Hebrew, the more likely it will contain a similar root or expression; but exceptions to this have been offered. For example, Ullendorff has given a number of examples in which he feels a language so distant as Ethiopic appears to preserve words and expressions found nowhere else outside OT Hebrew. This illustrates the need to make use of all possible sources.

Barr emphasized the requirement of regarding the normative phonetic correspondences (CPTOT, 81ff). He outlined the problems involved and how complicated the question can be. No one can deny that disregard for this elementary principle has resulted in many an unacceptable elucidation based on comparative philology. However, further study needs to be done in delineating the criteria necessary for a suggestion to receive credence; viz., must all deviations from the regular sound correlations be dismissed, or are there occasions when they may be acceptable? The current consensus of historical linguists is important here.

General Works

Encyclopaedia Judaica, The (1971).

Fronzaroli, Pelio (ed.). *Studies on Semitic Lexicography* (1973).

Hospers, J. H. (ed.). *A Basic Bibliography for the Study of the Semitic Languages* (vols. 1-2; 1973-4).

Moscati, S. (ed.). *An Introduction to the Comparative Grammar of the Semitic Languages* (1964).

Sebeok, T. (ed.). *Current Trends in Linguistics* (vol. 6; 1970).

Spuler, B. (ed.). *Semitistik* (Handbuch der Orientalistik, Abteilung 1, Band 3; 1964).

Vida, G. della (ed.). *Linguistica Semitica: Presente e Futuro* (1961).

These works give a good deal of useful general information and bibliographical material on the Semitic languages as a whole. The bibliography by Hospers is especially useful. Its major lack is an author index. It also has no annotations and such information must be supplied from some of the other works listed. HAL (see next section) has a useful discussion in its preface. Its section on abbreviations gives a list of important Semitic materials. Since the works given here have sections on individual languages, these need to be consulted in addition to the material listed below (the works cited here are not repeated in the following lists). The new *Encyclopaedia Judaica* has several useful articles on the individual Semitic languages (e.g., Kutscher's classic treatment of Aramaic and Mishnaic Hebrew).

Biblical Hebrew

Bauer, H., and P. Leander. *Historische Grammatik der hebräischen Sprache* (1922).

Baumgartner, W., et al. *Hebräisches und aramäisches Lexikon zum Alten Testament* (1967-).

Bergsträsser, G. *Hebräische Grammatik* (1918).

Blau, J. *A Grammar of Biblical Hebrew* (1976).

Brown, F., et al. *A Hebrew and English Lexicon of the Old Testament* (corrected reprint 1953).

Buhl, F. *Wilhelm Gesenius' hebräisches und aramäisches Handwörterbuch über das Alte Testament* (1915).

Cowley, A. *Gesenius' Hebrew Grammar* (1910).

Koehler, L., and W. Baumgartner. *Lexicon in Veteris Testamenti libros* (vols. 1-3; 1953-8).

Lisowsky, G., and L. Rost. *Konkordanz zum hebräischen Alten Testament* (2nd edition, 1958).

Mandelkern, S. *Veteris Testamenti concordantiae hebraicae atque chaldaicae* (corrected edition, 1959).

Noth, Martin. *Die israelitischen Personennamen im Rahmen der gemeinsemitischen Namengebung* (1928).

Zorell, F., et al. *Lexicon hebraicum et aramaicum Veteris Testamenti* (reprinted 1968).

The most recent lexicon is HAL, of which the first two fascicles (*'* through *M*) were available for this study. Important supplements were BDB, GB, and Zorell. The two concordances are sufficient to meet most needs. Unfortunately, the most recent grammar, that of Blau, appeared too late to use (it is also not intended to be exhaustive); Bergsträsser, GKC, and

BL had to suffice. Noth's study on proper names in the OT is still the classic one.

Post-Biblical and Epigraphic Hebrew

Discoveries in the Judaean Desert, The (vol. I- ; 1955-).

Donner, H., and W. Röllig. *Kanaanäische und aramäische Inschriften* (2nd edition; vols. 1-3; 1969).

Fitzmyer, J. *The Dead Sea Scrolls, Major Publications and Tools for Study* (1975).

Gibson, J. *Hebrew and Moabite Inscriptions* (Textbook of Syrian Semitic Inscriptions, 1; corrected reprint, 1973).

Gordis, R. "On Methodology in Biblical Exegesis," JQR 61 (1970-1), 93-118.

______. "Studies in the Relationship of Biblical and Rabbinic Hebrew," *Louis Ginzberg Jubilee Volume* (1945), 173-99.

Jastrow, M. *A Dictionary of the Targumim, the Talmud Babli and Yerushalmi, and the Midrashic Literature* (vols. 1-2; 1903).

Jongeling, B. *Classified Bibliography of the Finds in the Desert of Judah 1958-1969* (1971).

Kuhn, K. *Konkordanz zu den Qumrantexten* (1960).

______. "Nachträge zur 'Konkordanz zu den Qumrantexten,'" RQ 4 (1963-4), 163-234.

LaSor, W. *Bibliography of the Dead Sea Scrolls 1948-1957* (1958).

Lévi, I. *The Hebrew Text of the Book of Ecclesiasticus* (reprinted 1969).

Levy, J. *Neuhebräisches und chaldäisches Wörterbuch über die Talmudim und Midraschim* (vols. 1-4; 1924).

Lohse, E. *Die Texte aus Qumran* (2nd edition, 1971).

Murtonen, A. *An Etymological Vocabulary to the Samaritan Pentateuch* (1960).

Townsend, J. T. "Rabbinic Sources," *The Study of Judaism* (1972), 35-80.

One might expect to find the most likely source of help within the Hebrew language itself, if not synchronically then diachronically. Perhaps one reason post-biblical Hebrew has been drawn upon less than other cognate languages is the lack of study of it by many Christian scholars. Rabbinic Hebrew has traditionally been the domain of rabbinic students, and these students have made up a minority of those having a wide impact in the area under discussion. There has also been the (now-disproved) assumption that Hebrew was forgotten as a spoken language during the intertestamental period while Mishnaic Hebrew was only an artificial school dialect. (For a further discussion, see CPTOT, 223-37; J. A. Fitzmyer, CBQ 32 [1970], 528-31).

The non-biblical Qumran material also offers a reservoir of post-biblical Hebrew, though already widely exploited. Further material (in MHeb) comes from the Bar-Kokhba period. (Some of this is yet to be published by Yigael Yadin.) Epigraphic Hebrew material is rather skimpy, but we are fortunate to have good editions and a proper lexicon. For Heb among the Samaritans, Murtonen is useful.

The lexica used for MHeb are those of Levy (NW) and Jastrow. Most of the necessary information is contained there. However, wherever I have consulted the Babylonian Talmud directly, the "Vilna-Romm" edition has been used. (See Townsend for a thorough listing and annotation of the editions and other source materials available for rabbinic material in both Heb and Aram.) For Qumran material a convenient edition for much of the non-biblical material is found in Lohse. Where necessary the original publications have been consulted (listed in LaSor and Jongeling; see also Fitzmyer). Kuhn has covered a good deal of the non-biblical material in his *Konkordanz* and the "Nachträge." But since only DJD I was available for the "Nachträge," the indices of the later volumes still have to be consulted. Lévi's edition has been used for the Heb of Ben Sira. The excellent lexicon DISO has been used for epigraphic Hebrew while KAI has the texts collected in one convenient reference work. In addition to KAI, other sources such as Gibson have been consulted for the inscriptional material.

<u>Phoenician and Punic</u>

Benz, F. *Personal Names in the Phoenician and Punic Inscriptions* (1972).

Donner, H., and W. Röllig. *Kanaanäische und aramäische Inschriften* (2nd edition, vols. 1-3; 1969).

Friedrich, J. *Phönizisch-punische Grammatik* (2nd edition, ed. W. Röllig, 1970).

Harris, Z. *A Grammar of the Phoenician Language* (1936).

Jean, C-F., and J. Hoftijzer. *Dictionnaire des inscriptions sémitiques de l'Ouest* (1965).

Lane, W. *A Handbook of Phoenician Inscriptions* (1962).

Segert, S. *A Grammar of Phoenician and Punic* (1976).

As a Canaanite dialect with very close affinity to Heb, Phoen has good potential for comparison with it. Furthermore, there seems to be no quarrel with classifying Heb and Phoen together as Canaanite dialects (classifying Ug as Canaanite is disputed). The major problem is the limited corpus of literature in Phoen. The later Punic material is also often heavily influenced by the indigenous North African Berber languages. But we now have the convenience of the Phoen and Punic vocabulary collected into one lexicon. Where not otherwise indicated I have used DISO. Any inscriptions quoted are taken from KAI. Since DISO does not cover proper names, Benz is a very useful supplement, especially considering the small amount of textual material in Phoen/Punic.

Aramaic

Aufrecht, W., and J. Hurd. *A Synoptic Concordance of Aramaic Inscriptions* (1975).

Ben-Ḥayyim, Z. *The Literary and Oral Tradition of Hebrew and Aramaic amongst the Samaritans* (Hebrew; vol. 1- ; 1957-).

Benoit, P., et al. *Les grottes de Murabba^cât* (DJD II; 1961).

Brockelmann, C. *Lexicon syriacum* (2nd edition, 1928).

Cowley, A. *The Samaritan Liturgy* (vols. 1-2; 1909).

Dalman, G. *Grammatik des jüdisch-palästinischen Aramäisch* and *Aramäische Dialektproben* (reprinted 1960).

Degen, R. *Altaramäische Grammatik* (1969).

Dion, P.-E. *La langue de Ya'udi* (1974).

Driver, G. "Hebrew Poetic Diction," VTS 1 (1953), 26-39.

Drower, E., and R. Macuch. *A Mandaic Dictionary* (1963).

Fitzmyer, J. *The Aramaic Inscriptions of Sefîre* (1967).

______. *The Genesis Apocryphon of Qumran Cave 1* (2nd edition, 1971).

Gibson, J. *Aramaic Inscriptions* (Textbook of Syrian Semitic Inscriptions, vol. 2; 1975).

Jongeling, B. "Contributions of the Qumran Job Targum to the Aramaic Vocabulary," JSS 17 (1972), 191-7.

Kutscher, E. Y. "Mittelhebräisch und Jüdisch-Aramäisch im neuen Köhler-Baumgartner," VTS 16 (1967), 158-75.

Levy, J. *Chaldäisches Wörterbuch über die Targumim . . .* (vols. 1-2; reprinted 1966).

______. *Neuhebräisches und chaldäisches Wörterbuch über die Targumim und Midraschim* (vols. 1-4; 1924).

Maclean, A. *Dictionary of the Dialects of Vernacular Syriac* (1901).

Macuch, R. *Handbook of Classical and Modern Mandaic* (1965).

______, and E. Panoussi. *Neusyrische Chrestomathie* (1974).

Margoliouth, J. *Supplement to the Thesaurus Syriacus of R. Payne Smith*, (1927).

______. *A Compendious Syriac Dictionary* (1903).

Margolis, M. *A Manual of the Aramaic Language of the Babylonian Talmud*, (1910).

Milik, J. T. *The Books of Enoch, Aramaic Fragments of Qumrân Cave 4* (1976).

Nöldeke, T. *Mandäische Grammatik* (reprint, 1964).

______. *Compendious Syriac Grammar* (English edition, 1904).

Payne Smith, R. *Thesaurus syriacus* (vols. 1-2; 1879-1901).

Ploeg, J. van der, and A. van der Woude. *Le targum de Job de la grotte XI de Qumrân* (1971).

Rosenthal, F. *Die aramaistische Forschung seit Th. Nöldeke's Veröffentlichungen* (reprint, 1964).

______. *A Grammar of Biblical Aramaic* (1961).

Schulthess, F. *Lexicon syropalaestinum* (1903).

Segert, S. *Altaramäische Grammatik* (1975).

Sokoloff, M. *The Targum to Job from Qumran Cave XI* (1974).

Stevenson, W. *Grammar of Palestinian Jewish Aramaic* (2nd edition, 1962).

Vogt, E. *Lexicon linguae aramaicae Veteris Testamenti* (1971).

Wagner, M. *Die lexikalischen und grammatikalischen Aramaismen im alttestamentlichen Hebräisch* (BZAW 96; 1966).

______. "Beiträge zur Aramaismenfrage im alttestamentlichen Hebräisch," VTS 16 (1967), 355-71.

Aramaic offers great potential for comparative purposes. An abundance of original literature in the various Aram dialects means that the vocabulary of Aram is generally quite well understood. This includes the vast "sea" of the Talmud and other rabbinic literature. We also have the translation of the Old Testament into various Aram dialects, viz., the targums and the Peshitta (see the section on targums above for additional information on these). No other cognate language offers the triple bonus of direct translation from the Hebrew, close contact with the Old Testament through much of its history, and an abundance of independent literature.

Naturally, the close connection of Aram speakers with the Old Testament is not an unmixed blessing. Sometimes the spoken and written Aram may have been influenced by the Hebrew text and vice versa. The question of Aramaisms in OT Hebrew is not always easy to answer (see Driver; Wagner; CPTOT, 50-8), but on the whole the problems are very small compared to the benefits.

The abundant linguistic tools available would seem the answer to some faithful Aram scholar's prayer. We have good lexica in several dialects, including those such as Brockelmann's and Drower-Macuch's (MD) done on a proper linguistic basis. Epigraphic Aram information appears in DISO and KAI (see also the useful concordance of Aufrecht and Hurd). Even so there is still some new material, such as the Neofiti MS, in a relatively unstudied state. Where not otherwise indicated the lexica used for the respective dialects in this thesis are NW, CW, and Jastrow; Brockelmann; Schulthess; MD: DISO; Maclean and Macuch; Vogt. For the Aram editions, etc., of rabbinic literature, see Townsend (listed above under Post-Biblical Hebrew).

Major published Aram texts from Qumran include 11QtgJob, 1QapGen, 4Q Enoch fragments, and material in DJD II. Unfortunately, Kuhn's concordance (see section on Post-Biblical Hebrew above) includes little Aram material (only a few fragments in DJD I), so one must depend on the indices in the major publications. The *editio princeps* of 11QtgJob (van der Ploeg and van der Woude) gives a complete listing of all passages for each Aram word in the index. However, no definitions occur. Sokoloff gives short definitions in his glossary and includes a brief grammar of the text. Fitzmyer gives a concordance of 1QapGen (only certain words defined) and a brief grammar of the text. Milik has an Aramaic-Greek-Ethiopic glossary with brief definitions. For Samaritan Aram one has to depend upon the glossary in Cowley and the medieval Aram-Heb-Ar glossary reproduced in Ben-Ḥayyim.

Ugaritic and Amorite

Barr, J. "Ugaritic and Hebrew *šbm*?" JSS 18 (1973), 17-39.

Bauer, T. *Die Ostkanaanäer* (1926).

Buccellati, G. *The Amorites of the Ur III Period* (1966).

Dahood, M. *Ugaritic-Hebrew Philology* (1965).

______. "Hebrew-Ugaritic Lexicography," *Biblica* 44-55 (1963-74).

______. "Ugaritic Lexicography," *Mélanges Eugène Tisserant*, I (1964), 81-104.

Dietrich, M., and O. Loretz. *Ugarit-Bibliographie der Jahre 1926-1966* (vols. 1-4; 1973).

______. "Zur ugaritischen Lexikographie," BO 23, 25 (1966, 1968); OLZ 62 (1967); UF 4 (1972). Continued in conjunction with J. Sanmartín, UF 5- (1973-).

______. "Das Ugaritische in den Wörterbüchern von L. Kohler und W. Baumgartner," BZ 13 (1969), 187-207.

Driver, G. *Canaanite Myths and Legends* (1956).

Fisher, L. *Ras Shamra Parallels* (vol. 1- , 1972-).

Gordon, C. *Ugaritic Textbook* (1965; Supplement, 1967).

Gröndahl, F. *Die Personennamen der Texte aus Ugarit* (1967).

Herdner, A. *Corpus des tablettes en cunéiformes alphabétiques* (vols. 1-2; 1963).

Huffmon, H. *Amorite Personal Names in the Mari Texts* (1965).

Leslau, W. "Observations on Semitic Cognates in Ugaritic," Or 37 (1968), 347-66.

Martinez, E. *Hebrew-Ugaritic Index to the Writings of Mitchell J. Dahood* (1967).

Moor, J. de. *The Seasonal Pattern in the Ugaritic Myth of Ba^{c}lu* (1971).

Palais royal d'Ugarit, Le (vols. 1- ; 1955-).

Ullendorff, E. "Ugaritic Marginalia," Or 20 (1951), 270-4; JSS 7 (1962), 339-51; IOS 2 (1972), 463-9.
Whitaker, R. *Concordance of the Ugaritic Literature* (1972).

In recent years Ugaritic has tended to displace the other Semitic languages as a source of lexical comparisons. Probably the bulk of these have come from the pen of Professor Dahood and his students. Listed are only a few more important of Dahood's publications on the subject. A complete index of his Hebrew-Ugaritic comparisons through 1966 has been done by Martinez. Blommerde adds a few more bibliographical references through part of 1968. Pope's commentary is a valuable source for the book of Job specifically as is Michel's dissertation. (See above under "Commentaries" for more information on Blommerde, Pope, and Michel.)

Studies on the Ug vocabulary itself have been done by various writers, the most important being those of Ullendorff, de Moor, who gives very complete bibliographies for those passages he treats (but has a particular theory to support--see my forthcoming review in UF 8), and Dietrich-Loretz-Sanmartín (Moshe Held's oft-cited thesis was unavailable to me). The standard lexica of WUS, UT, and Driver need to be supplemented by these detailed studies on individual words. Leslau adds useful etymologies from Southeast Semitic. Further bibliography for Ug can be found in the Dietrich-Loretz bibliography and that of Hospers on the Semitic languages in general (see above under the "General" section). Fisher, as yet incomplete, has excellent indices. The standard editions of Ug texts are CTA and PRU (especially vols. 2 and 5). UT provides a convenient collection of the material published up through about 1966. Gröndahl's study on personal names is not complete but still provides a useful reference.

Amorite is known mainly from personal names in the Akkadian texts. The basic studies and collections are Huffmon, Bauer, and Buccellati. The new Eblaite tablets have only been reported on in the more popular media, and the contents of these new texts were naturally unavailable for this study. Although labeled "Old Canaanite," the exact place of Eblaite in Northwest Semitic is likely to be disputed just as that of Ug still is.

Arabic

Barthélemy, A. *Dictionnaire arabe-français: dialectes de Syrie* (1935-69).

Blachère, R., et al. *Dictionnaire arabe-français-anglais* (1964-).

Blau, J. *The Emergence and Linguistic Background of Judaeo-Arabic*, (1965).

______. *A Grammar of Christian Arabic* (vols. 1-3; 1966-7).

______. "Arabic Lexicographical Miscellanies," JSS 17 (1972), 173-90.

Boris, G. *Lexique du parler arabe des Marazig* (1958).

Denizeau, C. *Dictionnaire des parlers arabes de Syrie* . . . (Supplément au Dictionnaire arabe-français de A. Barthélemy, 1960).

Dozy, R. *Supplément aux dictionnaires arabes* (vols. 1-2; 1881).

Freytag, G. *Lexicon arabico-latinum* (vols. 1-4; 1830-37).

Friedlaender, I. *Arabisch-deutsches Lexikon zum Sprachgebrauch des Maimonides* (1902).

Fück, J. "Zur arabischen Wörterbuchfrage," ZDMG 107 (1957), 340-7.

Guillaume, A. *Studies in the Book of Job* (1968).

______. "Hebrew and Arabic Lexicography, A Comparative Study," *Abr-Nahrain* 1 (1959-60), 3-35; 2 (1960-1), 5-35; 3 (1961-2), 1-10; 4 (1963-4), 1-18.

______. "The Arabic Background of the Book of Job," *Promise and Fulfilment* (1963), 106-27.

Harrell, R. (ed.). *A Dictionary of Moroccan Arabic: Moroccan-English* (1966).

Hirschberg, H. "Some Additional Arabic Etymologies in Old Testament Lexicography," VT 11 (1961), 373-85.

Kazimirsky, A. de B. *Dictionnaire arabe-français* (vols. 1-2; 1860).

Kopf, L. "Arabische Etymologien und Parallelen zum Bibelwörterbuch," VT 8 (1958), 161-215; 9 (1959), 247-87.

______. "Das arabische Wörterbuch als Hilfsmittel für die hebräische Lexikographie," VT 6 (1956), 286-302.

Kraemer, J. *Theodor Nöldekes Belegwörterbuch zur klassischen arabischen Sprache* (letter Alif only; 1952).

Kraemer, J., et al. *Wörterbuch der klassischen arabischen Sprache* (1970).

Landberg, C. de. *Glossaire daṯînois* (vols. 1-3; 1920-42).

Lane, E. *Arabic-English Lexicon* (1863-93).

Marçais, W., and A. Guīga. *Textes arabes de Takroûna: 2. Glossaire* (vols. 1-8; 1958-61).

Rabin, C. *Ancient West-Arabian* (1951).

Roth-Laly, A. *Lexique des parlers arabes tchado-soudanais* (vols. 1-4; 1969-72).

Wehr, H. *A Dictionary of Modern Written Arabic* (1961).

Wild, S. *Das Kitāb al-ᶜAin und die arabische Lexikographie* (1965).

______. "Neues zur ältesten arabischen Lexikographie," ZDMG 112 (1962), 291-8.

Woodhead, D. R., and W. Beene, *Dictionary of Iraqi Arabic: Arabic-English* (1967).

Wright, W. *A Grammar of the Arabic Language* (3rd edition, 1898).

Arabic has been a favorite language for comparative philological treatments for a number of reasons: its familiarity, its huge vocabulary, and the notion that it remained more conservative to PS than many of the other languages. But the problems with using it are only now becoming generally recognized, primarily the improper methods used in producing the standard lexica. See especially the writings of Fück and Kopf on this subject. Blau has given examples of "ghost words" in such standard lexica as those of Freytag and Lane. Progress is being made in the production of scientifically constructed lexica, notably Wehr, WKAS, and DAFA, but much of the classical vocabulary has yet to be covered. WKAS, for example, covers only the letter *K* and part of *L*. DAFA is through the letter *Ḫ*.

Middle Arabic is a source not extensively used in the past. Blau has probably done more than anyone else in recent times to advance our knowledge of this stage of the language. No lexicon devoted to Middle Ar is presently available. However, Dozy covers quite a bit of Middle Ar material, and Friedlaender treats the large vocabulary of Maimonides. For the various modern dialects we have some good dictionaries. French scholars especially have contributed to this area of studies.

A number of aids have been devised by Ar specialists for relating Ar to the OT. Kopf's three articles plus the supplementary article by Hirschberg are very helpful. A number of word studies by competent scholars also take into account Ar information. Unfortunately, the studies by Guillaume, while often very suggestive, cannot necessarily be trusted.

For the classical language WKAS, DAFA, and Kraemer were used for the part of the alphabet for which they were available, otherwise Lane. Other lexica for classical and middle Ar are cited where used. For the dialects I used the following: Iraqi, Woodhead; Arabian peninsula, Landberg; Syria, Barthélemy and Denizeau; North Africa, Boris, Marçais, Roth-Laly, and Harrell. Although all these dialects were checked consistently, they are not usually cited when they add nothing to the classical and modern written languages.

Ethiopic and South Arabian

Armbruster, C. *Initia Amharica* (Part III, vol. 1; 1920).

Baeteman, J. *Dictionnaire amarigna-français* (1929).

Beeston, A. *A Descriptive Grammar of Epigraphic South Arabian* (1962).

______. *Sabaean Inscriptions* (1937).

______. "Notes on Old South Arabian Lexicography," *Le Muséon* 63-7, 85 (1950-4, 1972).

Conti Rossini, K. *Chrestomathia Arabica meridionalis epigraphica* (1931).

Dillmann, A. *Ethiopic Grammar* (English tr., 1907).

______. *Lexicon linguae aethiopicae* (1865).

Grébaut, S. *Supplément au Lexicon linguae aethiopicae de A. Dillmann* (1952).

Harding, G. *An Index and Concordance of Pre-Islamic Arabian Names and Inscriptions* (1971).

Jahn, A. *Die Mehri-Sprache in Südarabien* (1902).

Jamme, A. *Sabaean Inscriptions from Maḥram Bilqîs (Mârib)*, (1962).

Leslau, Wolf. *Lexique Soqoṭri* (1938).

______. *Gafat Documents* (1945).

______. *Etude descriptive et comparative du Gafat* (1956).

______. *Ethiopic and South Arabic Contributions to the Hebrew Lexicon* (1958).

______. *Etymological Dictionary of Harari* (1963).

______. *Hebrew Cognates in Amharic* (1969).

______. *Concise Amharic Dictionary* (1976).

______. "Observations on Semitic Cognates in Ugaritic," Or 37 (1968), 347-66.

______. "Vocabulary Common to Akkadian and South-east Semitic," JAOS 64 (1944), 53-8.

______. "Southeast Semitic Cognates to the Akkadian Vocabulary," JAOS 82 (1962), 1-4; 84 (1964), 115-18; 89 (1969), 18-22.

Littmann, E., and M. Höfner. *Wörterbuch der Tigrē-Sprache* (1962).

Müller, W. *Die Wurzeln Mediae und Tertiae Y/W im Altsüdarabischen* (1962).

______. "Altsüdarabische Beiträge zum hebräischen Lexikon," ZAW 75 (1963), 304-16.

Ryckmans, G. *Les noms propres sud-sémitiques* (1934-5).

Ullendorff, E. "The Contribution of South Semitics to Hebrew Lexicography," VT 6 (1956), 190-98.

______. "The Semitic Languages of Ethiopia and their Contribution to General Semitic Studies," *Africa* 25 (1955), 154-60.

The Southeast Semitic languages have received much less attention than their northern cousins, mainly because there are fewer specialists in them who also have an interest in the OT. There are usable lexica for many of the Eth languages, but the South Arabic dialects are much less accessible. So far there is no ESA lexicon. Conti Rossini's glossary must be supplemented from a variety of scattered sources. Jamme is very helpful in this regard as are Beeston and Müller. Leslau has gone out of his way to make the Southeast Semitic linguistic sources available for the OT scholar. (Unfortunately, his works specifically aimed at the OT and Heb often omit rare words.) Harding and Ryckmans are both important for names.

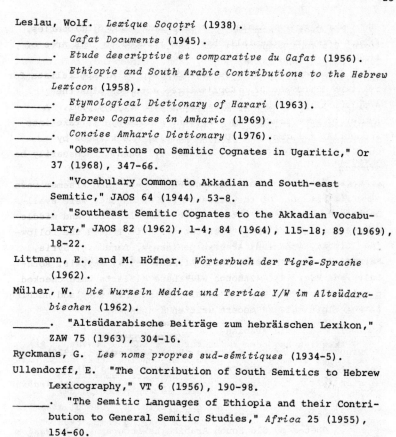

For Geez I have used Dillmann supplemented by Grebaut; Tigre, Littmann/Höfner; Harari, Leslau; Soqotri, Leslau; ESA, Conti Rossini and Jamme; Mehri, Jahn. Otherwise, references are quoted wherever used. When Leslau is referred to by name only, it means I have checked both his *Contributions* and *Hebrew Cognates in Amharic* (unless reference is obviously to his supplementary articles to UT and AHW). Leslau's new Amharic dictionary appeared too late to be used.

Akkadian

Assyrian Dictionary of the Oriental Institute of Chicago, The (1956-).

Delitzsch, F. *Assyrisches Handwörterbuch* (1896).

Muss-Arnolt, W. *Assyrisch-englisch-deutsches Handwörterbuch* (vols. 1-2; 1894-1905).

Reiner, E. *A Linguistic Analysis of Akkadian* (1966).

Soden, W. von. *Akkadisches Handwörterbuch* (1959-).

______. *Grundriss der akkadischen Grammatik* (1969).

Zimmern, H. *Akkadische Fremdwörter als Beweis für babylonischen Kultureinfluss* (1917).

Akkadian has been known for more than a century. Akk etymologies already appeared in BDB. On the other hand, the use of Akk has not been so widely used for comparative purposes. Perhaps the main reason is the phonological difficulties involved in making comparisons. Useful grammars are GAG and that of Reiner. AHW is nearing completion while CAD covers a good portion of the alphabet. I have used AHW and CAD, comparing them wherever they overlap. Where they are both lacking, I have had to resort to older lexica such as Muss-Arnolt and Delitzsch (these are cited whenever used). Zimmern is a useful collection of Akk cognates to Heb even though the thesis he attempted to defend has long been rejected.

CHAPTER II

STUDY OF SELECTED PASSAGES FROM JOB

§ 1. 3:5

Barr, J. "Philology and Exegesis," *Questions disputées d'Ancien Testament* (1974), 50-7.

Clines, D. J. A. "The Etymology of Hebrew *Ṣelem*" JNSL 3 (1974), 23-5.

Cowley, A. E. *The Samaritan Liturgy*.

Lewy, H. *Die semitischen Fremdwörter im Griechischen*, 157.

Mansoor, M. "The Massoretic Text in the Light of Qumran," VTS 9 (1963), 316-7.

Masson, E. *Recherches sur les plus anciens emprunts sémitiques en grec*, 16-17.

Nöldeke, Th. "צלמות und צלם," ZAW 17 (1897), 183-7.

Sawyer, J. F. A. Review of W. Holladay, *Concise Hebrew and Aramaic Lexicon*, JSS 17 (1972), 258.

______. *Semantics in Biblical Research*, 14 and 90.

Thomas, D. W. "A Consideration of Some Unusual Ways of Expressing the Superlative in Hebrew," VT 3 (1953), 219-22.

______. "צלמות in the Old Testament," JSS 7 (1962), 191-200.

Let darkness וצלמות claim it,
Let a cloud lie over it,
Let them terrify it כמרירי יום.

Ṣalmāwet

For the past century or more commentaries have connected this word with the PS root **ẓlm*, generally revocalizing it to *ṣalmût*. Although the root *ṢLM* has tentatively been identified elsewhere in Hebrew by some scholars, the identification primarily comes from a comparison with other Semitic languages, notably Akk, Ar, and Eth. Many modern works no longer mention the older interpretation, "shadow of death" (cf. Sawyer).

The word occurs in the following passages in the MT: Isa 9:1; Jer 2:6; 13:16; Amos 5:8; Ps 23:4; 44:20; 107:10, 14; Job 3:5; 10:21, 22; 12:22; 16:16; 24:17 (*bis*); 28:3; 34:22;

38:17. Of these 18 occurrences, the older versions overwhelmingly support the traditional rendering "shadow of death":

LXX: some form of σκιὰ θανάτου appears 9 times (Thomas lists 12 but seems to have overlooked the fact that Job 24:17 and 28:3 are Hexaplaric additions). Other renderings include σκιά alone, γνοφερός "gloomy," ᾅδης, and ἄκαρπος "barren."

MV: these are extant only at 10 of the 18 occurrences. Of these 10, σκιὰ θανάτου is in one or more of the versions 7 times. Σκεπομένη θανάτῳ "covered by death" is used by Sym at Job 10:21 and Ps 23:4, while βιασθεὶς θανάτου is his rendering in Job 24:17b. Note "death" occurs each time even if the rest of the phrase is different.

Tg: 16 times the translation is טולא דמותא or טולי מותא. Only at Jer 13:16 and Amos 5:8 is any reference to death omitted.

Syr: some form of טללי מותא or טללא דמותא is used consistently each time.

Vg: *umbra mortis* translates the word 11 times, while *mortis* is found in the translation of 3 other passages.

The much more detailed and lengthy studies of others (primarily that of Thomas) can only be summarized here with the reader referred to those for many points not touched on or discussed in detail. Thomas' major contention is that the use of the word "death" is one more means of emphasis (in his words, "means of expressing the superlative," an expression to which Barr, 53, n. 33, takes exception). Just as in English such hyperboles as "embarrassed to death" may be used, the "shadow of death" was a way of saying "fearsome shadow" or "deep darkness." The resulting meaning would not differ from that understood by most commentators, though "shadow of death" might not be an inappropriate understanding in some passages.

As for the form of the word, there are a number of analogous forms which might serve to explain it. Two place names with comparable patterns are עזמות and חצרמות. These could very well be compounds of the divine name Mot. (Cassuto, *Goddess Anath*, 64, n. 14, suggests as much for the first one.) A "shadow of Mot" is not otherwise known but could certainly explain the form in the MT. Dahood notes that in UT 51.2.27 (CTA 4.2.27) *ẓl* is parallel to *ngh* (RSP II, p. 14). Since *ṣalmāwet* is also parallel to *nāgah* in Isa 9:1, he analyzes the first word as *ṣal* + *māwet*--at least for Isa 9:1. However, the root *ngh* is a restoration in the Ug passage and not at all certain.

A question which must be asked is how much of a time gap separates some of these passages from the translation of the LXX. One could argue an original *ṣalmût* became assimilated to *ṣalmāwet* by folk etymology, but this is problematic. While such a midrashic analysis by the readers is not unlikely, its influence on the actual pronunciation of the word does not necessarily follow. Further, *ṣalmût* could also be analyzed into "shadow" and "dying" (from the infinitive absolute). If *ṣalmût* should indeed be the original form, we still have to say the interpretation "shadow of death" had displaced it as the dominant understanding already during the intertestamental period. This brings us to the question of which stage of the text we are dealing with. Are we trying at all points to push back as close to the original as possible, or are we trying to understand the form of the text as it was finalized? The answer will partially determine the weight one gives to the various arguments.

Kim^e rîrê yôm

Traditionally, the phrase was translated something like "as the bitter things of the day." But most modern commentators emend the vocalization to *kamrîrê*, deriving the word from the root *KMR* rather than *MRR* and taking the *K* as a radical rather than as the preposition k^e. The root *KMR* is not new to Hebrew. HAL and BDB list three such roots while GB has four. But this particular word is thought to have a root unique to it. The identification depends upon cognate evidence in classical Syriac.

With the exception of the LXX all the early versions agree with the MT, though sometimes ignoring the prefixed k^e:

Aq--ὡς πικραμμοὶ (ἡμέρας).

Vg--*amaritudine* (here the word "day" is ignored).

Tg--היך מרירי יומא.

Syr--מרירי יומא.

The LXX reads καταραθείη ἡ ἡμέρα but connects it with the beginning of v. 6, to read "may that day and night be accursed." According to Schleusner (II, 208) this renders not *kim*^{e}*rîrê* but *y*^{e}*ba*^{c}*ătuhû*, though the LXX seems corrupt here. Dhorme agrees with this. If this is correct, the LXX either ignored the word in question or had a different *Vorlage*.

The expression *BMRYRY YWM* is found in the Hebrew text of Ben Sira (11:4) and *BMRWRY YWM* in the Thanksgiving Hymns from Qumran 1QH 5:34. The use of *B* instead of *K* leaves no alternative for any root other than *MRR* in these expressions. One could perhaps argue that they are borrowed from Job in both instances. That is possible though difficult to establish one way or the other. (The *Hodayot* passage seems based on Ps 31:10, at least for the first part.) On the other hand, the way the phrase is used suggests it carried meaning for the writers. Even if borrowed it was not a meaningless quote, though this would not preclude a different interpretation for the phrase than might have been in the mind of the author of Job.

Later Jewish tradition connects this and similar expressions with demonic spirits. *B. Pesaḥim* 111b refers to a certain demon called *QṬB MRYRY*, of which there were two types, one ruling before noon and one after (cf. also *Num. r.*, s. 12). Both Deut 32:24 and Ps 91:6 are obviously in mind at this point. Rashi interprets Job 3:5 as a reference to demons ruling at noon and quotes Ps 91:6. Both Saadiah and Ibn Ezra, while referring to Deut 32:24, mention the hot wind *samūm*. The expression evidently had meaning from the intertestamental period all the way through medieval times, even though some variation of connotation according to the age and commentator has to be allowed for.

As evidence for the root *KMR* here, Dhorme cites the Akk *kamāru*. But this means "heap" rather than his suggested "overshadow" or "darken." GB, BDB, and Zorell all list only the Syriac cognate. HAL adds in addition a reference to Cowley (vol. 2, p. lviii). In the glossary Cowley lists the meaning "wretched, feeble" for the word *KMRYN*. But in the actual text (vol. 1, p. 31), a MS variant is noted. This is also the only passage cited by Cowley for this root. On the other hand, even if the reading *KMRYN* is correct, the meaning still accords only with the basic Syriac connotation "be sad, mourn" and does not add any support to the meaning "black."

Lewy compares the Greek word κάμμερος with a Hebrew root *KMR* meaning "dark." However, he is postulating a Semitic loanword into Greek based on the evidence of the assumed Heb root. Thus, his information can hardly be used to prove such a Heb root. Furthermore, he notes that Indo-European scholars give a purely Indo-European etymology for this Greek word. (While Lewy often gives interesting suggestions, many of his etymologies are sheer speculation. See the critique in Masson.) A root *KMR* meaning "dark, black" does not appear to occur elsewhere in the Semitic languages. The cognates in Phoen, Akk, Eth, and Ar relate only to other *KMR* roots in Heb. Ug does not have any such root as yet attested. The Syriac meaning seems unique to the Aram dialects.

Even in the various East Aram dialects which include Syriac, the meaning "dark, black" is not widely attested. It is not found in Mandaic, Babylonian Aram, or the modern dialects. (Neither does it occur in Christian Palestinian Aram; however, while this dialect is written in Syriac characters, it is actually a branch of West Aram.) One would gather from these data that the meaning "dark, black" is a unique development in Syriac. Barr suggests the meaning "sad" is more basic than "black" since Syriac normally uses other words for the color black (55, n. 41).

Because the comparative evidence is so skimpy and problematic, it seems better to turn back to the MT form and work from there. One of Mansoor's suggested translations, "the most bitter day," is quite interesting and fits well in the context. Many have compared Amos 8:10 which may be referring to an eclipse. There is also the question of *'RRY-YWM* in Job 3:8. The construction is very similar to that in v 5, both employing an objective genitive. As pointed out to me by Professor Brownlee, a verbal play involving *MRR* and *'RR* is found in Num 5:23, 27. Was the author of Job consciously drawing on that? Whether any of the understandings of early and medieval rabbinic sources were in the mind of the original writer is hard to say. In any event an attempt to elucidate the form as perpetuated by the Masoretes seems more in order in the light of the present evidence.

§ 2. 3:6

Dahood, M. "Hebrew-Ugaritic Lexicography II," *Biblica* 45 (1964), 407-8.

______. "A New Translation of Genesis 49,6a," *Biblica* 36 (1955), 229.

Ginsberg, H. L. "Lexicographical Notes," VTS 16 (1967), 71-3.

______. "A Ugaritic Parallel to 2 Sam 1 21," JBL 57 (1938), 210, n. 3.

Loewenstamm, S. E. "The Ugaritic Fertility Myth--the Result of a Mistranslation," IEJ 12 (1962), 87-8.

Moor, J. de. *The Seasonal Pattern in the Ugaritic Myth of Ba^c lu*, 210-11.

Let it not יחד- with the days of the year,
Into the number of the months let it not go.

It has long been customary to emend *yiḥadd*, from the root *ḤDH* "to rejoice," to *yeḥad* "be united" from the root *YḤD*. More recently Dahood has explained the word as being from a root *ḤDH* which he explains as "to see." This root in fact finds an entry in HAL. (Dahood takes the form here as a *nifal*, which also requires emendation to *yēḥad*.)

The early versions are practically unanimous in translating the word in such a way to suggest they understood the root *YḤD* "join":

Sym: μηδὲ συναφθείη.

Vg: *non conputetur in diebus anni.*

Tg: לא יתיחד עם יומין טבין דשתא "let it not be joined with the good days (festival days) of the year."

Syr: לא נתחשב במנינא דיומתא דשנתא "let it not be reckoned in the number of the days of the year."

The LXX μὴ εἴη εἰς ἡμέρας ἐνιαυτοῦ evidently means something along the lines of "let it not come into the days of the year," which also seems to read the root *YḤD* (cf. Schleusner, I, 683-4). Saadiah agrees with the other earlier versions: לא יגתמע פי איאב אלסנה.

One of the major questions is the PS original of *ḥdw* "to see" in Ug. UT takes it as **ḥ̱dw* but is not sure whether to compare the Heb *ḥāzāh* with it or with Syriac *ḤZ'* and Ar *ḥāzin*.

Ginsberg has no reservations on the subject. He is certain the PS root of both Ug and Heb is **ḥḏw*. Of course, if that is the case, the Heb and Ug fit into the normal pattern of sound correspondence but Aram does not. Ginsberg explains this by arguing for an Aram borrowing of the Heb and Phoen root.

Ginsberg's proposed etymology is certainly possible. To be correct it requires Aram to have borrowed the word very early while at the same time losing its counterpart of the PS **ḥḏw/y*. The reason it must have been early is that *ḤZY* is spread throughout the Aram dialects, suggesting the root was a part of "Proto-Aramaic." It is already found in the Sefire and Zakir inscriptions and occurs in almost all the historical dialects, including the modern spoken ones. Any expected **ḥdy* with this meaning is absent, though *ḤDY* "rejoice" is widespread throughout Aram.

If we assume a PS root **ḥzw/y*, on the other hand, the Aram evidence fits and only the Ug word fails to conform to normal phonetic correspondence. In this case one would see the Ar cognate in *ḥzw/y* rather than *ḥḏw/y*. This seems to be the more probable situation for the following reasons: Neither Ar *ḥḏw/y* nor *ḥzw/y* mean "see" in the same sense as the normal Heb usage. *Ḥḏw/y* in both the classical language and various modern dialects means "to face, be opposite to, cut." One could postulate some sort of connection with the meaning "see," but the semantic content is somewhat different. *Ḥzw/y* has the basic senses "to divine, augur, consider." While this, too, is not exactly the same as "to see," the sense seems to be closer. As an analogy one can think of Heb *ḥōzeh* "seer, one who has inner vision" which is a development of the normal *ḥāzāh* "see." If this argument is correct, one has to postulate an irregular development in Ug which produced an exception to the expected phonetic quality. However, we already have another deviation which has caused similar problems in *dr*^{c}. Some contexts of this word have suggested the meaning "sow" to a number of scholars, but the expected Ug cognate for the common Semitic "sow" should be **zr*^{c}. (See UT § 5.4 and the Loewenstamm article; also M. Dietrich, Or 26 [1957], 64; J. Blau, *Pseudo-Corrections*, 48 n. 9; and J. de Moor. The word appears in some texts as *ḏr*^{c}--UT 2059.17, 19.) If *dr*^{c} is indeed "sow," and *ḥdy* is indeed to be related to Hebrew *ḥāzāh* and its cognates, we have two examples of an exception to the normal rule that PS **z* remains *z* in Ug.

The weight of linguistic evidence seems slightly in favor of the PS **ḥzy*. But in any case as Ginsberg points out, it is difficult to explain how the Ug root *ḥdy* ended up in Heb. The only possibility is a direct loan since none of the other Semitic languages is likely to have been the mediator. Of course, a direct loan cannot be ruled impossible. But when we consider the passages in which this new root *ḤDH* is supposed to occur, each of them is perfectly understandable as it stands according to the traditional reading. HAL lists Ps 33:15; 49:11; Gen 49:6; and Job 34:29. (A number of emendations have been suggested for the last passage, "none of which carries conviction" according to Pope.) Therefore, the argument from the OT usage is also rather weak.

The standard emendation to "let it not be united with the days of the year" is an attractive one because of parallelism, not to mention the practically united reading of the versions. However, what is logical to us and to the early translators was equally logical to the Masoretes. That they recorded the word as "rejoice" means they must have had some well-established reading tradition. A consideration of the structure of the passage at this point may help to clarify how the MT arose. The parallel between Jer 20:14-18 and this section of Job 3 is obvious. Some commentators feel the author of Job is even dependent upon Jeremiah here (e.g. Fohrer). In Jeremiah the one being cursed is the messenger who brought the news of birth. In Job the personified night (of conception) speaks. The birth of a male child was normally a time of rejoicing; Jeremiah's father rejoiced at the news of the birth of his son (Jer 20:15b). Although the word used in Jer 20:15b is *ŚMḤ*, the basic sense is the same. It would be hardly surprising to find this thought taken up in Job 3:6--only instead of the rejoicing father, it is the rejoicing day which is spoken of: Let not this day of rejoicing--this day when everyone rejoices at the birth of a male child--rejoice among the days of the year. A similar type of thinking seems to have influenced the Tg translator who referred to the festival days of the year.

While this may not be the actual origin of the MT form, it is one possibility and illustrates why the MT should not be emended lightly. We also have a case of *difficilior lectio* which cannot easily be dismissed. Although it would be hard to say which is more likely to be original, two traditions have clearly been preserved for this verse, the one attested in the versions and accepted by most critics and the other in the MT.

§ 3. 3:8

Barr, J. "Philology and Exegesis," 56-7.

Fishbane, M. "Jeremiah IV 23-26 and Job III 3-13: A Recovered Use of the Creation Pattern," VT 21 (1971), 151-67.

Gunkel, H. *Schöpfung und Chaos*, 59-61.

Kraus, H.-J. *Psalmen*, 512-19.

McCarthy, D. J. "'Creation' Motifs in Ancient Hebrew Poetry," CBQ 29 (1967), 393-406.

Rainey, A. "The Word 'Day' in Ugaritic and Hebrew," *Leshonenu* 36 (1971-2), 186-9 (Heb with English summary).

Let curse it the cursers of יום-,
The ones prepared to arouse Leviathan.

Gunkel suggested the reading *yām* because of the parallelism with Leviathan in the second half of the verse. This has become widely accepted, especially since the Ras Shamra texts showed both Yam and Leviathan to be part of an elaborate mythology only hinted at by the few references in the OT.

Without exception the early versions all translate by "day" (LXX, Aq, Vg, Tg, Syr). With the exception of the Tg they also seem to recognize the figure of Leviathan at the end of the verse:

LXX: τὸ μέγα κῆτος "the great sea-monster."
Aq, Sym: Λευιαθάν
Th: δράκοντα
Vg: *Leviathan*.
Syr: ללויתן.
(Tg: "let curse it the prophets who curse the day of recompense, who are ready when aroused to remember their lament.")

Yām and Leviathan occur together in two passages of the Old Testament. In Isa 27:1 *yām* occurs only in the phrase, "the Tannin which is in the sea." Ps 74:13-14a reads, "By your strength you divided Sea; you broke the heads of Tanninim upon the waters. You smashed the heads of Leviathan. . . ." Here *yām* could be considered parallel to both Leviathan and Tanninim. Ps 74 is dated anywhere from 587 to 168 B.C. (Kraus; Weiser, *Psalms*, 518). However, it is more likely during the period 587-520, closer to 520 than 587 (Kraus). Not only is this psalm not likely to be much earlier than Job, it is probably later. Therefore, the MT "cursers of the day" does not appear to come from a time after any import of Yam in connection with Leviathan had been forgotten. In both passages the mythology does not dominate the setting but only forms elements of the language for the purpose of expressing another thought. In Ps 74 the mythical languages serves as the vehicle for expressing the early Israelite *Heilsgeschichte* in the experience of the Red Sea and the crossing of the Jordan (Kraus). In Job the language serves to express Job's vehemence against the day of his birth.

The context of Job 3:8 is the curse of the day of birth and the night of conception. Of course, one could argue the alternation of day and night was responsible for the substitution of *yôm* for an original *yām*. The argument that the phrase was originally a standard mythological phrase or formula appears cogent to me. The poet undoubtedly used such a formula which he found at hand rather than inventing his own. One might compare the Aramaic curse which refers to the "spell of Sea and the spell of Leviathan" (Montgomery, *Aramaic Incantation Texts*, p. 121; Isbell, *Corpus*, p. 19, text 2.4). But in doing so the poet changed the formula to suit his purpose, substituting *yôm* for *yām*. This substitution is not only clear from the context but required by it. Dhorme notes that to change *yôm* to *yām* at this point, as some have suggested, "would result in a meaning diametrically opposite to the one expected and expressed. It is the supporters, not the cursers, of the sea, who are the enemies of the day (9:13)." Fohrer similarly argues that Job is calling on the magicians who can place a curse on a part of the godly creation. He calls upon the "arousers of Leviathan" (= magicians) because that monster of chaos is required to engulf the offending day and night. Fishbane (161) argues that a deliberate wordplay is in operation so that the use of *yôm* parallel to Leviathan is "a clever paratactic device for preserving two mythologems of the Dragon," viz., sea monster and eclipse dragon. (Whether Leviathan is an eclipse figure here is a question. Fohrer argues that it is not, but eclipse dragons were known in the ancient Near East. Possibly the figure of Leviathan had added this symbol to his older one of the watery chaos by this time. Fishbane evidently believes so--159.)

Thus, questions of form criticism and context favor the retention of the MT at this point. It has become a question not of which is right (*yām* or *yôm*) but of the literary level on which we are working. As this section of the poem left the hand of its final redactor, it seems fairly certain it already contained *yôm*.

At this point one would need to consider the claims of McCarthy and others who feel the *Chaoskampf* language of the OT has been greatly "demythologized." Gunkel himself made an interesting observation in this regard (61):

> Genauer ist zu sagen: Leviathan erscheint Job 3_8 noch deutlich als das personificierte Meer, was Job 40f und Ψ 104 nicht mehr der Fall war. Das bedeutet, dass Job 3 den Mythus in ursprünglicherer Form enthält als die beiden andern Recensionen.
>
> More precisely, Leviathan appears in Job 3:8 still clearly as the personified Sea, which was no longer the case in Job 40f and Ps 104. This means that Job 3 retains the myth in its more original form than the other two recensions.

If my arguments are correct, Job 3:8 also alters the image of the "personified Sea" in the same way that Gunkel claims has already happened in chap. 40.

One might solidify this argument with a reference to the use of vowel letters. The system of internal *matres lectionis* did not become well developed in Hebrew until the post-exilic period although vowel letters occur sporadically in the 6th century (Cross and Freedman, *Orthography*, 56-9). With "day," however, we are dealing with a word of which the original form was most likely **yawm* (see Rainey's article). In those dialects in which **yawm* had not reduced to *yôm*, this diphthong required the writing of a medial *waw*. Thus the early Aramaic inscriptions such as those of Sefire (KAI 222-3) and Zinčirli (KAI 214-15) have *YWM*. The Yavneh-Yam inscription from about the late seventh century (KAI 200.4) evidently also uses the orthography *YWM*. (KAI has this though Gibson, I, p. 28, reads differently, following Naveh, IEJ 10 [1960], 131.) If the dialect in which Job was written used the pronunciation **yawm*, the presence or absence of a *waw* would have helped keep the correct meaning clear, apart from any scribal corruption.

In sum, one must consider a number of factors when trying to decide the original reading here. Most commentators are aware of the mythological elements. Yet the equally important questions of form criticism and orthography are often overlooked. This amply illustrates the need for a combination of disciplines in doing text critical work.

§ 4. 3:22

Guillaume, A. "The Arabic Background of the Book of Job," *Promise and Fulfilment*, 110.
Wolff, H. W. *Hosea* (English translation), 149ff.

> The ones rejoicing unto גיל-,
> They are joyful because they have found a grave.

This has been commonly emended to *gal* which is then interpreted as "burial heap." The reason is an effort to find a parallel with "grave" in the second half of the verse. This emendation has been objected to (e.g., Driver) because *gal* by itself never means "grave" in the OT. Even the whole expression *gal-'ăbānîm* (Josh 7:26; 8:29; II Sam 18:17) does not refer to an ordinary grave. Guillaume agrees with this but compares the Ar word *jāl* which means "inside of the grave." He is followed in this interpretation by Pope.

Most of the versions follow the MT to a greater or lesser extent:

LXX: περιχαρεῖς δὲ ἐγένοντο, ἐὰν κατατύχωσιν "and become exceedingly glad if they are successful."

Vg: *gaudentque vehementer cum invenerint sepulchrum* "and they rejoice greatly when they have found a sepulcher."

Tg: דהוו חדיין לדיצא השתא יחדון ארום ישכחון בית קבורתא "(those) who rejoiced with joy now rejoice that they have found the sepulcher."

The Syr gives a reading which has been used to justify the emendation mentioned above: דחדין ומתכנשין ודיצין כד משכחין קברא "who rejoice and are gathered and leap for joy at finding the grave." However, there is quite a difference between the suggested reading for the Hebrew text and the Syriac rendering. The Syr translator is more likely to be indulging in one of his favorite habits, that of paraphrasing. Dhorme suggests the Syr translator understood the Hebrew phrase as "in a heap," which is still a far cry from "grave." Actually, the root *KNŠ* can mean simply "to die" and does not necessarily imply gathering into a heap. (Lamsa's translation omits the phrase and translates the verse, "Who rejoice exceedingly, and are glad when they can find the grave?" We have no way of knowing what his particular original read, but in any case he seems to be heavily influenced by the AV as his translation so often is.)

While there seems ample evidence of the meaning "side of the interior of a grave" for Ar *jāl*, the other meanings of the word suggest this is a development unique to Ar: "wall of a well, sea wall, slope of a mountain." Both Heb and Ar derive a wide variety of subforms from the basic roots *GLL* and *GWL*, both of which cover the broad semantic area of "go around." Since there is no comparable meaning of "grave" for any of the sub-forms in Heb or the other Semitic languages (even though "heap" is frequent), the most probable inference is that this is an isolated meaning in Ar alone.

MHeb has a noun *gôlēl* which refers to "the gravestone placed before the mouth of the grave," used primarily in reference to a grave tunneled horizontally into a hillside (cf. the stone of Jesus' grave in the Gospels). There appears to be no evidence of such a word in BHeb; consequently, it is quite possible the word was only a post-biblical development.

The traditional interpretation of Job 3:22, "who rejoice to exaltation," itself causes no problem of sense. It seems simply a way of emphasizing the degree of rejoicing, viz., "who rejoice exceedingly." One could perhaps compare the common form of expressing emphasis by using the infinitive absolute with the finite verb. Hos 9:1 also has virtually the same wording. The Hosea passage is commonly emended to "do not rejoice," mainly because of assumed parallelism and the LXX (e.g. Wolff). However, it seems to me one could argue for climactic parallelism in Hosea, with the expected repetition of *'al-tiśmaḥ* elided (cf. similar examples in Ug, UT §§ 13.105, 110, 116). Dhorme, although admitting that the suggested emendation for Job 3:22 is an attractive one, ends up keeping the MT and cites Hos 9:1 with which he apparently finds no difficulty as it stands.

Guillaume offers an interesting suggestion. He mentions an Arabic rhetorical device known as *taurīya* in which a homonym is used as a pivot between two parts of a verse so that one meaning connects with the first part and the other meaning with the second. Thus *gîl* would connect with *haśś^{e}mēḥîm* as a logical follow-up while anticipating the *qeber* which follows. While his own particular connection of the word with Ar *jāl* is rather problematic, the suggestion of a wordplay is still interesting. Wordplays do not require homonyms or even exact phonetic correspondences. The author might very well have written *gîl* for the basic purpose of expressing the idea of "rejoicing" yet have expected that it would suggest *gal* or *gôlēl* or some other word which the reader would then connect--even if rather obliquely--with "grave." Many of the subtleties of ancient Hebrew poetry undoubtedly escape us with the limitations of our present knowledge. Facile emendation could hinder us from doing the necessary probing to discover these literary devices. Whether this is the case here perhaps needs further study. But the emendations thus far suggested, whether based on intra-Hebrew considerations or on Ar cognates, seem to carry less conviction than the text as it stands.

A recent article discusses this passage of Job in the context of trying to solve a similar difficulty in Ps 2:11 (A. A. Macintosh, "The Problems of Psalm II. 11 and 12," JTS 27 [1976], 1-14, esp. 2-8). Arguing on the basis of statements by Saadiah and Ibn Janaḥ, he concludes that *gîl* is an example of *aḍdad*, the use of a word with (apparently) opposite meanings. While Job 3:22 is only a subsidiary example, he suggests the translation, "Which rejoice when they come to (mortal) distress, and are glad when they can find the grave." Without trying to discuss Macintosh' arguments in detail, a couple of comments seem in order. First, Ps 2:11-12 is a notorious *crux*. Even with his lengthy comparative philological arguments, Macintosh cannot avoid resorting to some emendation. (Cf. CPTOT, 284, where emendation is still considered the best solution for this verse.) Second, whatever the merits of the case in regard to Ps 2, I think the arguments advanced above still stand for Job 3:22; i.e., it makes good sense when *gîl* is taken in its well-attested meaning of "rejoicing."

§ 5. 4:18

Behold, he does not put trust in his servants,
And in his messengers he notes תהלה.

This *hapax legomenon* is frequently emended to *tiplāh* ("madness") on the basis of such other passages as Job 24:12. Dillmann compared it with the Geez word *täḥalä* "wander," taking the root to be *THL*. Others have explained it on the basis of Ar *wahila* which can also mean "commit error."

The versions all give a rendering which suggests "folly" or "transgression":

LXX: κατὰ δὲ ἀγγέλων αὐτοῦ σκολιόν τι ἐπενόησεν "and against his angels he observed some crookedness."

Sym: καὶ ἐν ἀγγέλοις αὐτοῦ εὑρήσει ματαιότητα "and in his angels he will find folly."

Vg: *et in angelis suis repperit pravitatem* "and in his angels he finds perverseness."

Tg: ובאזגדוי ישוי עילא "and against his messengers he imputes unrighteousness."

Syr: ובמלאכוהי נסים תמהא "and in his angels he produces amazement."

This rather unified understanding of the versions could be taken as a sign they all understood the correct meaning of the word. On the other hand, the context itself greatly limits the probabilities of meaning, and the versions could simply be guessing from the context. The traditional understanding (e.g. Rashi, Ibn Ezra, David Kimchi) takes the word from the root *HLL* meaning "be deceived, a fool" (*HLL* III in HAL). This fact combined with the specific translations of the versions suggests that most or all of them understood the word to be from that root. Thus, their unity would appear to be more than accidental.

The usual objection to deriving *tohŏlāh* from *HLL* is its peculiar form. Any connection with *HLL* has been labeled "impossible" by Driver and a number of other commentators. BL says the form is "*unsicher*" (497z η). GKC does not appear to comment on it at all. However, Dhorme sees no difficulty with deriving the form from *HLL* since other geminate verbs have peculiar *t*- noun derivatives (cf. the examples given by BL 497z η).

The form could easily come from a root **hly*. Finding such a root, though, is rather difficult. JAram has the word *hălî* or *hălā'* with the meaning "to labor, be faint, be weak." Delitzsch draws on this form to resolve the problem, translating, "And His angels He chargeth with imperfection." There are two problems with this. First, we do not know the origin of the word itself. Both CW and Jastrow compare it with the synonyms *l^ehî* and *l^e'î*. One suspects a case of metathesis. This suspicion becomes further confirmed when a fairly thorough check fails to turn up any other examples of a root **hly* in Semitic. Perhaps the form was somehow influenced by *ḥālāh* whose meaning overlaps it.

Dillmann's comparison with Geez *täḥalä* is interesting and widely cited. But it too has problems. One is the *ḥ* where an *h* should be. This could be simply an intra-Ethiopic problem--perhaps only of orthography--since he also lists the form *tähalä* in his commentary. Yet, secondly, a search through the other Semitic languages fails to turn up a root **thl* anywhere else. This suggests that the root--if indeed *thl*--is an isolated development in Geez.

It would not be too surprising to find the form in question derived from a root **whl*. Ar has such a root in *wahila*, one of whose meanings is "err" (Kazimirsky, 1616). (Dillmann himself compared this Ar word with the Geez *täḥalä*. While the meanings may overlap to some degree, any other connection would seem rather unlikely.) The question is whether this root and meaning is unique to classical Ar. Wehr lists no such meaning in modern written Ar, though the major classical meaning "to fear" is still retained. Nothing turned up in the other Ar dialects checked (though Syrian Ar also has a root with the meaning "to frighten"). In fact the root seems to be missing from all the other major Semitic dialects with the exception of Tigre *wähalā* "wander about." A note in the Littmann-Höfner lexicon reads "Vgl. Ar. *wahila*." One would gather from this note that the authors do not consider this an Ar loanword. If not, this second occurrence of the root would lend more credence to the possibility that it is part of the common Semitic stock.

Yet the one word well attested with a meaning "be foolish" is still *hll*. The drawback is whether the form under discussion could be derived from it. If Dhorme is correct that the derivation is perfectly credible, the traditional connection with *HLL* seems best. This also is the derivation most likely supported by the versions. Otherwise, the connection with Ar *wahila*, while somewhat tenuous from the information thus far available, is another possibility.

§ 6. 5:26; 30:2

Dahood, M. "Northwest Semitic Philology and Job," *The Bible in Current Catholic Thought*, 56.

> You will go בכלח to the grave,
> As a sheaf goes up at its time.
>
> Also what to me is the strength of hands of those
> Upon whom has perished כלח.

The root *KLḤ* occurs only in these two verses in the OT. In both cases the context limits the meaning to something in the range of "old age" or "strength, vigor." Thus, the possibilities of translation have been rather limited. The question to be determined is first of all whether the form is even a legitimate one. Only when this is done can any attempt be made to narrow the meaning further. Dahood has suggested the form in both passages is a "congeneric assimilation of the two words *kōaḥ*, 'strength' and *lēaḥ*, 'freshness.'" Many of the older lexica and commentaries mention Ar *kalaḥa* "contract the face, look hard." Some suggest a "strengthened" (!) form of *KLH*. Tur-Sinai connects with MHeb *qelaḥ* "stalk."

The versions vary widely from one another:

LXX: ἐλεύσῃ δὲ ἐν τάφῳ ὥσπερ σῖτος ὥριμος κατὰ καιρὸν θεριζόμενος "you will come to the grave as ripe grain at the time of harvest."

Vg: *ingredieris in abundantia sepulchrum* "you will go to the grave in abundance," apparently taking the problem word as a form of *KLH*.

Tg: תיעול בשלימות שנייך בכוכא לקבורתא "you will enter the sepulchre chamber in fullness of your years."

Syr: ותעול ניחאית לקברא "and you will go gently to the grave."

The versions at 30:2 likewise seem to be guessing at the meaning of the passage:

LXX (Hexaplaric addition): ἐπ' αὐτοὺς ἀπώλετο συντέλεια "for them has perished completion (of life)."

Aq: ἐπ' αὐτοὺς ἀπώλετο παντελὲς ἐν ὑστερήσει "for them has perished everything in poverty." This seems to take *KLḤ* with the meaning of *KLH*. The last two words translate the first word of v 3 in the MT.

Sym: ἀπώλετο αὐτοῖς πᾶν τὸ πρὸς ζωήν "everything toward life is destroyed for them." Note the similarity with Aquila's verse division, though the word in question seems analyzed as "all" plus "life."

Vg: *et vita ipsa putabantur indigni* "and of life itself they were thought unworthy."

Tg: עילויהון הוביד כוך "upon them is destruction of the grave."

Tg II: אין אתגזר להון להובדא בכוך קבורתא "when they are cut off from perishing in the sepulchre chamber" (see CW I, 357 for an explanation of this statement).

Syr: דעליהון אביד כלה עושנא "upon whom perishes all vigor."

Finding a root *KLḤ* elsewhere in Semitic is not easy. It does not seem to occur in MHeb, in the various Aram dialects, or in Ug. The Ar dialects have the root: In classical and modern written Ar it means "to frown, scowl, look gloomy." As an adjective it seems to refer to a dull coloring. In Syrian Ar it means "be tarnished" and also "to pilfer." A *kalḥûn* noun form means "branch of a vine." The Ar of Marazig has the verbal root with the meaning, "dry up, wither." None of these by itself seems to help us too much.

When we turn to Tur-Sinai's suggestion, however, we find some interesting parallels. The root *QLḤ* is found both in MHeb and JAram with the meaning "tube, stalk, jet of liquid" from which are derived denominative verbs. In Ug what seems to be a divine name occurs in UT 611 but the meaning is uncertain. Various explanations have been offered. Compare "unknown to us and apparently unexplained" ("*nous est inconnu et paraît inexplicable*," Virolleaud in the original publication in *Ugaritica* V, 588), "deified cooking-pot" (De Moor, "Studies . . . II,", 317), "very difficult, but it may be related to the Egyptian *ḳrḥ.t* which was a 'Schutzgott' of a temple or king" (Fisher, "An Ugaritic Ritual," 198, n. 8). Modern written Ar has *qalaḥ* "yellowness of the teeth" and *qaulaḥa* "cob (of corn, and the like)." According to Kazimirski, classical Ar *qalḥama* means "be very old and decrepit." In Syrian Ar *qạlḥan* means "cut the branches of a tree." Along side the *kalḥûn* mentioned above, we also see *qalḥûn* "new, tender branch." In Yemen a *maqlaḥ* is a rod used in measuring the height of a heap of grain to estimate its volume (Landberg, *Glossaire Daṯinois*, 2521-2).

The parallels seem more than accidental. The possible connection between color in classical Ar *kalaḥa* and *qalaḥa* could be pure coincidence. But when we find a similar type of phonetic alternation between Syrian Ar *qalḥûn* and *kalḥûn*, this suggests either two possible pronunciations for this word or perhaps the confusion of two words with somewhat similar meanings which were originally separate. Granted, the phonetic evidence is in Ar alone, though it is well-known Syrian Ar has borrowed quite a bit from Aram. Further, MHeb and JAram have *QLḤ* even if not *KLḤ*. The meaning "be old" for one of the Ar words is itself rather suggestive though very possibly a derived meaning. While the identification may be less direct than normal, it is not just an arbitrary one. It is made on the basis of several semantic connections ("old, stalk, color"), a phonetic variation for which we have attested examples, and the fact that it all fits the imagery of Job 5:26.

The evidence seems strong enough in any case to make us hesitate about emending the text here. The meaning "stalk" as proposed by Tur-Sinai fits 5:26 but seems inappropriate for 30:2. "Old age" would fit both quite well while the similarity in sound (if not a homonym or the same polysemic word) would fit well with the harvesting metaphor. "Stalk" with the idea of ripeness could also be used with the obvious implication of old age.

Dahood's suggestion would not be impossible. Unfortunately, there seems to be no way to prove or disprove it, though one might claim some support in the versions. Considering the linguistic evidence from the whole range of Semitic languages, however, it would seem better to consider the word a legitimate three-radical root. Also while "manly vigor" seems perhaps a bit better for 30:2, it does not go so well in 5:26. Of course, one could accept one solution for one verse and another for the other, but the least complicated explanation is usually the most convincing one. *KLḤ* seems a true variant of the well-known *QLḤ*--not *ex hypothesi* but because of what appear to be actually attested examples of such variants for this root. Though the exact connotation in Job is still tenuous, "old age" seems quite possible for the word and certainly the best meaning for the context of 5:26.

§ 7. 6:10

> And it will still be my comfort,
> ואסלדה in pain which spares not,
> For I have not rejected the words of the
> Holy One.

This word has not usually been rejected outright by recent commentators, though many still express some doubt about its exact meaning. The usual treatment is to compare it with the identical word found in MHeb. Occasionally it has been compared with Ar *ṣalada* ("of a galloping horse which stamps hard with its fore-feet"--Delitzsch).

The versions all translate rather diversely. The LXX, though quite different in part, seems to support the MHeb meaning for this word:

LXX: εἴη δέ μου πόλις τάφος, ἐφ᾽ ἧς ἐπὶ τειχέων ἡλλόμην ἐπ᾽ αὐτῆς, οὐ μὴ φείσωμαι "but let my city upon whose walls I leapt be a grave; I would not draw back."

Vg: *et haec mihi sit consolatio ut adfligens me dolore non parcat* "and this will be my consolation that he spare not in afflicting me with pain."

Tg: ואבוע ברתיתא ולא יחוס על רשיעא "and I will rejoice with trembling that (and) he not spare the wicked." This also gives the idea of quick bodily movement.

Syr: ואשתמלא תוב בחילא דלא חוסן "and I will become perfected again in strength without lack."

The *ṢLD* comparison with Ar has two problems. The first is the irregular phonetic correspondence. The second is its meaning: it would appear the use of the word in reference to a galloping horse is only a derived meaning. The other meanings seem to refer to the idea of being hard, such as "hard soil." It would appear the definition which includes a running horse came about through the sound on the soil rather than the motion of the legs. Unless more convincing evidence can be found, the connection of *SLD* with *ṢLD* seems illegitimate.

In MHeb *SLD* is well-attested in the *qal*. A number of contexts seem to carry some idea of reaction to stimulus, giving the meanings "shrink, rebound, retract." Otherwise, the root appears to be unattested in the rest of the Semitic languages. (However, the word or name *šld* occurs in UT 2041.15. Astour connects this with our Heb word in RSP II, p. 307.) Driver and Tur-Sinai both wish to reject any use of the MHeb to elucidate the biblical word, arguing that the later word originated only in a misunderstanding of this passage (cf. CPTOT, 227f). Four considerations tend to weight the evidence against the negative conclusions of Driver and Tur-Sinai: (1) the word is used most frequently in the *qal* in MHeb and seldom in the *piel* whereas the single occurrence of the word in the OT is a *piel*; (2) none of the instances where used in later Heb seem to have any reference to the biblical passage; (3) the root is sufficiently frequent and diverse in the literature to suggest a common usage rather than a deliberate literary adoption of a word known otherwise only from this passage in Job; (4) the personal name *seled* occurs in 1 Chr 2:30, suggesting that a textual corruption is unlikely.

The translations in the versions could be the result of guessing. Dhorme considers the attestations of the LXX and Tg helpful because they somewhat coincide with the MHeb meaning. Whether they really help us or only suggest possibilities is still a question to me. In any case the MHeb evidence seems strong enough to confirm the correctness of the text at this point, and the context itself narrows the field sufficiently to understand the basic sentence even if the exact connotation of the word may still be uncertain.

§ 8. 6:14; 7:16; 36:5

למס from his friends mercy,
And he forsakes the fear of Shaddai.

מאסתי I will not live forever,
Cease from me for my days are nothingness.

Behold, God is mighty and ימאס not,
Mighty, strong of heart.

Job 6:14 has long been a problem both because of the first word in the verse and because of the awkward syntax. The two other passages have the root *M'S* but the usual meaning "reject, despise" does not seem to fit since neither has an object. Therefore, a number of commentators have connected them with *MSS* or *MSH* with the connotation "melt" or "pine away." The difficult word in 6:14 is also usually taken to be from *MSS*. Pope connects the word of that passage with an Ar root *MSS* meaning "be seized with madness, possessed with a demon."

For 6:14 the versions read as follows:

LXX: ἀπείπατό με ἔλεος, ἐπισκοπὴ δὲ κυρίου ὑπερεῖδέν με "mercy has renounced me, and the visitation of the Lord has disregarded me."

Vg: *qui tollit ab amico suo misericordiam timorem Domini derelinquit* "who takes away mercy from his friend has abandoned fear of the lord."

Tg: לגברא דמנע מן חבריה חסדא ודחלת שדי ישבוק "concerning the man who withholds mercy from his companion, he also forsakes fear of Shaddai."

Syr: דכלא שלמא מן חברה דחלתה דעליא שבק "who withholds peace from his companion abandons fear of the High One."

The versions for 7:16 are the following:

LXX: οὐ γὰρ εἰς τὸν αἰῶνα ζήσομαι "for I will not live forever." No translation is given for *mā'astî*.

Vg: *desperavi nequaquam ultra iam vivam* "I have absolutely no hope; I will live no longer."

Tg: רחיקית דלא לעלם איחי "I loathe that I will not live forever."

Syr: קטעת לי ולא הוא לעלם חי אנא "I am weary and will not live forever."

Here are the versions for 36:5:

LXX: γίγνωσκε δὲ ὅτι ὁ κύριος οὐ μὴ ἀποποιήσηται τὸν ἄκακον "know that the Lord will not reject the innocent."

Vg: *Deus potentes non abicit* "God does not cast away the powerful."

Tg: הא אלהא רבא לא ידחק צדיקא "for God is mighty, he will not press upon the righteous." A textual variant is ירחק "remove."

Syr: הא אלהא עשינא לא מסלא לאינא דדכא איך חלבא "for God is powerful; he will not cast away the one who is pure as milk."

The major lexica tend to connect the forms *M'S* and *MSH* with *MSS*. HAL for example under both *M'S* II and *MSH* states, "By-form of *MSS*." When we turn to MHeb and especially JAram we indeed find that the three roots overlap a great deal. For MHeb the following information can be summarized: *M'S*--"loathe, cast away, reject"; *MSY*--"melt, flow"; *MSS*--"melt, dissolve." All three JAram cognates have the meaning "melt, dissolve, flow" among their definitions. In Syriac and Mandaic only the root *MS'*(Mandaic *MSA*) occurs; it has the meaning "melt, dissolve." Akk appears to have only the one word *mesû* "wash, clean." The existence of any of these roots in Ug is uncertain, partly because of difficulties of determining semantic content. In classical Ar we find *maswat* "flowing milk"; and in Dathina Ar, *mws* "wash, dissolve." Eth has *mäsäwä* "dissolve." Soqotri *myr* is "waste away"; Leslau connects this with the Eth word just listed. (Ar *msy* also means "make lean.")

These data suggest the basic root *MS* carries the connotation "melt, dissolve, waste away," but was filled out in more than one way with a weak radical. Another explanation is that originally distinct roots later became confused because of similar meanings. In any event there seems some justification for assuming the roots *MSS*, *M'S*, and *MSH* can all mean "melt, dissolve" in some contexts.

This knowledge will not necessarily solve all the problems in the three verses in question, but at least the possibility seems supported by the comparative evidence, both in post-biblical Heb and in the other Semitic languages. However, it is only with the connotation "melt" that the terms may be interchangeable; one cannot substitute one for the other indiscriminately. Dhorme at 6:14 claims the meaning of "reject" which is usually associated with *M'S*. He translates, "His friend has scorned compassion and forsaken the fear of Shaddai." This would be an illegitimate connection if he is attempting to relate the root *MSS* to the meaning of *M'S*. (However, though he is not entirely clear, he may be emending to *M'S* rather than attempting to bridge the gap by philology alone.)

Regarding 6:14 Pope states, "The great difficulties commentators find in this line are of their own making. It is a straightforward and simple statement." This may be true, yet his connection with the Ar root *MSS* meaning "be seized with madness; possessed by a demon" is somewhat problematic. The basic idea of the Ar word seems to do with touch and the seizing by madness or a demon a development from that (cf. the colloquial English "be touched" or "touched in the head" for madness). The reason a special development is postulated is that no such meaning for *MSS* in the rest of the Semitic languages is evident. In any case Pope's translation "unfortunate" (see his commentary to the verse) or "sick man" could probably as easily be derived from a word meaning "melt, waste away, despair" as from one meaning "go mad." If so, the net result would be much the same.

The versions in all three passages seem generally to understand the basic idea "reject, withhold, withdraw." This sometimes requires adding an object when there is none in the Heb text. Therefore, with the possible exception of Syr for 7:16, they appear to give no support to the comparative suggestion offered here.

§ 9. 6:16

Dahood, M. "Canaanite-Phoenician Influence in Qoheleth," *Biblica* 33 (1952), 206.

Dietrich, M., and O. Loretz. "Untersuchungen zur Schrift- und Lautlehre des Ugaritischen (I)," WO 4 (1968), 308.

Gaster, T. "The Canaanite Epic of Keret" (review), JQR 37 (1946-7), 289-90.

Ginsberg, H. L. *The Legend of King Keret; a Canaanite Epic of the Bronze Age*, 34 and 45.

Skehan, P. W. "Second Thoughts on Job 6:16 and 6:25," CBQ 31 (1969), 210-12 (= *Studies in Israelite Poetry*, 83-4).

The ones black from ice,
Upon which snow -יתעלם.

The word is often connected with the root ^{c}*RM* "heap up," either by emendation or philology. In the most recent edition of his commentary, Pope takes the word to mean "dark," citing mainly the writings of Dahood.

The versions seem to read according to the Aram meaning of ^{c}*LM* "be strong" (cf. Dhorme):

LXX: οἵτινές με διευλαβοῦντο, νῦν ἐπιπεπτώκασίν μοι ὥσπερ χιὼν ἢ κρύσταλλος πεπηγώς "the ones who (once) respected me now fall upon me as snow or freezing ice."

Vg: *qui timent pruinam inruet super eos nix* "those who fear the hoarfrost, snow pours on them."

Tg: דשחימין מן צינתא עליהון יתחייל תלגא "upon those who are black from the cold the snow is strengthened."

Syr: דדחלין הוו מן גלידא עליהון סגי תלגא "upon those who fear the ice snow increases."

The normal meaning of ᶜ*LM* is somewhat problematic in the verse, at least according to a number of commentators. However, it is accepted with little discussion by Gray ("When the snow hideth itself upon them" which the commentary explains further as "falls upon them, and disappears in them"), Delitzsch ("The melting blocks of ice darken the water of such a wady, and the snow falling together is quickly hidden in its bosom"), and Dillmann (*der schmelzende Schnee verbirgt sich gleichsam, indem er auf . . . die Bäche herabläuft als Wasser* "the melting snow hides itself as it were, in that it runs down into . . . the streams as water"). In the first edition of his commentary, Pope also saw no need for emendation, taking the word snow as the "accusative of material," and translating, "Covered by the melted snow."

Pope's more recent translation, "Darkened with snow," comes from the connection of the word with *ǧlm* in Ug which is supposed to mean "become dark" in some contexts (see Gaster, Ginsberg, Dahood, and apparently Dietrich-Loretz). This meaning for *ǧlm* does not, however, meet with universal approval among Ug scholars. No such definition is found in the glossary of UT, in WUS, or in the glossary of Driver's *Canaanite Myths* (though *ǧlmt* is translated "deep darkness" in this last work). The first identification of the word in Ug, that of Ginsberg, compared it with the Ar *ẓlmt*. (Ug *ǧ* sometimes corresponds to *ẓ* in other Semitic languages--UT § 5:8 and Dietrich-Loretz). The main identification seems to have been made because it appeared to be parallel with Ug *ẓlmt* in UT 51 Frag. 7-8 and 51.7.54-5 (= CTA 8.7-8 and 4.7.54-5). *Ẓlmt* was itself identified by some scholars by comparing it with Ar *ẓlm* and its cognates. Again, though, neither UT nor WUS understand it this way. UT (no. 1053) gives no rendering while Gordon's translations in *Ugarit and Minoan Crete* take both *ẓlmt* and *ǧlmt* as proper names. This does not mean, therefore, that Gordon and Aistleitner are right while Pope, Ginsberg, etc. are wrong; but it shows the difficulty involved with the Ug evidence.

When we turn to the other Semitic languages, we find the

root *$\breve{g}lm$ widespread. None of the other languages appear to show any meaning "dark" or "black" for it, though. (My studies turned up no cognates not already listed in UT, no. 1969, and Brockelmann, 528.) On the other hand, the root *$\d{z}lm$ was also widespread with normal sound correspondences. *$\d{z}lm$ or *$\d{z}ll$ occurs in all the major Semitic languages with the meaning "dark, shadow, black" or something similar. Some have both roots. *$\d{z}lm$: Akk ($\d{s}al\bar{a}mu$), Ar ($\d{z}alima$), Eth ($\d{s}\ddot{a}lm\ddot{a}$), ESA ($\d{z}lm$), Aram (ṬLM?). *$\d{z}ll$: Heb ($\d{s}\bar{a}lal$), Aram (ṬLL', ṬWL'), Ar ($\d{z}alla$), Ug ($\d{z}l$), Akk ($\d{s}illu$), Eth ($\d{s}\ddot{a}l\ddot{a}l\ddot{a}$). Considering the abundant use of these roots throughout Semitic, it is not surprising we do not find another root $\breve{g}lm$ to express the same idea. Since Ug has the root $\d{z}ll$, one might also hesitate to ascribe the same meaning to $\breve{g}lm$ without good evidence. Again, this is not to say that such does not exist in Ug but only to point out the uncertainty of the identification. These data also go against the suggestion that $\breve{g}lm$ is cognate with the root *$\d{z}lm$ in other Semitic languages.

As already noted the versions seem to understand ^{C}LM in the sense of "be strong" which it has in Aram. This fits English idiom but is less likely to be used in Aram in reference to snow. The reason is that the word is a denominative verb from the noun "youth" or adjective "youthful." The notion of "be strong, sturdy" develops from this and would thus appear to be inappropriate as a reference to snow. This possibility would probably also require an Aram borrowing since that meaning is otherwise unattested in Heb. Unless examples can be found which would illustrate the use of ^{C}LM "be strong" in this type of context, this suggestion would have to be considered unlikely.

The translation of ^{C}LM in Job 6:17 as "be dark," while suggestive and fitting to the context, seems best abandoned unless firmer evidence for a root *$\breve{g}lm$ meaning "be dark" can be adduced. Some plausible reasons can be given for keeping the normal meaning "hide" as mentioned above. Skehan has made what seems a good case for believing the poet wanted the meaning of ^{C}RM "heap up" but used the somewhat similar ^{C}LM because it better suited the phonetic effect he desired. (Skehan seems to have been anticipated in this by Dhorme but discusses the subject at greater length.) If he is correct, this illustrates how a better understanding of the various devices used in Hebrew poetry could solve many of the *cruces* we now find in the text. Of course, we cannot rule out an aural confusion between *L* and *R*, or even some dialectical variation such as apparently occurs between normal *'arm^{e}nôtâw'* and *'alm^{e}nôtâw* in Ezek 19:7 and Isa 13:22.

§ 10. 6:17

Driver, G. R. "Some Hebrew Medical Expressions," ZAW 65 (1953), 261.

> In the time יזרבו they are exterminated,
> When it is hot they are extinquished from
> their place.

This *hapax legomenon* is often related to *ṢRB* "scorch," especially among the older commentators. One reason is the parallelism created between it and *b^{e}ḥummô* when this is done. Dhorme, along with a number of commentators including Driver and Pope, refers to the Ar *zariba* "flow away."

The versions do not give much help since there is no consistent rendering:

LXX: καθὼς τακεῖσα θέρμης γενομένης οὐκ ἐπεγνώσθη ὅπερ ἦν "when it melts away at the coming of heat, it is not recognized what it was."

Vg: *tempore quo fuerint dissipati peribunt* "at the time that they are dispersed, they will perish."

Tg: בעידן דחבו דר טובענא אישתרבבו. There seems to be some disagreement about how to translate this verse when the lexica of Jastrow (1627) and CW (II, 516) are compared. One possibility seems to be, "In the time of the Flood when they sinned, they were scorched (by the sun)." Another is, "In the time of the Flood when they sinned, they sank (below the surface)."

Syr: ובשעתא דדנח בהון פשרין "in the time when (the sun) arises over them, they melt."

The connection with *ṢRB* is somewhat dubious, the major problem being the irregular phonetic correspondence for the first radical. When we come to *ZRB*, on the other hand, we have no trouble finding cognates. In JAram the *itpeal* of the root means "overflow, be poured out." Syriac has *zarbā'* "rush of water." In modern written Ar, *zariba* "flow (water)" and *mizrāb* "spout" occur. The same verb form is found in classical Ar along with *zirb* "conduit." Dathina Ar has the verb ("flow") and the noun *mazrāb* "gutter, channel." Leslau (*Contributions*) cites Tigrinya *'an-zärbäbä* "collect water falling from the roof." In what appears to be a case of metathesis, we find the root *RZB* in several of the branches of Semitic: JAram--*marzēb* "canal"; Syriac--*marzibā'* "conduit"; modern written Ar--*mirzāb* "waterspout, gargoyle"; classical Ar--*mirzāb* "conduit"; Dathina Ar--*marzāb* "gutter." The only major branch where the root is apparently lacking is East Semitic. Driver and others have cited a word *zarābu* with the meaning "press, squeeze" which they related to the Heb. But CAD simply refers the reader to *ṣarāpu*, by which I assume that any identification of a root *zarābu* has been abandoned. Under *ṣarāpu* is the following note in CAD: "There seems to be no reason to assume a mng. 'to press' or the like . . . on the basis of an Arabic etymology. All the refs. are shown to belong to *ṣarāpu*, 'to burn,' by the Sum[erian] correspondences attested in vocabulary and bilingual passages" (pp. 103-4).

There is no question of the existence of a root *ZRB* with the meaning "flow" or something similar as a part of common Semitic. The root *RZB* also seems sufficiently attested to be considered a metathesis of the same root. While the meaning "scorch" makes nice parallelism, it does not seem to have enough evidence to back it up. Perhaps again we have a word play in which the poet used *ZRB* because of its similarity in sound to *ṢRB*. The comparative evidence, though, strongly favors the meaning, "In the time of their flowing, they perish," for 6:17a. This is possibly supported by the Vg rendering.

§ 11. 7:12

Barr, J. "Ugaritic and Hebrew *šbm*?" JSS 18 (1973), 17-39.

Dahood, M. "*mišmār* 'muzzle' in Job 7,12," JBL 80 (1961), 270-1.

Loewenstamm, S. "The Muzzling of the Tannin in Ugaritic Myth," IEJ 9 (1959), 260-1.

______. "Anat's Victory over the Tunnanu," JSS 20 (1975), 22-7.

Am I the sea or Tannin,
That you set over me משמר.

The basic meaning of this passage seems never to have been in question until very recently. On the basis of the identification of a root *šbm* meaning "muzzle" in Ug, Dahood suggested an identical Heb root for several pasages. One of these was Ps 68:23. Dahood compared the imagery of that passage with Job 7:12 and suggested *mišmār* should also be translated "muzzle."

The versions all more or less support the MT:

LXX: ὅτι κατέταξας ἐπ' ἐμὲ φυλακήν; "that you set over me a guard?"

Vg: *quia circumdedisti me carcere* "that you have enclosed me in a prison?"

Tg: ארום תמני עלי מטרא. Tg II: ארום תשוי עלי נטירא. Both translate essentially as "that you place a guard over me." Tg I refers to Pharaoh and the event at the Red Sea for comparison. Tg II, while also somewhat paraphrastic, is closer to the MT. But in both cases the specific clause in question is translated quite literally.

Syr is also very literal: דמקים אנת עלי נטורא.

Barr's article seems an exemplary piece of comparative philological work to which I have little to add. Therefore, primarily only a summary of the major points is given here. No attempted rebuttal of Barr's arguments by Dahood has come to my attention.

The root *šbm* occurs in three passages of Ug literature: UT Anat (= CTA 3) 2.16 and 3.37; 1003.8. (It may also occur in UT 49.1.2 = CTA 6.1.29, but this is disputed because of a damaged text.) The word is usually taken to mean "muzzle" in the latter two. Its meaning in the first passage is, to quote Gordon, "problematic." In the initial translation by Virolleaud, it was compared with Ar *šibām*. In Part II of his article Barr calls into question the Ar evidence on which basis the Ug word was first translated. Without my repeating his arguments, Barr adduces reasons for doubting the existence --or at least any significant use--of an Ar word *šibām* meaning "muzzle." To quote him, "Thus, to sum up the argument so far, the Arabic evidence upon which the original identification in Ugaritic was made is very weak, so weak indeed that an identification made purely on the basis of the context in Ugaritic, and thus depending on no cognate evidence whatever, could hardly be said to be weaker" (24). (Barr does not mention the modern dialects in this part of the article, but none of the dialect sources used for the present thesis has a *šbm* "muzzle.")

In Part III Barr discusses the earlier article of Loewenstamm which, while showing some weaknesses of the initial defining of *šbm*, attempted to support it with Akk evidence. The Akk evidence also turned out to be as problematic as the Ar, depending on three unusual sound correspondences for one root (a metathesis, a *p* for a *b*, and an *s* for an expected *š*), a doubtful semantic argument, and a reconstruction of a text which other Akkadian scholars regard as erroneous. (In his 1975 article Loewenstamm noted that "Barr's criticism of the present writer's paper on the muzzling of the Tannin is basically sound," 24.)

Part IV is an attempt to find the meaning of Ug *šbm* through comparative philology. There is no need for discussion on this here except to note that "muzzle" does not seem the most appropriate sense for the Ug contexts, anyway, and some other possible cognates have meanings which are more suitable. Part V is a reinvestigation of the Ug passages, the state of the text and the semantics of the individual contexts. Part VI gives Barr's concluding remarks. The major one which concerns us here is that to reconstruct a Hebrew root *ŠBM* "on the basis of this Ugaritic, must be deemed precarious" when the Ug itself is very uncertain. (In his latest article Loewenstamm argues for a meaning along the lines of "bind, tie," perhaps with a net-type ensnarement. This new proposal does not, however, remove the difficulties from Dahood's suggestion for a new reading of Job 7:12.)

Interestingly enough, Pope does not accept Dahood's proposal even though he is convinced of a Hebrew root *ŠBM* "muzzle" for other passages in the OT. He writes: "The consideration which deters the present writer from accepting this interpretation here is the impression that it does not suit the context. There is nothing to suggest that God is attempting to silence Job. What Job complains of is the constant harassment and surveillance which God maintains (cf. vss. 18-20) and this accords perfectly with the normal meaning of *mišmār* as 'guard, watch.'"

§ 12. 8:14

Reider, Joseph. "Etymological Studies in Biblical Hebrew," VT 4 (1954), 288-9.

> Whose confidence יקוט,
> And his trust is a spider's house.

This *hapax* is often emended. Some have accepted Saadiah's famous translation "gossamer" or a similar rendering which forms a parallel with "spider's house." Tur-Sinai connects with Ar *waqṭ* "hole which collects rainwater." There is also the question of whether the word is a noun or a verb.

With the exception of the LXX the versions all seem to take the word as a verb, but there is considerable diversity in translation:

LXX: ἀοίκητος γὰρ αὐτοῦ ἔσται ὁ οἶκος "for his house will be uninhabited."

Vg: *non ei placebit vecordia sua* "his senselessness will not please him." This seems to understand the root *QWṬ* "loathe" and *KSL* in the sense of "foolish."

Tg: די תזוח סבריה "whose hope gives way."

Syr: ונתפסק תוכלנה "whose confidence will be broken."

The question of the root of the word is a problem. Some take it to be *QWṬ* but *QṬṬ* seems equally possible (cf. HAL, Delitzsch, GB). In fact the root *QWṬ* is somewhat scarce in the Semitic languages; however, *QṬṬ* is widespread. *QṬṬ* occurs with the meaning "cut" in MHeb. The root does not appear to occur in any of the Aram dialects, though *QṬH* is found in JAram with the meaning "bite off, eat" (also in MHeb with the meaning "cut off, shorten, make small"). The root also seems to be absent from Akk. In Ug we find *qṭṭ* "transgress" according to UT. WUS lists a root *qṭṭ* "break up" but takes it only from an obscure context in a hippic text (UT 56.22); thus the identification seems uncertain. Both classical and modern written Ar have *qaṭṭa* "cut, carve." In Southeast Semitic, no root seems to occur in ESA. Mehri has a word *qôṭa'* "cut, hack" but it seems to be more directly related to Ar *qṭ*^{c}. In the Eth languages are several words which seem likely to be related to a Heb *QṬṬ*. Geez has *qäṭqäṭä* "break, break in pieces"; Tigre, *qēṭäṭä* "strike a blow" and *qäṭqäṭa* "push, knock, crush"; Harari, *qiṭäqäṭa* "hammer, pound." All of these may not ultimately be directly related to *QṬṬ*, but some of them seem definitely cognates.

Tur-Sinai's suggested connection with Ar *waqṭ* has several problems with it. First, the root seems to be unique to Ar. The noun form itself may also be a later development in Ar since the verb means "throw something violently to the ground" (Kazimirsky, 1585). Finally, his translation, "Whose hope shall be a water-hole," does not itself make the best sense.

Saadiah's reading חבל אלשמס "thread of the sun" is intriguing. Reider is probably correct in supposing Saadiah took the etymology of *yāqôṭ* from biblical Aram *qayiṭ* "summer," cognate to Hebrew *qayiṣ*. Yet Saadiah's rendering is a further interpretation since the Aram word means only "summer" by itself (Vogt, 150) and not "gossamer." Fleischer, in a footnote to the passage in Delitzsch, further discounts any connection between Saadiah's translation and Ar parallel expressions. According to him no expression "thread of the sun" is used in Ar.

Ultimately, the connection with a spider's gossamer is a desire to find a parallel to the second half of the verse. Is this looking for a parallel which the poet did not put there? From the cognate evidence, any emendation of the word seems baseless. A basic meaning "cut" makes sense in the verse. This does not settle the question of whether the word is a verb or noun. The versions generally take it as a verb, but a noun would also make sense. Yet the basic meaning should be the same in either case. However, it seems that Saadiah's interesting translation does not have enough of a philological basis to make it acceptable. The most probable translation is, "Whose confidence breaks," or "Whose confidence is fragile." This appears to be the way the Tg and Syr take it.

§ 13. 9:12

Dahood, M. "Some Northwest-Semitic Words in Job," *Biblica* 38 (1957), 310.

______. "Ugaritic and Phoenician or Qumran and the Versions," *Orient and Occident*, 55.

Wheeler, S. B. "The Infixed -*t*- in Biblical Hebrew," JANESCU 3 (1970-1), 20-31.

If he יחתף, who will turn him back,
Who will say to him, "What are you doing?"

It is fairly common to relate the root *ḤTP* to *ḤṬP*, if not actually to emend to the latter. Dahood (1957 article) as "a mere possibility" proposed to emend the clause to *hēn yaḥat pāmî yešîbennû*, translating, "If He should snatch away, who could resist Him?" He was followed in this by Blommerde. In the later article Dahood suggested *YḤTP* might be an infixed -*t*- form of *ḤPP* "surround, enclose."

The versions differ somewhat, though Sym and Tg translate as if they understand *ḤTP* to mean the same as *ḤṬP*:

LXX: ἐὰν ἀπαλλάξῃ, τίς ἀποστρέψει; "if he takes away (sets free), who will turn (him) back?"

Sym: ἰδοὺ ἀναρπάσει "behold, he will snatch away."

Vg: *si repente interroget quis respondebit ei* "if he unexpectedly inquires, who will reply to him?"

Tg: הא יחתף אינש בעלמא "behold, he merely snatches a man." According to the lexica, the Tg root *ḤTP* means the same as *ḤṬP*. One might suspect the translator of the Tg simply took over the Heb word since the root occurs only here in targumic literature. However, *ḤTP* is also used by Syr to translate Heb *ŠBR* (e. g. Ps 29:5). Although the Qumran targum is not extant for this section of the book, *ḤTPWHY* "his snatchers" occurs in 11QtgJob 2:2 and seems to translate Heb *gedûdâw* "his bands" of

Job 19:12. The root also exists in Mandaic (see below). This indicates the root is common Aram.

Syr: הא אן תבר מנו נפקוד באידה "behold, if he smashes, who will require it from his hand."

A root *ḤTP* seems too well attested to be dismissed lightly. It occurs in Prov 23:28 with the meaning something like "thief, robber" (cf. HAL and GB, though BDB takes it as "prey"). The root also occurs several times in the Hebrew fragments of Ben Sira (15:14; 32:21; 50:4) and is found at Qumran (IQH 5:10). One might argue that the *Hodayot* and Ben Sira use is a literary borrowing from the OT text. That is possible though none of the passages appear to contain direct allusions to the verse here in Job.

The lexica of JAram take the root *ḤTP* as equivalent to *ḤṬP*. Although the root does not appear to occur outside the one place in the Tg to Job 9:12, it seems to be genuine Aram (see the discussion above in reference to Tg). A word *ḤTPY* of uncertain meaning is found in DISO. In Syriac both roots are attested, *ḤTP* with the meaning "break." Mandaic has primarily the spelling *ḤṬP* for "snatch away, carry off" but occasionally *HTP* (for the shift of initial *Ḥ* to *H* in Mandaic, see Macuch, *Handbook*, p. 80). This could be a simple orthographic variant but may possibly represent two separate roots with similar meanings (Nöldeke, *Mandäische Gram.*, p.42 n., thinks this an old variant). Akk *ḫaṭāpu* is uncertain in meaning according to AHW, while *ḫatāpu* means "slaughter." Ug does not seem to have either root. Ar has no root *ḫtf*. *Ḫaṭafa* means "snatch, seize." (The word *ḥatf* "death" has been suggested as a cognate of Heb *ḤTP*.)

The data are not what one would call overwhelming, yet there is some evidence of either a phonetic variation between *Ṭ* and *T* in the root *ḤṬP* or two roots (*ḤṬP* and *ḤTP*) with an overlap of semantic area. The meanings "break" and "slaughter" may not be too closely related to "seize, plunder." However, in the realm of gross semantics--which is the only area we can deal with in questions of etymology--they are not necessarily so far apart. Whether the Ar *ḥatf* "death" is also a cognate is a question. If so, the existence of Ar *ḫaṭafa* along side it might argue against a simple phonetic variation

ḤṬP, *ḤTP*. But the other possibility cannot be ruled out from the data so far seen. The Northwest Semitic evidence (JAram, Syr, extra-biblical Hebrew) is the strongest, a point of no little weight.

While Dahood's suggestion that *YḤTP* is from *ḤPP* is not couched in dogmatic terms, he still defends the identification of infixed -*t*- forms in Heb. Wheeler's article has examined the major passages and words in which an identification had been made and demonstrated that such is very unlikely for most of them (cf. also CPTOT, 253). As a passing rebuttal Dahood cited Isa 50:6 which has *HSTRTY* (claimed as an infixed -*t*- form of *SWR*) in the MT whereas 1QIs[a] has *HSYRWTY*. Dahood concludes this supports his argument about infixed -*t*- forms in Heb even though he does not say exactly how it is supposed to do so.

However, there is no reason to see anything unusual in the 1QIs[a] form as compared with the MT. II Chr 30:9 reads "he will not turn (his) face from you" (*wᵉlō̄'-yāsîr pānîm mikkem*) which is very similar to the wording of Isa 50:6 in 1QIs[a] (*PNY LW' HSYRWTY*). To "turn the face from the smiters" is semantically equivalent to "hide the face from the smiters" in the context. It is not surprising to find two slightly different traditions of wording at this point. This in no way implies the MT consonantal text conceals an original infixed -*t*- form. Wheeler and Barr have already demonstrated that *STR* with "face" is the root *STR* and not an infixed -*t*- form of *SWR*. The citation of 1QIs[a] adds nothing to Dahood's argument. This is not to say there may not be a few such forms, but they seem rare. Any proposed identification must be carefully scrutinized individually and hasty generalizations avoided.

The identification based on an infixed -*t*- form must be rejected in the absence of clear demonstration for the existence of the form in Heb generally and for this root specifically. Dahood's suggestion would also require a revocalization of the MT *yaḥṭōp*, though he does not comment on that. His earlier suggestion (1957 article) would require even more changes. It may involve "no consonantal changes," but one could hardly see what advantage that is when both pointing and word division are drastically altered. Could one in any sense of the word label his rearrangement "simpler" or "less drastic" than the one change of *ḤTP* to *ḤṬP*?

Yet the comparative philological evidence seems strong enough to keep the MT *ḤTP* without change. Several translations are possible in the context, including "snatch," "break," "slaughter," all of which could receive some support from the cognate languages. Sym, Tg, Syr, and possibly LXX seem to support the MT in this basic sense as well.

§ 14. 10:17

Dahood, Mitchell. *Psalms I*, 197.

> You renew עדיך against me;
> And you increase your anger at me,
> Relief troops upon me.

The traditional understanding of the word has been "your witnesses." However, this has been thought not to fit the supposed parallelism and other imagery in the verse. Ehrlich compared with Ar ^{c}*dy* "be hostile," in which he was followed by Dhorme and Pope. Dahood compared with Ar and Ug *ǧadda* "swell up, be irritated."

The versions read as follows:

LXX: ἐπανακαινίζων ἐπ᾽ ἐμὲ τὴν ἔτασίν μου "renewing my trial against me." A variant reading is "your trial."

Aq and Th (from Syro-Hexapla): ἀνεκαίνισας μάρτυράς σου κατέναντί μου "you renewed your witnesses against me."

Sym (from Syro-Hexapla): καὶ ἀνακανίζεις σεαυτῷ ἀντικείμενον (s. ὑπεναντίον) μοι "and you renew for yourself an adversary against me."

Vg: *instauras testes tuos contra me* "you renew your witnesses against me."

Tg: תחדית סהדיך לקבלי "you renew your witnesses against me."

Syr: ומחרא אנת זינך לוקבלי "you prepare your weapon to fight against me."

A root *^{c}*dw* with some approximation to the meaning "snatch" seems to exist in several of the Semitic languages.

JAram has ^{c}*DY* "plunder" (in the *afel*). Similarly the Syr verb means "lay hold, snatch" in the *afel*. Mandaic *ADA* (II) means "sever, remove." Imperial Aram has ^{c}*DY* "remove" in the *hafel* (Vogt, 123-4). Ar (including both classical and the modern written language) has ^{c}*dw* meaning "treat as an enemy" in the III and other stems. There are also noun forms such as ^{c}*adāwa* "enmity, hostility." Geez has ^{c}*adäwä* "pass by" while the root ^{c}*dy/w* is found in a number of Eth dialects with a similar meaning. In ESA is ^{c}*dw* "pass over." It is interesting that the meaning "rob, plunder" or "be hostile" seems to occur only in the derived stems rather than as the more general meaning (which is usually something like "pass"). Perhaps there is a connection between Heb ^{c}*ad* "prey, booty" and the *afel/hafel* forms of the Aram words meaning "snatch, plunder." One could even conceive of a connection between those and the Ar "be hostile." But this latter is stretching things a bit, and GB specifically rejects such a connection (565). A secondary development in Ar seems much more likely. Thus, the argument based on the Ar evidence seems extremely weak.

The attestation of a root **ǧdd* as common to the Semitic stock is rather skimpy. Ar definitely has it, primarily with the idea of glandular swelling because of disease. It has also been generally accepted as existing in Ug. However, it must be noted that the only actual occurrence is once in UT Anat (= CTA 3).2.25. In UT 131 (= CTA 7.1).7 it is a restoration. In the Anat passage the first two letters of the word are damaged though still clearly visible according to the autograph. The photograph in CTA was illegible to me at this point. The question could perhaps be settled by a direct examination of the actual tablet, but one must at least wonder whether *ǧdd* is as certain in Ug as is sometimes assumed. If not, any attempt to find it in Heb is that much more precarious.

Even if one granted that the proposed cognate evidence was unquestionable, it would still be necessary to ask whether the MT reading "witness" is not perfectly acceptable for Job 10:17. The comparative material is usually adduced because "witnesses" is thought to be out of place with "anger" and "troops." This brings up the question of parallelism which will be dealt with in further detail in Chapter III. However, the last part of the verse is a bit of a problem to translate, anyway. It is, furthermore, important to note that form critics have tended to find "witness" quite fitting for the context. Forensic language is widely used, court imagery being generally accepted as one of the major forms in the book. For example, G. Fohrer comments on v 17 as follows, beginning with the end of v 16:

> Selbst wenn Hiob im Recht wäre, ginge Gott in erschreckender Weise gegen ihn vor, um ihn für schuldig zu erklären. 17 Zu diesem Zweck stellte Gott immer neue Zeugen gegen Hiob auf, wie vor Gericht derartige Zeugen beizubringen sind, um Schuld oder Unschuld zu erweisen . . . . So brächte Gott Zeugen für die Schuld Hiobs bei. Das besagt, dass er neue Leiden über Hiob heraufführte, die nach der Vorstellung des Vergeltungsglaubens als Strafe für eine Schuld und damit zugleich als Zeugen für diese Schuld gelten. So fürchtet Hiob, Gott werde, um ihn unter allen Umständen für schuldig zu befinden, seinen Zorn (<<Unmut>>; vgl. zu 5,2) noch steigern und immer neuen mühseligen <<Frondienst>> über ihn verhängen. Die Unzahl der Leiden Hiobs erfüllte schliesslich den Zweck, den Gott seit jeher beabsichtigt hat: Hiob wäre als schuldig hingestellt.

> Even if Job were in the right, God would still procede against him in an alarming manner to show him guilty. 17 For this purpose God continually brings forward new witnesses as such witnesses are customarily arraigned to prove guilt or innocence . . . . So God produces witnesses for Job's guilt. This means that he lays on Job new sufferings which, according to the belief in recompense, serve both as punishment for guilt and as proof of it. Thus, Job fears that God would increase his anger ("displeasure"; cf. 5:2) and continually add new harsh "drudgery" in order to find him guilty under any circumstances. The unlimited sufferings of Job ultimately fulfill this purpose which God had in mind all along: Job is to be considered guilty.

Compare also Westermann (*Der Aufbau des Buches Hiob*, 49) and Horst on the passage.

The MT "witnesses" causes no real linguistic problems since the verse is perfectly understandable with this reading. It also fits in quite well with the overall structure and literary forms of the book. Of course, one might argue this caused the corruption of an original "hostilities" or "petulance." However, the cognate evidence produced to back up the proposed change is itself skimpy and problematic. Ultimately, the real reason for a change seemed the desire to find a parallel with "anger." One would gather the Ar words were brought forward to keep from being totally arbitrary in emending or retranslating the text. Thus, it is not surprising the evidence seems rather contrived when scrutinized more closely. Aq, Th, Vg, and Tg all support the normal reading of the MT.

§ 15. 15:12

Why does your heart take you away,
And why do your eyes ירזמון-?

The word is often compared with the root *rmz* in cognate languages and thought to be a case of metathesis or a simple transcriptional error. The versions seem to understand it that way for the most part, assuming they had the same reading as the MT:

LXX: ἢ τί ἐπήνεγκα οἱ ὀφθαλμοί σου "or upon what have your eyes laid?" This may presume a different Heb text (cf. Schleusner I, 892, and Dhorme).

Vg: *et quasi magna cogitans adtonitos habes oculos* "and (why) do you have astonished eyes as if thinking great things?"

Tg: ומה מרמזין עינך "and why are your eyes winking?"

Syr: ומנא מרמזן עיניך "and why do your eyes wink?"

A root *rmz* is found in several major branches of Semitic with the meaning "wink" or some similar movement of the eyes: MHeb, JAram, Syriac, Mandaic, classical and modern written Ar. It seems to be unattested in Ug, Akk, and the Southeast Semitic languages.

We look for a root **rzm* with some disappointment. Ar (both classical and modern) has *razama* with a variety of meanings but none relating to the eyes. Any connection with Heb *RZM* in Job 15:12 would appear somewhat doubtful. Geez has the noun *märzäm* or *märz^{e}m* with the meaning "staggering, turning, trembling." One might argue this is a borrowing of the OT Heb root, but that seems unlikely. The possible support from Eth is interesting, but even without it one would hesitate to eliminate the peculiar reading of Job 15:12. The fact that a few manuscripts have *RMZ* only reinforces the antiquity of the reading since scribes would tend to assimilate to the better-known root.

At this point we need to consider briefly a subject which will be dealt with at greater length in Chapter III. If a root is sufficiently well attested to be considered common to the Semitic languages, we should expect to find it in each major language or certainly in each major branch of Semitic. If it does not appear, we have to ask why. A word may not appear for several reasons. For example, it may not appear in Ug simply because our corpus of literature is so small. It may not appear in Akk because Sumerian influence helped to uproot it. But if it appears in MHeb and a number of the Aram dialects, we should not be surprised to see it in BHeb. Yet instead of an expected *RMZ*, we find *RZM* with the very meaning we would suppose the sought-after *RMZ* to have. Furthermore, we find no *RMZ* along side this *RZM*. One would therefore assume a metathesis with a good deal of confidence. We are not comparing two isolated forms and postulating a metathesis. We are, rather, looking at the whole system and filling in an obvious gap. When the broad picture is considered, *RZM* seems clearly a metathesis of a common root PS **rmz*. This picture is reinforced by the Geez form.

§ 16. 15:29

Dahood, M. "Northwest Semitic Philology and Job," 60-1.

> He will not be rich and his strength will
> not rise,
> And מנלם will not stretch to the earth.

The word as a hapax is often emended. Dahood, however, takes *'ereṣ* as "netherworld" and compares *minlām* with Ar *nāla* "give, donate" (following the suggested etymologies in Zorell). He revocalizes to *m^e^nōlem* and translates, "And his possessions will not go down to the nether world."

LXX: οὐ μὴ βάλῃ ἐπὶ τὴν γῆν σκιάν "he will not cast a shadow upon the earth." Orlinsky has convincingly argued that σκιάν here is a corruption of ῥίζαν "root" (HUCA 33 [1962], 136-9).

Vg: *nec mittet in terra radicem suam* "neither does he send his root into the earth." Jerome is probably following the original text of the LXX at this point (so Orlinsky, *ibid.*).

Tg: ולא יתמתח לארעא מנהון ולהלהון טבתא דדתן ואבירם "and nothing from them will be extended to the earth and to these (belong) the goods of Dathan and Abiram."

Syr: ולא נרמא מלא על ארעא "and he will not set words upon the earth."

The Hebrew root of *minlām* would appear to be *NLH* from the MT vocalization. However, it is difficult to find such a root elsewhere. Isa 33:1 appears to have this root though often thought to be corrupt. Otherwise, I could find no **nly* or **nlw* elsewhere in Semitic. Ar has *nāla* which means "to obtain, possess" in both the classical and modern written languages. The noun *nail* means "favor, attainment, acquisition." The semantics of the root would fit well in Job 15:29, but the MT pointing seems to think of a final *yod* rather than a medial *yod*. Even if one decides to revocalize as Dahood does, the problems are not solved. The reason is that we have no corroboration of the Ar data. Is this perhaps only a special development within Ar? If one has to revocalize the attested form, why not simply emend to an easier reading all around? One could of course postulate a root which is medial *yod* in Heb but appears as final *yod* in Ar, thus eliminating the need for any sort of change.

Dahood suggests the root may also occur in the Phoen inscription of Tabnit (KAI 13.7). However, the reading *YNL* is generally taken to be an error for *YKN LK* (see KAI commentary; Rosenthal's translation in ANET, 662). Both Torrey (JAOS 57 [1937], 405) and Gevirtz (VT 11 [1961], 149, n. 4) argue the Phoen word does indeed contain the root *NWL*. If correct, this is evidence outside Ar and would certainly strengthen the case. Yet one must not overlook the difficulties with the Phoen (and Akk?--so Gevirtz) material. Aram has one or more *NWL* roots (JAram, Syriac, modern dialects) but the various senses do not seem appropriate ("to be weak, suffer pain," "nightmare," "loom, weaver's beam"). One could no doubt imagine an idiom in which "stretching their weaver's beam on the earth" had meaning. However, if we stick to substance rather than conjecture, the Aram material seems of little help.

The evidence is very skimpy, no matter how it is viewed. One must also consider whether it is more credible to keep the consonantal text but revocalize on the basis of cognate evidence as Dahood does, or simply to consider the text corrupt and emend more boldly as has generally been done in the past. Is the revocalized form any more acceptable than the MT form as it stands? However, a consideration of the versions also suggests caution about emending. The original LXX, the Tg (though somewhat midrashic here), and the Vg all seem to have had the same reading as our present MT consonantal form. The Syr also may have had the same text as well. The diverse renderings appear as simply the result of trying to make sense out of a difficult form on the basis of context alone. While not proving the correctness of the forementioned comparative suggestion, the versions tend to bolster the legitmacy of using comparative philology at this point. This is an example of how the versions may be of definite value simply by helping confirm the pristine character of the MT. (If the MT is retained, one might think of a translation such as, "Their possessions will not spread upon the earth.")

§ 17. 16:18

Dahood, M. "Northwest Semitic Philology and Job," *The Bible in Current Catholic Thought*, 61-2.

Nida, E. "Implications of Contemporary Linguistics for Biblical Scholarship," JBL 91 (1972), 73-89.

_____. "Semantic Structure and Translating," BT 26 (1975), 120-32.

Earth, do not cover my blood,
And let there be no מקום for my cry.

Although the word has usually been taken in its more usual sense of "place," Dahood proposed the meaning "burial-place" because of Aramaic inscriptions which also used *māqôm* in that sense. Dahood is followed in this interpretation by Pope who translates "tomb."

The versions all render with general words which usually have the broad connotation "place" in the respective languages: LXX--τόπος; Sym--στάσις; Tg--אתר; Syr--אתרא. The Vg is less literal with *neque inveniat locum in te latendi clamor meus* "neither let my complaint find a hiding place in you." If they understood the sense "tomb" or "burial-place," the versions did not indicate by any sort of word which would normally fit such a narrow sense.

The definition "tomb" for *MQM/MQWM* is found in DISO as a "specific sense" of the more general "place" (cf. also Gibson, II, p. 72). The glossaries of Harris (*Phoenician Grammar*), Segert (*Altaram. Gram.*; *Gram. of Phoen.*), and KAI, however, give only the definition "place" for Phoenician and/or Aram. The root occurs in Ug only in the Keret text in the stereotyped phrase *yd.mqmh* of uncertain meaning (e. g., Keret 2.54 = CTA 14.2.54). Sample translations are "a portion of her estate" (Gordon, *Ugarit*, 102), "a portion of his estate" (Driver, *Canaanite Myths*, 30-1), "token of her value" (Gray *Krt Text*, 12; also 50-1 for a discussion). Otherwise, the word is attested only in Ar *maqām*, with a usage somewhat similar to Heb.

Barr has already discussed the question briefly (CPTOT, 291-2). He distinguishes between the "reference" and "information" of a word. A person may refer to a tomb by the term *māqôm*. This does not mean that one can give the definition "tomb" to *māqôm* if the word carries only the more general information of "place." To this observation might be added those of Eugene Nida. In his 1975 article Nida discusses the various ways of relating different lexical units. One of these he calls "included" (123). That is, one lexical unit includes one or more lexical units within itself. The word "animal" includes "dog." In the same way *māqôm* includes "tomb," along with an almost infinite number of other specific entities within itself. Only the context reveals what the more specific *māqôm* in question is.

The question of context is of upmost importance: "The individual word is thus largely meaningless apart from context and it is only within the various contexts that the semantic structure of any word or semantic unit can and must be defined" ("Contemporary Linguistics," 77). Furthermore, "the correct meaning of any term is that which contributes least to the total context, or in other terms, that which fits the context most perfectly" (*ibid.*, 86). Thus, if the context of *māqôm* does not define it more specifically, we do violence to the principles of language operation to try to apply any but its broad connotation.

These are general principles. When we look at the specific contexts where *māqôm* is supposed to mean "tomb," there is no compelling evidence for such a meaning. For example, the references in DISO are to KAI 9, 14, and 214. As well as *MQM* KAI 9.3 also contains the more specific word *MŠKB* "resting place." KAI 14 in addition to *MQM* (line 4) has *QBR* twice (lines 3 and 8) and *MŠKB* several times (lines 4-8, 10, and 21). With specific words used so often, there is no reason to think *MQM* has taken on a narrower meaning. As for KAI 214.14, is it even referring to a tomb? A memorial, yes, but a memorial is not always set up at the place of burial. Dahood cites Greek *topos*, giving a reference to Mark 16:6. Without having done a detailed study of the Greek usage, I can at least point out that Mark 16:6 does not refer to Jesus' tomb as a whole. In context *topos* clearly designates the exact spot within the tomb where the body had been. If the reference were to the whole tomb, what evidence would that be for the statement "he has risen"?

There are two situations in which *māqôm*--without other qualifiers such as "burial," "holy," "resting," etc.--might take on the limited denotation "tomb." One would be a special development in which the word became the word for "tomb" and another word was used for "place." So far as I know we have no record of such a development within any of the Semitic languages. The other situation would be its use as a euphemism, such as might be represented in English by capitalization (the Place). But if this latter were true, we would expect to see it used consistently in certain situations (such as funerary inscriptions). (As an example, one might think of the expressions "pass away," "die," and "kick the bucket."

Only the former is usually used in funeral homes while the latter would always be found in a comic situation.) Yet in the Phoenician inscriptions used to support the case, we find other, presumably more blunt, words used along side *MQM*. So the case of euphemism seems also eliminated. I am in no way denying that a generic term could not take on a specialized meaning in certain contexts (as will be further discussed in Chapter III). This is plainly evident, for example, in the use of *māqôm* as a term for God in MHeb. I am only saying that such has to be clearly demonstrated from transparent contexts and that the specialized meaning has to be demanded by the particular context in question. Such is not the case here.

In the context of Job 16:18 Job wishes to make sure his exorbitant sufferings do not go unnoticed. Therefore, he calls out for his blood to remain uncovered; i.e., to remain as a witness for God to see. He also calls out for his cry of anguish and injustice to be noticed rather than to disappear without being heard (cf. Fohrer). There is very likely an allusion to Gen 4:10 here, or certainly to the concept embodied in it. Both "blood" and "cry" occur in each passage. (Perhaps "cry" alludes to the cry of the uncovered blood to God; i.e., "my cry" means "the cry of my blood.") Several possible expressions would bring out this point (though "tomb" in my opinion does not seem to fit very well in any case, regardless of the other factors already mentioned). "Let there be no (resting) place" or "let there be no (hiding) place" would be two of the first to come to mind, but in context "place" by itself is sufficient. That would explain why the poet used it rather than some more specific term.

§ 18. 18:3

Why are we regarded as cattle,
נטמינו in your eyes.

The word has often been compared with the root *ṬMM* in cognate languages and translated something on the order, "we are stopped up" or "we are stupid." Others have related to *ṬM'* "be unclean." Blommerde revocalizes the word to *niṭmannû*, from the root *ṬMN* "to hide." The versions read:

LXX: διὰ τί ὥσπερ τετράποδα σεσιωπήκαμεν ἐναντίον σου; "for what reason have we been silent like quadrapeds before you?"

Vg: *quare reputati sumus ut iumenta et sorduimus coram vobis* "why have we been thought of as beasts of burden and considered filthy in your presence?"

Tg: מא דין אתחשבנא היך בעירא טמענא במחמיכון

The lexica of Jastrow and CW differ as to the exact significance of the key word. According to Jastrow's definition, the last clause would read something like, "(why are we regarded as cattle,) dull in your sight?" CW detaches the final alef from *B*^{C}*YR'* and attaches it to the next word to form an *itpael*, translating "*wir sind versenkt (in die Gruft, begraben) in euren Augen* we are submerged (in the tomb, buried) in your eyes" (I, 308).

Syr: למנא אתחשבן איך בעירא ואתטמאן בעיניך קטל נפשה ברוגזה "why are we regarded as cattle and polluted in your eyes, one killing himself in his anger?"

The 11QtgJob preserves part of v 3a but nothing for the problematic word.

The MT form of the verb in question is easily related to *ṬM'* though one might have to assume an Aramaism. JAram for example has *ṬMY* with the same meaning as the normal Heb *ṬM'*. To relate it to *ṬMM* is more difficult. One could postulate a biradical verb which became a geminate verb outside Heb but *ṬMH* in Heb. This is possible but not likely since the roots *ṭmm* and *ṭmy* exist side by side in several languages: JAram, Syriac, Ar. (Both are also found in Southeast Semitic though not always in the same languages. ESA has *ṭm'* according to HAL, while Tigrinya has *ṭmm* according to Brockelmann. Akk seems to have only *ṭmm*--Delitzsch, *Assyr. Handwörterbuch*, 302.) This suggests we are dealing with two roots which were generally kept distinct. The only way to obtain "be stopped up, stupid" would be to revocalize the form.

There is no doubt the expression, "we are stupid in your eyes," to our way of thinking better fits Job 18:3. Furthermore, the use of cattle as a metaphor for stupidity is found in Ps 73:22. On the other hand, the phrase "we are defiled/unclean" is not unintelligible. It is possible for a *b^e hēmāh* to be ritually unclean (cf. Lev 5:2; 7:21). We cannot dismiss this as completely unacceptable since we do not know exactly what connotation the expression would have had at the time of the poet. It is also supported by Vg and Syr. One might note that matters of uncleanness have already been mentioned in Job 14:4; 15:15-6; 17:9. Perhaps this is what the poet had in mind, or this fact may have caused a later assimilation of *ṬMM* toward *ṬM'* in the MT. Blommerde's suggestion not only requires a revocalization of the word but also, as Pope points out, does not clarify the passage in any way. If we wish to revocalize, we might as well go over to *ṬMM* (*n^e ṭammōnû*).

§ 19. 18:11

Driver, G. R. "Some Hebrew Medical Expressions," ZAW 65 (1953), 259-60.

Hillers, D. R. "A Convention in Hebrew Literature: The Reaction to Bad News," ZAW 77 (1965), 86-90.

Round about terrors frighten him,
והפיצהו at/upon his feet.

The root *PWṢ* in the broad sense of "scatter" does not fit English idiom very well since we do not usually refer to "scattering one's feet." Various means, including emendation and paraphrastic translation, have been resorted to in order to solve the problem. Driver compares with Ar *fāṣa* "make water." This seems to be the basis of the NEB rendering, "The terrors of death suddenly beset him and make him piss over his feet." The versions mostly seem to have understood *PWṢ* in the sense of "scatter" which they then rendered as well as they could according to the context:

LXX: κύκλῳ ὀλέσαισαν αὐτὸν ὀδύναι, πολλοὶ δὲ περὶ πόδας αὐτοῦ ἔλθοισαν ἐν λιμῷ στενῷ "let distresses destroy him round about, and let many come around his feet with the pinch of hunger."

Aq, Th (from Syro-Hexapla): διεσκόρπισαν αὐτὸν ἐν τοῖς ποσὶν αὐτοῦ "They scatter (confound) him in his feet."

Vg: *et involvent pedes eius* "and assail his feet."

Tg: ומבדרין יתיה לריגלוי "and they scatter him at his feet."

Syr: ובדרו אנין לרגלוהי "and they scatter (put in disorder) (him) at his feet."

Physical reaction to frightening events is often described in ancient Near Eastern literature (see the Hillers article), but the exact bodily reaction is not always clear. We find cognates of the root *PṢṢ* in practically every language, usually with the meaning "break, shatter." There does not seem any way to derive the MT form from *PṢṢ*, though some of the lexica suggest that *PṢṢ* and its cognates are akin to *PWṢ*. Yet we have already seen examples in which a correspondence between geminate and middle *waw/yod* roots may occur (§§ 8, 12, 16).

When we look at Driver's suggestion of comparing Ar *fāṣa*, some problems emerge. The phonetics would fit the Heb word, but the required meaning "urinate" occurs only in stem IV and would seem an internally derived meaning rather than one likely to be found in its cognates. If this were the only evidence, I think we would have to abandon Driver's interpretation for lack of data. However, the Ar verb *fāḍa* (*fyḍ*) "flood, overflow" is well-attested in both classical and modern written Ar. (Driver mentions this verb but only in a footnote and only as one of the "cognate [!] verbs" to *fāṣa*.) Syriac also has a verb *PY*^{c} (*PW*^{c} according to Margoliouth, 438) meaning "wash out." Brockelmann lists no cognates, so perhaps there is some intra-Syriac consideration I am not aware of. Otherwise, this seems further evidence to add to that of Ar. Finally, within the OT itself there are several passages which seem to use *PWṢ* in the sense of "overflow" (cf. BDB which lists these under a second root *PWṢ*). These include Prov 5:16 and Zech 1:17. Driver also lists Akk *pâṣu* "to stream (the eyes with tears)," but I was not able to confirm this.

Thus, there seems to be evidence of a root *PWṢ* (whether the same as the root meaning "scatter" or not) with the meaning "overflow." This would give confirmation of Driver's argument for the bold metaphor for fear in Job 18:11, though his own argument seems based on the wrong evidence. To this one might add a similar reaction described in Ezek 7:17; 21:12.

However, this presumes that "scatter" is meaningless in the passage. Granted, we have no Heb parallel for such an expression that I am aware of, but that does not mean ancient Heb did not have an idiom "scatter the feet" which had a special meaning in that language. All the versions, with the possible exception of LXX, seem to understand this meaning. Professor Brownlee brought to my attention the Syriac *BDRTY 'WRḤTKY* "you have scattered your ways" = "you have wandered in many directions" (Margoliouth, 36). This is a suggestive example to illustrate the possibilities. Any language abounds with idioms which would be meaningless from the individual words alone (examples in English are "pull one's leg" and "up the creek"). We must always remember our most ingenious of suggestions may be rendered utterly worthless by new linguistic information.

§ 20. 20:23

Dahood, M. "Some Northwest-Semitic Words in Job," *Biblica* 38 (1957), 314-15.

Nöldeke, T. Review of Friedrich Delitzsch, *Prolegomena eines neuen hebräisch-aramäischen Wörterbuchs*, ZDMG 40 (1886), 721.

He sends against him the anger of his wrath,
And rains upon him בלחומו.

If they did not resort to emendation, scholars in the past have compared with Ar *laḥm* "flesh." Dahood redivided and revocalized the last part of the verse to read *ᶜālāw mabbēl ḥammô* and translated 23b, "and may he rain upon him the fire of his wrath." He was followed in this by Blommerde.

With the exception of the LXX, the versions seem to have understood a root *LḤM*:

LXX: νίψαι ἐπ' αὐτὸν ὀδύνας "let him wash pains over him." This seems to presuppose a different Heb text (cf. Dhorme).

Vg: *et pluat super illum bellum suum* "and rain upon that one his war."

Tg: ויחית עלוי מיטרין בשלדיה "and will make it rain upon him in his body."

Syr: ונמטר עלוהי בקרבתנותה "and he will rain upon him in warlike strength."

Cognates for *LḤM* are found throughout Semitic. The meanings tend to fall in the range of "food, meat, flesh, eat." This root or a homonym also refers to anger and fighting. (A listing of the cognates is superfluous since they can be found in HAL and other lexica.) There seem to be ample data for the common explanation "into/against his flesh." However, one could also take the meaning "anger, war" which is equally well attested and translate "in his fury" (cf. Nöldeke who rejects a comparison with "flesh"). This would form more of a parallel with 23a.

Dahood's suggestion gives the stichs nice synonymous parallelism. The question is whether the poet wrote it that way. Dahood's reconstruction of the text requires revocalization, word redivision, and elimination of some vowel letters. He should plainly admit he has emended the text--as drastically as many of his predecessors who did not pretend to use comparative philology. The disarming statements, "the consonantal text is eminently sound" and "no emendations are necessary," completely belie the rather drastic reshuffling done. One might also note that there are no preformative *m*- nouns of the root *nbl* in Ug, Akk, Ar, or Eth, a fact which makes Dahood's reconstruction even more hypothetical.

When we come back to choosing between "in his flesh" and "in his anger," the problem is not one of finding ample cognate evidence but choosing between two suggestions, each of which has a good deal to be said for it. Comparative philology has produced possibilities of solution but a choice must be based on other considerations. The versions also show a division, with Tg supporting "flesh" and Vg and Syr understanding "war."

§ 21. 21:20

Dahood, M. "Some Northwest-Semitic Words in Job," *Biblica* 38 (1957), 316.

His eyes will see כידו,
And from the wrath of Shaddai he will drink.

This *hapax legomenon* has been almost universally emended, often to *pîdô* "his ruin." Dahood revocalized it to *kaddô*, translating, "His eyes shall behold his cup of fate." Pope compares with Ar *kayd* to retain the MT and translates "his calamity."

LXX: ἴδοισαν οἱ ὀφθαλμοὶ αὐτοῦ τὴν ἑαυτοῦ σφαγήν "let his eyes see his own slaughter."

Sym: πτῶσιν "fall." Only this one word is preserved.

Vg: *videbúnt oculi eius interfectionem suam* "his eyes will see his destruction (killing)."

Tg: יחמון עינוי תבריה "his eyes will observe his misfortune (breach)."

Syr: ונחזין עינוהי אבדנה "and his eyes will see his destruction."

11QtgJob: ע]י̊נ̊ו̊הי במפלתה ומ̊["his eyes in his downfall" or "his eyes [look] upon his downfall."

Evidence for a Heb word *kîd* outside this passage is skimpy. Only in South Semitic do we find some help. Geez and Tigre both have a word *kēdo* meaning "walk, tread, tread down." Ar has *kāda* "deceive, dupe, outwit." (Pope also claims the meaning "punishment" for the noun form *kaid* but does not cite his source. WKAS gives no such information. The closest is "strategm of war.") This suggests some meaning such as "his oppression/downfall/treading down." A. F. L. Beeston (*Le Muséon* 67 [1954], 313-16) identified a root *kyd* in ESA (in a votive text--R. 3992) which he conjecturally rendered "to be condemned." He thought this might possibly be related to the problem word here in Job 21:20. But then the question is why the root is not attested outside South Semitic. Is the parallel with Heb purely accidental or does Heb preserve a form which has not otherwise survived in North Semitic? Of course, one could postulate an Ar borrowing, but there seems no way to prove it.

Dahood's suggestion is interesting. The word *KD* for "cup" or some other container of liquid is BHeb and also widely attested elsewhere in Semitic. (Most of the cognates are listed by HAL. To these one should add Punic and Imperial Aram--DISO 115. Whether the Ar *kadd* "mortar" is a cognate is a question. Gordon lists it in UT § 19:1195 but Leslau disputes that.) The reference to drinking in Job 21:20b makes the suggestion more attractive. But as usual Dahood does not attempt to explain the origin of the MT form; he simply revocalizes with no further comment. However, in Samaritan Hebrew the form *kid* or *kidda* occurs according to Murtonen (*Etymological Vocabulary*, 116). If correct, this would provide a parallel to both the meaning and part of the form of the MT here. One could then think of a dialectical form in Job which differs from that found elsewhere in the OT (e.g., Gen 24 *passim*; 1 Kgs 18:34; Judg 7:16). The one problem is the gemination of the *-d-* which occurs in the Samaritan and normal MT forms. There is no gemination in the word in Job. One has to weigh these possibilities against those of a simple graphic error as suggested by many of the older commentaries. The versions all read "fall" or the like, which could be taken to presuppose *pîdô*. It is possible, however, that they read *kîdô* as in the MT and thus give support to the comparative suggestion mentioned first. None of them understand "cup."

<u>§ 22. 21:24</u>

עטיניו are full of milk,
And the marrow of his bones is moist.

This word has been explained by an appeal to the MHeb root which has to do with pressing oil from olives. Others have connected with Ar *ᶜaṭina* "resting place around a waterhole." The common emendation to *ᶜṬM* itself appeals to cognate words which mean "hip, thigh" since no such root is otherwise known in BHeb.

The versions give the impression of working back from the word they take as "milk" or "fat." Also the "bones" of v 24b may have suggested some part of the body:

LXX: τὰ δὲ ἔγκατα αὐτοῦ πλήρη στέατος "his intestines are full of fat."

Vg: *viscera eius plena sunt adipe* "his inwards are full of fat."

Tg: ביזוי אתמליאו חלבא "his breasts are full of milk."

Syr: וגבוהי מלין תרבא "his sides (humps?) are full of fat."

11QtgJob: ו]הוא רמיא מדין [24]אב°] The restoration of the word at the beginning of v 24 is a tantalizing enigma, enough remaining to whet the appetite but not enough to bite on with confidence. Indeed, the editors of the *editio princeps* point out that something seems to be missing from vv 23-4. If 23b-24a are missing, they would suggest reading *'B[D]* "perish," a suggestion which they take as less likely. If the whole of v 23 is the missing part, they would read *'BR[WHY]* "his limbs." Sokoloff seems to take the surviving words of this line as all part of v 23. Pope cites the suggestion of his student Bruce Zuckerman that the partially preserved word is *'B[WZ]* "buttocks"; he himself offers the alternative *'K[WZ]*, also "buttocks." These suggestions would, of course, have to assume that the word in question is indeed part of v 24. Thus, the fragment preserved at this point gives us no more information for our purpose than if it did not exist.

Suitable cognates are hard to find for the word under discussion. BDB suggests the meaning "buckets," apparently based on MHeb. The basic meaning of the root ^{c}*ṬN* would be something like "lay in." The verb in MHeb refers to laying olives into a press or vat while *ma*^{c}*ǎṭān* is an olive vat. Ar ^{c}*aṭana* has reference to treating a hide in tanning solution. The noun ^{c}*aṭan* is a resting place near a watering hole. Tigre ^{c}*aṭnä* is suggestive. It basically means "fumigate," but the derived form *m*^{ec}*ṭ*^{e}*n* refers to a watering place, while *m*^{ec}*ṭān* refers to the place where the milk pans are fumigated, viz., at the watering place of the cattle. Perhaps the connection with Heb is just coincidence. If not, however, it would explain why the MT has "milk" instead of "fat" as is often read by commentators. Whether there is a common denominator between the MHeb, Ar, and Tigre evidence is not certain. But perhaps it would not be too far-fetched to point out that animals would usually be milked around their resting place, which would be the watering hole. The tubs or jars of milk might bring to mind these watering places, even if the specific reference is only to the storage vessels of milk. Certainly the cognate evidence tends away from reference to any part of the body. It is also strong enough to make us wary of changing the MT even if a translation on the order of "storage vessels" may not be completely certain. (As already noted, the versions all indicate a part of the body, though none of them agree on which part. The impression given is that they translated from context rather than having a specific knowledge of the word.)

§ 23. 22:25

And Shaddai will be your gold,
And silver תועפות to you.

This word is used in reference to wild oxen (Num 23:22; 24:8) and mountains (Ps 95:4) as well as to silver here. If not emended, it is often taken as "mountains" or "piles" or something which suggests the idea of being high. This translation usually has been influenced by the Ar *yafa*^{c}*a* "go up a hill," *yafa*^{c} "hill."

LXX: καθαρὸν δὲ ἀποδώσει σε ὥσπερ ἀργύριον πεπυρωμένον "and he will restore you pure as refined silver."

Vg: *et argentum coacervabitur tibi* "and silver will be heaped up for you."

Tg: ומן כסף תקוף רומא דילך "and exalted power (will be) yours more than silver."

Syr: וכסף חושבנין נהוא לך "and money will be counted out for you."

One would expect the root of this word to be *Y*^{c}*P*. But finding such a root is difficult; at least, finding one with a usable semantic content is difficult. The root *yp*^{c} with a meaning "rise" or the like occurs in Ar, ESA, and probably Ug (see UT § 19.1133). Whether the root *YP*^{c} "shine" in Heb belongs to it as well is not certain. A problem with using this root is that of metathesis. If the Heb *YP*^{c} has no connection with the Semitic *yp*^{c} "rise," assuming a metathesis would not cause a great deal of difficulty. If both are from the same root, however, this presents a problem since *YP*^{c} occurs in

BHeb without metathesis, including several places in Job. Thus, one would have to assume a metathesis which affected *tô*^{c}*āpôt* only.

If we look for another root, we find an interesting one in ^{c}*WP*. It exists along side the well-known ^{c}*WP* meaning "fly." JAram has ^{c}*YP* and ^{c}*WP* meaning "to double." (*B. Ber*. 63a explains Job 22:25 as meaning "doubled silver.") Syriac has both ^{c}*WP* and ^{c}*PP* "double, fold over, multiply, increase." The verb is used with *'agrā'* "wages, reward" and *yûtrānā'* "gain, profit" (Margoliouth, 422). Mandaic *APP* and *AUP* similarly mean "double." Classical Ar ^{c}*āfa* refers to an animal hunting prey while ^{c}*uwāf* is used for "prey, profit, gain." In South Semitic, Tigre ^{c}*ōpū* means "to be complete, brimfull." ESA has ^{c}*wp* "profit" (Jamme 616.21 [*Sab. Inscrip.*, p. 114]).

There is, however, a complicating factor. Ar *ḍa*^{c}*afa* means "double, redouble, multiply" in both the classical and modern written languages. It is a cognate of Heb *Ṣ*^{c}*P* from which comes "wrapper, shawl." Brockelmann also lists this as a cognate of Syr ^{c}*ap* "double." The proposed development of the Aram form is **Ṣ*^{c}*P*> *^{cc}*P*> ^{c}*P*. (Cf. BDB under *Ṣ*^{c}*P*; see also Blau, *Pseudo-Corrections*, 47-8, n. 8.) If this is correct, some of the forms listed in the previous paragraph are probably not cognate. Others may have been originally separate but became assimilated when phonetic changes made them homonyms of roots already in the language. (Of course, one might explain the form in Job 22:25 as an Aram borrowing though it is not otherwise known in Aram.) Yet when all the various forms are considered, there still seems sufficient evidence for a root ^{c}*WP* or perhaps ^{c}*PP* in Semitic with the meaning "increase" or the like.

The proposed root ^{c}*WP* seems to have stronger linguistic arguments behind it than the proposed *YP*^{c}, though either is certainly a possibility. (The use of either root requires the assumption of a metathesis for the form *tô*^{c}*āpôt*.) On the other hand, the intra-Heb evidence for the word *TW*^{c}*PWT*-- regardless of its ultimate root--is quite strong. As already noted it occurs in Num 23:22; 24:8 in reference to something on wild oxen (perhaps "horns" though "humps" is another suggestion). In Ps 95:4 it is used for the peaks of mountains.

It also occurs in 4Q184 1:4 in the expression *TW^{c}PWT LYLH* "depths of night" (DJD V, p. 82). The general meaning of the word seems clear from these passages alone. The specific context and construction of Job 22:25 make the general thrust of the verse plain. The only real problem is what specific rendering to use. If one assumed the root ^{c}*WP*, a translation such as "silver will be your profits" or possibly even "silver (will be) yours (in) double (portions)" would be acceptable. The versions appear to have had the same problem we have and to have translated from the context. Whatever particular solution one ultimately takes, emendation is totally unwarranted. Considerations of both the intra-Heb and the cognate evidence support the correctness of the MT at this point.

§ 24. 22:30

Gordis, Robert, "Corporate Personality in Job: A Note on 22:29-30," JNES 4 (1945), 54-5.

Sarna, Nahum. "A *Crux Interpretum* in Job 22:30," JNES 15 (1956), 118-9.

And אי- innocent will escape,
He will be delivered by the cleanness of your hands.

The word in question has sometimes been kept with the attested Heb meaning "island" (e.g., Tur-Sinai). But since this is not thought to fit the context, it is often taken to be a negative particle meaning "not." Sarna repointed it to the indefinite pronoun *'ê* which he identified in Heb on the basis of cognates. The versions give the impression of being as puzzled by the verse as some modern commentators:

LXX (Hexaplaric addition): ῥύσεται ἀθῷον, καὶ διασώθητι ἐν καθαραῖς χερσίν σου "he will rescue the guiltless, and you save (yourself) by your clean hands."

Vg: *salvabitur innocens salvabitur autem munditia manuum suarum* "the innocent one will be saved, but he will be saved by the cleanness of his hands."

Tg: ישיזיב גבר דליתוי זכאי בזכותך ואשתיזיב בברירות ידך "a man who is not pure will be saved by your purity, and he will be saved by the purity of your hand."

Syr: נתפלט זכיא איכא דאיתוהי ונתפלט בדכיותא דאידוהי "the innocent will be delivered wherever he is, and he will be saved by the purity of his hands."

Cognates of both *'î* and *'ê* are frequent within Semitic (there is no need to list them since HAL does). In most languages the cognates of *'ê* include a function as an indefinite or relative pronoun as well as a *Fragewort*. Thus Sarna's suggestions can be backed up with cognates which have the function he wishes to give to the word in Job 22:30. However, while he claims his suggestion incorporates only "a slight vowel change to yield perfect sense and that emendation is therefore unnecessary," he fails to recognize that his vowel change *is* emendation. It involves a change of the linguistic evidence which has come down to us. Obviously, it is not as drastic as some, yet it is emendation nonetheless and should be called what it is.

Sarna's basic arguments against taking *'î* as the negative are (1) the existence of such a negative in BHeb is doubtful, and (2) it goes against the context. The second argument seems very subjective. For example, Gordis argues that Job 22:30 is in perfect alignment with ancient Hebrew thought on corporate personality. He cites the obvious examples of Abraham and Sodom and of Ezek 14:14-20. Note also Pope's comments on the passage (which include a reference to Gordis' article).

The first argument too loses some of its force when we see that it occurs in every major branch of Semitic including the Canaanite dialect of Phoen and MHeb. Thus, it would not appear unlikely that the word would turn up in Heb. Indeed, it does appear in the name *'î-kābôd* in I Sam 4:21. The particle *'Y* in Northwest Semitic names is generally thought to be the interrogative adverb "where" (see, for example, Benz, *Personal Names*, 265, and Albright, "Northwest-Semitic Names," JAOS 74 [1954], 226-7). Thus, the name Ichabod would originally have meant "Where is honor/the Honored one?" The explanation, "The glory of Israel has fled from Israel," is undoubtedly a folk etymology. But it would testify to the meaning of the name to Israelites at some time during the period of the monarchy. Furthermore, it would testify to the fact that *'î* was understood as a negative particle. It is also to be noted that the constructions of *'î-kābôd* and *'î-nāqî* are the same. Perhaps the particle survived in Heb only in certain stereotyped constructions, but the evidence that it did exist seems strong enough. (There is certainly as much evidence for a negative *'î* as there is for a relative *'ê*!) The reading of the Tg strengthens the case. The traditional interpretation "one not innocent" stands up to linguistic investigation.

Two further points to note. One, the change of person in the LXX, Vg, and Syr as compared to the MT was required to fit their translation, "innocent one." The grammatical person had to be reshuffled; otherwise, what could Job's clean hands have to do with the delivery of the innocent? Thus, the change by the LXX from "he will be saved" to "you will be saved" and by the Vg and Syr from "the cleanness of your hands" to "the cleanness of his hands" further attests to the real meaning, "not innocent." (Sarna's suggestion has a similar problem on which he fails to comment. What does the translation, "He delivers whosoever is innocent, and he is delivered by the cleanness of your hands," mean?) Two, chap. 42 is the exact fulfillment of this prediction: The guilty ones (Job's friends) are forgiven when Job (the innocent one) prays for them. Any slight incongruity with the rest of Eliphaz' argument would be amply covered by poetic license while the suggested meaning of Job 22:30 is in overall harmony with the message of the book if the final form is taken seriously. (Cf. J. William Whedbee, "The Comedy of Job," in a forthcoming issue of *Semeia*. A persuasive argument will there be given for including the epilogue with the book to understand its ultimate import.)

Tur-Sinai's suggestion "island" has the normal meaning of the Heb *'î* behind it. Considering our limited corpus of Heb literature, it is indeed possible that a reference to "island" may have had a meaning for the author of this passage which now escapes us. On the other hand, we have to work with the facts presently at our disposal. (It might also be noted in passing that *'î* in the sense of "island" is not otherwise used in Job, so a clash of homonyms is not necessarily being postulated.) The weight of probability seems to lie with *'î* =

"not" for this phrase.

§ 25. 23:9

Driver, G. R. "Difficult Words in the Hebrew Prophets," *Studies in Old Testament Prophecy*, 53-5.

Eitan, Israel. *A Contribution to Biblical Lexicography*, 56-7.

Guillaume, A. "The Arabic Background of the Book of Job," *Promise and Fulfilment*, 115-6.

Rad, G. von. "Das Werk Jahwes," *Studia Biblica et Semitica*, 290-8.

Yellin, David. "Forgotten Meanings of Hebrew Roots in the Bible," *Jewish Studies in Memory of Israel Abrahams*, 453-5.

On the left בעשתו and I do not behold,
He turns aside to the right and I do not see.

The expected meaning "in his working" (="when he works") is thought not to fit the parallelism of vv 8-9. Eitan, Guillaume, and Yellin compare with the Ar *ǧašā*, the first two taking it in the sense "turn, go to," the last in the sense "to cover." Driver compares with Ar ^{c}*ašā* which has the meaning "turn aside."

LXX (Hexaplaric addition): ἀριστερὰ ποιήσαντος αὐτοῦ καὶ οὐ κατέσχον "when he worked on the left, I did not observe."

Vg: *si ad sinistram quid agat non adprehendam eum* "if to the left, what is there to do? I do not take hold of him?"

Tg: בציפונא במעבדיה ולא אחמי "in the north in his doings and I do not see."

Syr: לסמלי בעית ולא אתחזי לי "on the left I seek but he is not seen by me."

Finding cognates other than in Ar is difficult. There seems no other witness than Ar (^{c}*šy/w*) for a presumed PS *^{c}*śy/w* with the meaning "turn away, turn aside" though this suggestion would seem the better fit for the passage in Job. If we postulate a root **ǧśw/y*, we can add to the Ar *ǧšw/y* ("deceive, cover, go") the Akk *ešû* "confuse." The question is whether a homonym for the frequent ^{c}*ŚH*, with its origin in one of these postulated roots, is borne out by the OT data. Passages other than Job which supposedly require this meaning are I Kgs 20:40, Ruth 2:19, and I Chr 4:10; but a translation such as "do, work, be busy" fits well for the first two. I Chr 4:10 may embody an idiomatic construction: A translation, "Make (me free) from evil," would probably approximate the general idea (cf. NAB, NEB, RSV). Certainly "turn me" is no more cogent than those translations based upon the general meaning of ^{c}*ŚH*.

The major argument for seeing another meaning for ^{c}*ŚH* in Job 23:9 is the supposed parallelism and the idea that "'Where/when he doth work' (KJ and JPS) makes little sense" (Pope). A consideration of the whole context, however, would seem to undermine these two objections. Vv 8-9 clearly involve the four basic directions from the point of view of the individual ("forward," "backward," "left," "right" or perhaps "east," "west," "north," "south"). Yet there is no other clear parallelism unless one emends to obtain it. In v 8 the action at the beginning of each hemistich concerns the first person ("I advance" and "[I go] backward"). In v 9 the first verbs in each hemistich concern the third person (though one or both are commonly emended to the first person). The end of the hemistich concerns the third person in v 8a but the first person in 8b, 9a, and 9b.

The two parts of v 9 could be taken as parallel to each other, but that still does not require synonymous parallelism. One could understand a progression of action for the first part of each colon: "he works on the left. . . he turns aside on the right." The second halves of the cola present no problem of understanding and are synonymously parallel. The concept of God working invisibly has already been presented by the poet in 9:5, 11-12 (cf. also the von Rad article on God's working generally). Naturally, other analyses are also possible from the text as it now stands, and the one given here is certainly not the only one. The point is that the text yields good sense if one takes the time to consider it rather than attempting to tell the poet how he should have written it.

In this discussion we have not considered in detail all the passages for which the identification of a new root ^{c}*ŚH* has been proposed. It may be that a detailed investigation would show evidence for the existence of such a homonym alongside the root so frequently found in the OT. Yet the arguments so far examined have not been very cogent. The cognate evidence itself is weak, being primarily from Ar. It could be useful if the intra-Heb evidence were strong, but that is also not the case. The versions support the traditional understanding of the verse as much as they contradict it. Finally, the proposed new root is not required for the verse to make sense if one has not already tried to fit the passage into an *a priori* straitjacket.

§ 26. 24:24

Löw, Immanuel. *Die Flora der Juden*, II, 231-2.
Reider, Joseph. "Contributions to the Hebrew Lexicon," ZAW 53 (1935), 273-5.
Thompsen, R. C. *Dictionary of Assyrian Botany*, 329.

They stand for a while, then are not,
They are brought down, ככל they dry up,
And they wither like a head of grain.

Traditionally taken to be "as all," the translation of the expression has been a problem. It has often been emended to the name of a plant, such as the mallow, because of the LXX. Reider, taking a clue from Ehrlich, proposed that the word *kōl* was itself the name of a plant and required no emendation so to translate.

LXX: ἐμαράνθη δὲ ὥσπερ μολόχη ἐν καύματι ἢ ὥσπερ στάχυς ἀπὸ καλάμης αὐτόματος ἀποπεσών "he is extinguished as a mallow in the heat or as a head falls by itself from the stalk."

Vg: *et humiliabuntur sicut omnia et auferentur et sicut summitates spicarum conterentur* "they will be brought down as everything and carried off and destroyed as the tops of grain heads."

Tg: ואתמכיאו בזמן דיסופהון יתקטעון "they are brought down, in the time of their end they are cut off."

Syr: ונתמככון ונאבדון כלהון מרגזנא "and all our troublers will be brought low and will perish."

11QtgJob: י/א/התכ]פפו כיבלא יתקפצון א] "they are bent, as dog grass they dry up."

A word with the base *kll* is used in a number of Semitic languages in reference to a type of plant. In JAram *KLYL'* by itself (or *KLYL* with *MLK'*) refers to the "melilot"; Syriac *KLYL MLK'* means the same thing. Ar has *'iklīl* which refers to the umbel of a plant, while with *'lmlk* it also means "melilot." Reider does not note that Akk has the word as well: *kilīli*. Thompsen says about the plant, "*Kililanu* must be connected with the late Heb. *k^elîlâ* 'crown', like *^šamkilili*, associated with the convolvulus . . . and consequently the tendril of the vine." According to both AHW and Brockelmann, the Aram forms are borrowed from Akk. The basic meaning of the root *kll* common to all these words is "crown." Evidently the name "crown of the king" or sometimes just "crown" became applied to a certain type of plant. Whether it was always the same plant in each of the native languages is irrelevant here.

The next question concerns the form of the word in the MT. Reider claimed the text had suffered no damage. Rather the "briefer or contracted form of the Hebrew word should not surprise us, since the Hebrew lexicon contains many such abbreviated nouns derived from" geminate roots. He cites *mōr* from *MRR* and *qōr* from *QRR*. These two examples might explain the vowel of the Heb word as well, but one might note that--as a probable loanward from Akk--the form borrowed may not have been *kilili* but *kulūlu* which also means "crown." The argument for a plant name here is especially strengthened by the reading of the 11QtgJob along with the LXX.

§ 27. 27:18

Dahood, M. *Ras Shamra Parallels* I, p. 155.

He builds his house כעש,
Even like a hut which the guard makes.

The normal and expected meaning of the expression is "as a moth." The problem is the imagery since moths are not usually thought of as house builders. A number of attempts have been made to find another meaning for *ᶜāš* on the basis of cognates. Ehrlich (followed by Dhorme) compares Ar $^{c}\check{s}\check{s}$ and translates "nest." Pope compares Ar $^{c}\bar{a}s$ "night watchman," and translates, "He builds his house like a watchman/Like a hut the guard makes."

The versions all appear to understand moth or some similar such creature: LXX--σῆτες; Vg--*tinea*; Tg--רקבוביתא (either "moth"--so CW--or "earthworm"--so Jastrow); Syr--גורגי ("spider"). Only one word of 18b is preserved in 11QtgJob, and it gives no information on this question.

The Heb word for moth has cognates in a number of the Semitic languages: Syriac and JAram--$^{c}\bar{a}\check{s}\bar{a}$'; Ar--^{c}<u>utt</u>; Eth--^{c}eḏē. Akk *ašašu* "fishmoth" is probably also cognate (so AHW; but cf. Pope's objections at this verse). Tigrinya has ^{c}*as*^{c}*asa* "become mouldy, musty" (Leslau, *Contributions*). However, it must be noted that the words do not always mean "moth." The Syriac word has reference to lice and the Eth and Ar words can refer to the larva of the moth as well as the adult stage. Thus, any imagery using the house of a moth could very likely have the pupa stage of the insect's development in mind.

The major problem with Ehrlich's suggestion is that it requires an exception to the normal phonological correspondences between Heb and Ar. Pope's suggestion has more merit. Possible cognates of Ar ^{c}*assa* "patrol by night, guard" appear in some of the other languages. Syriac ^{c}*S* "examine" seems to be related to the Ar word. Brockelmann also notes Mehri *eysūs* "investigators." Mandaic has *ASS* = *ASA* "press, tread down." However, these all suggest a PS root *^{c}*ss* which appears in Heb as ^{c}*SS*, not the attested root $^{c}\check{S}\check{S}$. If the words just listed are cognate, the Ar word is thus very unlikely to have any connection with Heb $^{c}a\check{s}$. If they are not actually cognates, Ar ^{c}*assa* seems unique to that language. Either way, the cogency of Pope's suggestion is greatly reduced.

Dahood discusses this passage as follows in commenting on a supposed parallel between *bt* and *nṣrt* in UT 127.3-5 (= CTA 16.6.3-5): "The Ugaritic parallelism casts doubt upon the correctness of the current translation and stylistic analysis of Job 27:18. Both texts are obscure, but a study of both together bids fair to dispel the obscurity." The use of *bt* and *nṣrt* is interesting in the light of this Job passage, and a thorough study might indeed bring up some useful comparisons. But at the moment there are some difficulties with Dahood's suggestion. The first is his supposing *bt* and *nṣrt* parallel in the passage from the Keret epic. Most scholars see *nṣrt* parallel to *bkt* (e.g., UT § 19.1691; Gray, *Krt Text*, p. 74-5). Gray translates the passage in the following manner: "At the house of *Krt* she arrives, /Weeping [*bkt*], she clears (the threshold) and enters./Shrieking [*nṣrt*], she enters the inmost chambers" (*ibid.*, pp. 27-8). Gordon and Driver render somewhat similarly. (See now also the review article by de Moor and van der Lugt in BO 31 [1974], esp. 11.) A second problem is that Job 27:18 is not so obscure as Dahood seems to think. The only troublesome part is the expression discussed above. But regardless of exactly what it is that he "builds his house like," the general thrust of the passage seems unlikely to become a point of debate.

The evidence brings us in a circle back to the more traditional "moth." Granted, it does not form the more exact synonymous parallelism that Pope's translation makes, but the imagery is perfectly understandable and hardly to be classified as inferior. It does not appear to strain credulity to consider a moth pupa as an apt figure for fragility. Are we attempting to force the poet into a rut by constantly demanding rigid synonymous parallelism? Unless more solid evidence for an alternative suggestion can be produced, we would seem to have a very usable and intelligible simile in "he builds his house as a moth (larva?)." Of course, the versions all understand some sort of small invertebrate.

§ 28. 28:8

Mowinckel, Sigmund. "שחל," *Hebrew and Semitic Studies Presented to Godfrey Rolles Driver*, 95-103.

> The sons of pride have not walked it,
> Upon it has not traveled שחל.

The word usually means "lion" as a number of passages in the OT show, but Mowinckel felt it did not fit all of them and rendered the word by "lizard" in his 1927 Norwegian translation of Job. Pope also accepts this interpretation in his commentary and translation of this verse.

LXX (Hexaplaric addition): οὐκ ἐπάτησαν αὐτὴν υἱοὶ ἀλαζόνων, οὐ παρῆλθεν ἐπ' αὐτῆς λέων "the sons of the boaster/vagabond did not tread it; the lion did not go by upon it."

Vg: *non calcaverunt eam filii institorum nec pertransivit per eam leaena* "the children of the merchants have not trodden it nor the lionness gone through it."

Tg I: לא טיילו בה בני אריוון לא זאר עלוי ליתא "the sons of the lion have not traveled it; the old lion has not passed upon it."

Tg II: לא הליכו בה בני אדם ולא סטא עלוהי חויא "the sons of man (Adam?) did not walk on it, and the serpent did not deviate upon it."

Syr: ולא דרשה חיותא ולא עבר עליה ארחא "and no animal trod it, and the merchant did not go past up on it." For "merchant" the Urmia edition has "lion."

The 11QtgJob is very fragmentary at this point. However, it does preserve the word חנין which seems to correspond to בני-שחץ of the MT. It is important to notice that 41:26, which has the same expression "sons of pride," has *RḤŠ* in the Qumran targum. These both indicate that some sort of reptilian figure (whether real or mythological is unimportant) was understood by the author of this targum.

Mowinckel's study needs only to be summarized here. His first and major argument is that certain passages require some other meaning for *šaḥal* than "lion." Argument 2 is the parallelism between "sons of pride" and *šaḥal* in Job 28:8. Since Leviathan is king of the "sons of pride" in 41:26, the expression would hardly suit the lion in context. Argument 3 is rather lengthy and parts of it seem to me to be prone to a good deal of subjective judgment. But Mowinckel does succeed in establishing that certain words for "serpent" and "lion" overlap at points within the Semitic languages. Thus it would not be unique to find *šaḥal* meaning "lion" in one context and "serpent" in another. Argument 5 seems to use questionable linguistic methods to establish a relationship between certain words. Nevertheless, one point is interesting: Mowinckel points out that the griffin of ancient Babylon combines features of both serpent and lion. The griffin myth does not seem to be confined to Babylon.

The argument from context appears the strongest one to me. The whole image of vv 1-11 is man's ability to search out that which is normally inaccessible to even the most clever of the animal kingdom. That which is searched out is deep within the earth; therefore, one is not likely to expect the lion here since one would not normally associate the lion with mining underground. (The mention of the falcon in v 7 is an illustration of keen-sightedness and does not negate the argument just given against lion in v 8.) Against this one can argue that the word appears in Job 4:10 and 10:16 with the normal meaning "lion." However, it is generally felt that chap 28 comes from a different hand than much of the earlier part of the poem. If so, this would account for the confusion of homonyms.

Direct cognate evidence is slim. JAram has *ŠḤL'* "lion." Ug has a word *šḥlmmt* but the meaning is very uncertain. Classical Ar, the modern written Ar of Egypt, and the Chad-Sudanese dialect have *siḥlīya* "a type of lizard." The Ar word is interesting. Other than that, the direct cognate evidence is not of much help. Yet the indirect linguistic evidence can be added to that, including the two passages from 11QtgJob and the rabbinic Tg II. Above all are the demands of the context itself. When all the evidence is totaled, there seems a solid argument for *šaḥal* meaning a real or mythical reptilian creature in Job 28:8.

§ 29. 28:11; 38:16; 31:39

Albright, W. F. *Archaeology and the Religion of Israel*, 191, n. 7.

Dahood, M. "Qoheleth and Northwest Semitic Philology," *Biblica* 43 (1962), 361-2.

Mansoor, M. "The Thanksgiving Hymns and the Massoretic Text (Part II)," RQ 3 (1961-2), 392-4.

Montgomery, J. A. "Notes on the Mythological Epic Texts from Ras Shamra," JAOS 53 (1933), 111.

Pope, M. *El in the Ugaritic Texts*, 61-81.

מבכי of the rivers חבש,
And her hidden thing he brings (to) the light.

Have you gone to the -נבכי of the sea,
Or walked around in the secret places of the
deep?

If I ate her strength without money,
Or snuffed out the life of בעליה.

For *mibb*^{e}*kî*--usually taken from *BKH* "weep"--Montgomery was the first to compare Ug *mbk.nhrm*. The Ug expression is discussed by Pope in his book on El and translated "the springs of the (two) rivers." Based on this Pope translates Job 28:11, "sources of the rivers," and 38:16, "springs of the sea." Pope compares the verb *ḥibbēš* in 28:11 with the root *ḤPŚ* "search." Blommerde does similarly, citing Pope. In 31:39 Pope takes *b*^{ec}*ālèhā* as a variant form of *P*^{c}*L* "work," following Dahood's example of doing this here and elsewhere (see further references in Blommerde and Dahood's article listed above).

The versions for 28:11 are the following:

LXX: βάθη δὲ ποταμῶν ἀνεκάλυψεν "the depths of the rivers he uncovered."

Aq/Th (for *ḤBŠ*): ἐξερεύνησεν "search out, examine."

Vg: *profunda quoque fluviorum scrutatus est* "he has also searched the depths of the rivers."

Tg: מן קלילי נהרייא זרז ומחרכא דתעלומא יפיק נהורא "who prepared the light things of the rivers and from the hidden windows brings out light."

Syr: ועושנא דנהרותא חבש "and the swellings of the rivers he bound."

For 38:16 the versions read:

LXX: ἦλθες δὲ ἐπὶ πηγὴν θαλάσσης "have you come upon the source of the sea?"

Sym: ἕως συνοχῆς πηγῆς "to the union of sources?"

Vg: *numquid ingressus es profunda maris* "have you entered the depths of the sea?"

Tg: איפשר דעלתא עד מערבלי סגור ימא "is it possible that you entered the hidden depths of the sea?"

Syr: עלת לעומקוהי דימא "have you entered the depths of the sea?"

The versions of 31:39 seem to understand the normal Heb, sense of *B*^{c}*L* as "master, owner": LXX--κυρίου; Aq (Syro-Hex)--ἐχόντων; Tg--דמרהא. The Syr reads דמרירא "bitter," which seems a corruption of דמריא or some other form of "lord" (cf. Dhorme). The Vg reads *agricolarum* "of (the) farmers" which could apply to the workers on the land. It seems doubtful, however, that Jerome understands anything but the sense of the MT, since an *agricola* could be an owner as well as a worker of the land.

Mibb^{e}*kî/Nib*^{e}*kê*

The previous connection of *MBKY* with *BKH* had some philological support. The semantic connection was possible and the vocalization seemed to presuppose that particular root. It also basically fitted the context. However, the discovery of *mbk.nhrm* as a sterotyped phrase in Ug gives a parallel too close to be mere coincidence. Further, the Ug phrase is used in conjunction with *apq.thmtm* "channel of the two deeps" in several passages, which is somewhat reminiscent of Job 38:16. One could postulate that *mbk* is not from the root *nbk* (cf. Whitaker who lists them separately), but the attestation of both *nbk* and *mbk* together in Heb and Ug compels one to think *mbk* is a derived form of *nbk*. The Ug evidence plus the context confirm the meaning "sources" or the like for Job 28:11 and 38:16. The root also occurs in the Qumran writings in the phrase ^{c}*L NBWKY MYM* "over the springs of waters" (1QH 3:15--see Mansoor for a discussion).

The question not answered, though, is that of the origin of the MT form in 28:11 since one would expect the form *mabb*^{e}*kê*. There are various ways one could explain it as an anomolous development. The *-i-* of the first syllable may be the result of the well-known Canaanite short *a>i* shift in closed, unaccented syllables (BL 193v-194y; GKC § 27s). An alternative explanation is as follows: Cognates in other languages are hard to find. Montgomery suggested it was connected with the name of the city Hierapolis in Syria, whose old name took the variant forms Bambyke, Mambuj, Mabbuj. He was followed in this by Albright. The origin of these various forms of the name was evidently the Syriac *NBG* "flow." This suggests the Heb form may have been borrowed and remained rather rare. The existence of the verb *Ḥ*B*Š* in 28:11 may have caused later readers who were not so familiar with the original expression to analyze it as the preposition *mi-* plus the more familiar *BKH*. According to this alternative hypothesis, folk etymology produced the reading now found in the MT but undoubtedly long before the time the Masoretes actually committed the traditional reading to written notation.

*Ḥibbēš/B*ᵉᶜ*ālēhā*

The proposals for both these words assume a *B/P* interchange. It cannot be denied that there are words in the Semitic stock which may have *B* where their cognates have *P*. Sometimes variant forms exist side by side within the same language. Ug *nbk* and *npk*, for example, seem alternate forms of the same root. On the other hand, such sporadic variants--far from being evidence for--are actually evidence *against* the free interchange of *B* and *P* in Heb, Ug, or any other Semitic language. The fact that only a few attested forms of unconditioned interchange can be produced is evidence that we have only sporadic variants. Such occasional variants can be found with practically any phoneme in the language; *B* and *P* are no more likely to freely interchange than ʼ and ᶜ, *G* and *K*, *K* and *Q*, *S* and *Š*, or any other two closely related sounds.

Interchange of phonemes sporadically happens from time to time in any language. Phonetically conditioned assimilation is more frequent and can be reduced to some clearly defined rules. Some sounds tend to shift in the environment of another particular sound. This is quite different from free interchange; the particular phonetic environment is very important. Yet Blommerde, for example, blithely ignores this in his discussion of the interchange of *B* and *P* (pp. 5-6). Notice certain cases in point:

He cites Brockelmann (*Grundriss* I, p. 166) as one of his bibliographical references. Yet Brockelmann is referring specifically to *bš>pš* in Akk. That is, Brockelmann is referring only to Akk (though it does occur elsewhere) and only to the change *B* to *P* before *Š*. Blommerde also cites several examples from the glossary of UT. Of the eight examples, three involve a *B>P* shift before *Š* or *T̲* (UT § 19.546, § 19.555, § 19.1353), two involve a shift before *K* (UT § 19.1597,

§ 19.2041a + § 19.2182; cf. Kühne, UF 7 [1975], 259-60), and one involves a word of non-Semitic origin (UT § 19.511). One more example (UT § 19.494) will be discussed below. This brings us down to two examples of a possible sporadic interchange. Thus, Blommerde's statement, "*b* and *p* are subject to reciprocal interchange in all the Semitic languages," needs some very specific qualifications. His actual practice of comparative philology also shows little regard for the specific conditions under which interchange takes place.

In the specific case *b*ᶜ*l* II in Ug, there is no doubt it is used much as *pā*ᶜ*al* is used in Heb. Gordon compares Heb and Phoen *P*ᶜ*L*. However, one must ask whether Ug *b*ᶜ*l* is actually a cognate of *P*ᶜ*L* or really a cognate of *B*ᶜ*L* with a special semantic development in Ug. The latter would appear to be the case, especially if the name *yp*ᶜ*l* in 2027:4 does indeed have *p*ᶜ*l* "make" as its base. Since the evidence of the Ug form is uncertain in its etymology, it seems rather precarious to postulate a meaning "work" for *B*ᶜ*L* in Heb. It is true a translation "workers" in Job 31:39 makes good sense in context. Yet one could obtain the same sense from the normal meaning of the Heb word. Ownership does not necessarily imply wealth or prosperity since the land owned may have been so small or poor the owner eked out only a bare existence. The owner and worker of the land were also often the same individual. While the expression "my land" is used in v 38, v 39a mentions payment for food. Job is not likely to pay for the fruit from his own personal property. "My land" could be understood metaphorically in the mouth of a patriarch even for the personal land of those under his charge. One might compare the example of Ahab and the vineyard of Naboth (I Kgs 21:1-16). Even the king was expected to respect individual ownership. Ahab's sin was doubly condemned since he took the land and its fruits without payment and he snuffed out the life of its owner.

The suggestion of Pope in regard to *ḥibbēš* is interesting and fits the context. However, the normal change is *B* to *P* before *Š*, not the reverse. Further, the cognates of the two Heb roots show no interchange. That is, all the cognates of *ḤBŠ* have a *B* (apparently Akk *epēšu* is no longer thought to be cognate with *ḤPŠ* as Brockelmann assumed) and all the cognates of *Ḥ*P*Ś* have a *P*. More important is that both the roots appear side by side in many of the other languages, as they do in Heb, and with much the same semantic content. (Pope does not note that his suggestion requires a *Ś*>*Š* for this same root as well.) If one feels the need for "search out" in Job 28:11, there seems no other way to obtain it than be emendation.

§ 30. 29:18

Broek, R. van den. *The Myth of the Phoenix according to Classical and Early Christian Traditions*.

Dahood, M. "Nest and Phoenix in Job 29,18," *Biblica* 48 (1967), 542-4.

_____. "*Ḥôl* 'Phoenix' in Job 29:18 and in Ugaritic," CBQ 36 (1974), 85-8.

Driver, G. R. "Birds in the Old Testament II," PEQ 87 (1955), 138-9.

Heras, H. "The Standard of Job's Immortality," CBQ 11 (1949), 263-79.

And I said, "With my nest I will perish,
וכחול I will multiply (my) days.

While most translations have adopted the rendering, "as sand," the interpretation, "as the phoenix," has been around a long time. Heras discusses three possible meanings of *ḥôl* in this verse, devoting most of the article to the phoenix myth. Dahood also accepts the translation "phoenix," followed by Blommerde (translating 18a, "Though I perish like its nest"). Pope discusses the problem at some length in his commentary. While translating "sand," he states the question "remains moot."

The versions also may have understood "palm tree" as well as the other two interpretations mentioned already:

LXX: ὥσπερ στέλεχος φοίνικος πολὺν χρόνον βιώσω "as the palm stump I will live a long time." It has been suggested the word "stump" is not original and "phoenix" instead of "palm" should be read (cf. Heras).

Vg: *et sicut palma multiplicabo dies* "and as the palm I will increase days."

Tg: והיך חלא אסגי יומיא "and as the sand/phoenix I will increase days." CW takes it as "sand" but mentions the interpretation "phoenix." Jastrow would translate it "phoenix."

Syr: ואיך חלא דיממא אסגא יומי "and as the sand of the seas I will increase my days."

The most immediate reason for looking for something other than "sand" in *ḥôl*--a perfectly good simile for years of long life--is the word *qēn* "nest" in the previous line. Some commentators have attempted to find a new meaning for *qēn*. Rowley mentioned the proposed reading "nestling" which occurs for *qēn* in such passages as Deut 32:11 and Isa 16:2 (see also Gray and cf. BDB), but observed, "Job scarcely thought he would die while his children were 'nestlings', i.e. unfledged." Driver compared *qēn* with Egyptian *qn* "strong" and *qn.t* "strength" and translated, "I shall die in my strength." This suggestion would remove any problem with taking *ḥôl* in its normal sense of "sand," but there appears to be no real evidence of such a loan word in Heb or elsewhere in Semitic.

If we read *qēn* as the usual "nest," the context seems to eliminate any other explanation than that of the phoenix myth. (While emending *qînnî* to *ZQNY*, Pope notes, "If 'nest' is retained here, one should probably, on the basis of parallelism, choose the 'phoenix' rather than 'sand' in the next line.") The whole of chap. 29 concerns Job's former prosperity. All his blessings and all his righteous deeds are described. Vv 19-20 refer to metaphors of health and vigor. What then does he mean when he refers to his thought during those days of prosperity, namely, the thought, "I will perish with my nest, I will multiply my days"? The reference to nest makes sense only in the light of one suggestion known to me--as a reference to the phoenix myth.

The history and form of the phoenix myth are complicated. The most recent lengthy treatment is that of R. van den Broek. The classical phoenix myth has often been related to the Egyptian bird *bennu* which played a prominent part in Egyptian mythology and was associated with the god Ra in the Book of the Dead. Van den Broek concludes that the classical myth is related to the Egyptian figure, but the former did not originate in the latter (20, 24). While there are a number of agreements between the phoenix and the *bennu*, there are also a number of significant differences (24-6). One important difference is that the *bennu* does not appear to be associated with any particular period time cycle. Thus, any use of phoenix imagery in Job could not be based on the Egyptian figure. However, the classical myth is also very old, going back at least to the time of Hesiod (about 700 B.C.--see A. Lesky, *History of Greek Literature*, 91). Further, there seems to be evidence that the Greek *phoinix* is to be traced back to Mycenaean (van den Broek, 62-5). It should not stretch one's credulity to suppose the myth known to the author of Job.

One of the reasons for assigning the meaning "phoenix" to *ḥôl* in this passage is the fact that the word certainly had that meaning in later Jewish writings. *Genesis rabbah*, s. 19, specifically relates Job 29:18 to the phoenix myth. This does not mean one could automatically read such a late account back into Job. Nevertheless, the antiquity of the myth has already been noted and the rabbinic account would indicate the persistence of the myth among the Jews of a much later time. The use of *ḥôl* for the phoenix appears to be not just a late development but a genuine reflex of older usage as the context and wording of Job 29:18 indicate.

Albright suggested that *ḥl* in Ug is also the phoenix (see references in the Dahood articles and Pope's commentary on the passage). Pope took exception to this and discussed it at some length. Dahood's 1974 article contains a partial answer to Pope's arguments. Dahood points out that the expression *rḥb.mknpt* in UT 125.9 (= CTA 16.1.9) finds an interesting parallel in Isa 8:8 where the two roots are used in proximity to each other though not as a syntactic unit. He translates the Ug passage *ḥl.rḥb.mknpt* as "O phoenix broad of wingspread!" Thus, if Job 29:18 associates "nest" with *ḥôl* and the Ug passage associates *ḥl* with "wingspread," only some sort of bird can be a question. At least "sand" would hardly fit. If correct, Dahood's explanation adds additional weight to the identification of "phoenix" in this Job passage.

A further indication that *ḥôl* was not just an invention of the later Jewish sages because of Job 29:18 is its possible etymology. The Semitic word does not of course appear in the

Egyptian or classical phoenix accounts. Heras suggests the myth originated in India. He offers evidence that *ḥôl* is itself a Dravidian word. If so, a confusion with the well-known word meaning "sand" would hardly be surprising. There is no doubt that a number of factors must be considered. Several alternative suggestions indeed have merit, but the weight of evidence available to me favors the phoenix interpretation. This again illustrates how a consideration of Semitic cognates alone may be insufficient. The whole literature and mythology of the ancient eastern Mediterranean may have to be considered before the correct explanation can be arrived at.

§ 31. 30:24

Guillaume, A. *Studies in the Book of Job*, 115.

Also let him not send his hand בעי-,
If in his ruin there is therefore a cry.

This verse is notoriously difficult ("regarded as one of the most difficult in the entire poem," Pope). Part of the problem is the word in question. Though it is usually translated "ruin," that imagery is felt by many commentators to be inappropriate here. Emendations for various parts of the verse are numerous, but a common one for *ᶜî* is *ᶜānî* "poor."

LXX: εἰ γὰρ ὄφελον δυναίμην ἐμαυτὸν χειρώσασθαι, ἤ δεητεὶς γε ἑτέρου, καὶ ποιήσει μοι τοῦτο "for were I able to lay hands upon myself (for) help, or beg another, and he will do this to me."

Aq (from Syr-Hex): πλὴν οὐκ εἰς τὸ ἐκπορθῆσαι (s. ἐξαναλῶσαι) ἐξαποστελεῖ (χεῖρα) "only that he does not send out (his) hands to plunder (destroy)."

Sym (from Syr-Hex): ἀλλ᾽ οὐκ ἐν ἰσχύϊ ἐχετείνετο χείρ "but he did not stretch out his hand in strength."

Th (from Syr-Hex): πλὴν οὐκ εἰκῆ ἐξέτεινε χεῖρα "only he did not stretch out (his) hands without purpose."

Vg: *verumtamen non ad consumptionem eorum emittis manum tuam et si conruerint ipse salvabis* "only you did not send your hand to their consumption, and if they fall, you yourself will save (them)."

Tg I: לחוד לא בריתחא ישדר מחתיה אין בעידן צעריה יקבל צלותהון "only not in rage let him send his plagues but in time of his pains let him receive their prayers."

Tg II: ברם לא לגרמיה יגרג מחתיה אין בחטטיה ישוי להון אספלניתא "therefore, let not his plague strike to his bones, but let him set them a plaster for his sores."

Syr: ברם לא עלי נושט אידה ומא דגעית לותה נפרקני "but let him not stretch out against me his hand and whenever I call out to him, let him save me."

Any ultimate solution to the problem is going to require a thorough syntactical analysis. However, comparative evidence produces two solutions which may eventually help solve the problem. Guillaume compares ^{c}*î* with Ar ^{c}*ayy* "weak, helpless" (but still has to supply a verb to the second half of the verse). This would produce the result of emending to "poor" without tampering at all with the MT. One could then translate along the lines, "One does not lift his hand against the helpless when in his calamity there is consequently a cry (for help)." (This requires taking the *lāhen* of 24b as equivalent to *lāhēn*, as is already done by many commentators.) The major question, though, is whether the Ar root ^{c}*yy* is unique to that language or has cognates in other branches of Semitic. My research did not turn up any clear cognates unless the Ar word is itself a cognate of Heb ^{c}*î* "ruin." If so, the sense "weak, helpless" seems a special semantic development in Ar and of little use to our inquiry.

MHeb hints at another possibility which would also seem conceivable from the BHeb usage alone. According to *b. Aboda Zara* 4a, Job 30:24 shows God will not destroy Israel in his punishment but will only punish like the pecking of a chicken. This indicates ^{c}*î* would mean something like "destruction" (cf. the OT usage "ruin"). Taking a clue from this, one could take the *b*^{e} as showing accompaniment and translate, "Indeed let him not send (his) hand with (complete) destruction/ruin if in his calamity there is accordingly a cry (for help)." Again, one could probably obtain such a meaning from a consideration of biblical usage alone, but the rabbinic comment reinforces the suggestion.

One further possibility takes into account the fact that

practically all the cognates of ${}^{c}WH$ (${}^{c}WH$ II in BDB) include the idea of going astray or sinning in their respective languages. Cognates with this meaning include: Heb, JAram, Ar (*ǧawā*), and Geez (^{c}*ayäyä*) (cf. also Akk *ewûm*). This could suggest God's sending his hand against "sin, error" and against the sinner by implication. A sample translation might be: "Also let him not send (his) hand against transgression if (the sinner) in his fall accordingly cries (for help)."

Both of these last two suggestions would explain the MT while still taking account of the grammatical problems involved and hopefully without straining the credibility too much. The suggestion of Guillaume was interesting but must be considered unlikely unless further cognate evidence can be found. Considering the diverse and generally paraphrastic rendering of the versions, they appear to have had the same difficulties modern commentators find.

§ 32. 33:18

Loretz, O. "Der Gott *šlḥ*, he. *šlḥ* I und *šlḥ* II," UF 7 (1975), 584-5.

Tsevat, M. "The Canaanite God *Šälaḥ*," VT 4 (1954), 41-9.

He will hold back his soul from the pit,
And his life from crossing בשלח.

Although *šelaḥ* definitely refers to weapons in a number of the passages where it is used in the OT, a need was felt for something parallel to *šaḥat*. This was achieved by some commentators by emending to "Sheol." Dhorme however suggested that *šelaḥ* in this passage and 36:12 meant the "Canal," a mythical term parallel to Sheol and Pit. He is followed in this by Pope and other modern translators.

LXX: καὶ μὴ πεσεῖν αὐτὸν ἐν πολέμῳ "and (he did) not (let him) fall in war."

Vg: *et vitam illius ut non transeat in gladium* "and his life that it not pass over by the sword."

Tg: וחיירי מן למעבר בשילחא "and his life from going over by the lance."

Syr: וחיוהי מן אבדנא "and his life from destruction/ Abaddon."

11QtgJob is not extant for this passage. But in 27:6 (= MT 36:12) is the expression בחרבא יפלון "they will fall by the sword" for MT בשלח יעברו. This suggests that "sword" would also be the rendering for Job 33:18.

The article by Tsevat demonstrates the existence of a Canaanite god *Šelaḥ*, associated with the river and the underworld. This deity can be equated with other river gods of the ancient Near East. (For example, Tsevat mentions Yamm of the Ugaritic myths who is also called Judge River. However, Yamm is not explicitly associated with the netherworld.) Tsevat also differs from Dhorme in seeing *šelaḥ* not just as the channel by which the netherworld is reached but as a designation of the underworld itself. One "passes over" or "through" the infernal river. (Cf. the River Styx of classical mythology.) At one point Tsevat quotes a passage from the "Babylonian Qohelet" about crossing the river Ḫuber (44). It is interesting that the expression is *na-a-ri ḫu-bur ib-bi-ri* (for text see Lambert, *Babylonian Wisdom Lit.*, 70). Note the last word contains the Akk cognate of Heb *ᶜābar* which is used in Job 33:18 and 36:12. Loretz adds some important data from Ug which Tsevat had overlooked.

The origin, then, of the expression "crossing the Channel" seems rather clear from the evidence offered by Tsevat and Loretz. Yet the homonym *šelaḥ* was also widely used in the context of a violent death. This coupled with a presumed pious shift away from direct references to pagan gods would explain why the expression *baššelaḥ* came to mean "by the sword." The question is when that came about. Apparently it had already taken place by the time of the Qumran targum, estimated to be about the 1st century B.C. at the latest. Yet the parallelism in 33:18 seems to warrant no other interpretation than that the poet understood *šelaḥ* as equivalent to Sheol. This is strengthened by the references to the netherworld in vv 22, 24, 28, 30. Note that v 28a uses the same verb syntactic construction as v 18 and the same verb, only "Pit" is substituted for *šelaḥ* and "soul" for "life."

§ 33. 33:24

Guillaume, A. "The Arabic Background of the Book of Job," *Promise and Fulfilment*, 121.

He grants him favor and says,
פדעהו from going down into the Pit;
I have found a ransom.

This *hapax* has no parallels in cognate languages to elucidate it--at least as listed by older commentaries and lexica. It is often emended to *PDH* whose meaning would fit here. Guillaume suggested the letter *P* was actually like the conjunction *fā* in Ar while the rest was to be explained from Ar *wada*^{c}*a* "allow, let off exempted."

LXX: ἀνθέξεται τοῦ μὴ πεσεῖν αὐτὸν εἰς θάνατον "he will support him that he might not fall in death."

Vg: *libera eum et non descendat in corruptionem* "free him and he will not go down into corruption."

Tg: פרוק יתיה מלמיחת בשוחתא "deliver him from going down into the grave."

Syr: פרוקיהי דלא נחות לחבלא "deliver him that he might not go down into destruction."

11QtgJob: פצהי מן חב]לא "rescue him from destr[uction]."

While some lexica such as BDB and KB give no cognates, others do (for example, Zorell and GB). The problem is whether the cognates are of any help (Zorell thinks not). A sense such as "deliver" is indicated by the versions and the context. *PD*^{c} occurs in both JAram and Syriac with the meaning "wound, break." *P. Kidd.* 61d refers to this passage in Job and interprets it as referring to saving Job from the Pit by means of expiatory punishment. (Jastrow defines the root as "redeem" but seems to be influenced by a comparison with *PDH*.) Classical Ar has two roots, *fada*^{c}*a* and *fadağa*, both of which seem related in meaning. *Fada*^{c}*a* refers to having a deformed member of the body. *Fadağa* means "break, shatter, crush." Similar ideas are found in other Ar dialects (Dozy; Denizeau; Landberg, *Glossaire daṯinois*). The idea of "break, wound" seems common to the root in Ar and Aram.

In considering these cognates, we must remember that

words can be cognates without necessarily having closely related semantic fields. But the fact that several cognates exist should deter us from assuming an error in the transmitted Heb text of Job. A second deterent is the fact that the emendation to *PDH* seems ruled out by v 28 of the same chapter. The tendency would be for scribes to assimilate *PD*^{c} to the more familiar reading of v 28. Also the poet is not likely to have used the same root so close together in such similar expressions. (The presence of *PDH* in v 28 is also an argument against *PD*^{c} being simply an orthographic variant of *PDH*.) Thus, if it does nothing else, the cognate evidence seems to give weight to the reliability of the MT reading at this point.

When we note the semantic field of the root *PD*^{c} in Ar and Aram, we might be tempted to conclude with Zorell that it gives no help. But that seems a hasty judgment. The explanation given in the Palestinian Talmud as mentioned above is not too convincing. It sounds rather contrived but perhaps should not be dismissed completely. The meaning of "break" needs consideration in the light of the various metaphors used for going to Sheol. One which seems important to me is the image of the "cords of death/Sheol." This type of expression is used in Ps 18:4, 5; 116:3, 16. Ps 116:16 refers to "opening" (*PTḤ*) these cords. Cords as symbols of death or suffering can also be "broken" (*NTQ*--Ps 107:14). Could Job 33:24 have reference to "breaking" or "dissolving" whatever it is that is taking Job down to the Pit--perhaps the "cords of the Pit"? One might compare *PRQ* which means "break, loosen" and by extension "redeem" (Jastrow 1238). This is only a suggestion. It is possible the root *PD*^{c} as used in Job had quite a different meaning from that of the cognates, but the cognates do testify to the existence of such a root elsewhere in Semitic. *PD*^{c} is not unique to this passage in Job and should not be blithely emended away.

The attestation of the root in other Semitic languages also tells against Guillaume's suggestion, ingenious as it is. One should note as well that his suggestion requires a change of the MT form. Proving the existence of a Heb cognate of *wada*^{c}*a* is another problem. Such cognates have been proposed and even find an entry in HAL under *YD*^{c} II (for a recent thorough study, see J. A. Emerton, JSS 15 [1970], 145-80). But the meaning is "set down, set forth" or "be quiet, at rest" and not "let off exempt" as Guillaume proposes. Much further evdience is needed for his suggestion to be persuasive.

§ 34. 33:25

רטפש his flesh than a youth's,
He will return to the days of his boyhood.

This unusual quadraliteral has been explained in various ways if not emended. BDB (936) suggests it may be a metathesis of *ṬRPŠ*, a word found in some cognate languages.

LXX: ἁπαλυνεῖ δὲ αὐτοῦ τὰς σάρκας ὥσπερ νηπίου "he makes his flesh soft as an infant's."

Vg: *consumpta est caro eius a suppliciis* "his flesh has been consumed by punishments."

Tg: איתחליש בסריה יתיר מן ריבותא "his flesh becomes more tender/weak than that of his childhood." Jastrow gives the reading "tender"; CW, "weak."

Syr: נתחלף בסרה איך דבטליותה "his flesh is renewed like that of his youth."

A quadraliteral verb is unusual enough that any cognates should stand out quite easily. One might assume the Heb word was a unique formation. Indeed, many quadraliterals have a liquid such as an *R* in them, though usually not as the first radical. Both JAram and Syr have such roots to compare but with a metathesis: *ṬRPŠ*. This forms a pattern more like many quadraliterals in having the *R* as the second radical. In both cases the meaning has to do with flesh. The JAram *ṬRPŠ'* refers to a lobe or membrane of fatty tissue which may cover certain organs such as the heart. The Syriac word *ṬRPŠT'* means "lean flesh." (Ar also has a word *ṭarfasa* but none of its meanings seem to fit.) The chance of coincidence between the JAram/Syr root and the Heb is very small. This militates against assuming a textual corruption. On the other hand, the presence of metathesis argues against a direct borrowing from this passage.

The next question is whether the quadraradical is expanded from a triliteral. Brockelmann, BDB, GB, and NW all suggest an expansion from *ṬPŠ*. A check of that word produces some interesting results. Both the BHeb and MHeb words mean "fat" and, by extension, "stupid." The Akk *ṭapāšu* also seems to mean "become fat" (see Muss-Arnold). The Christian Palestinian Syriac root refers to being unclean, as does Ar *ṭafisa*. Yet in Mandaic the same root means both "be dirty" and "be fat." The semantic range in the various Northwest Semitic languages (the root seems still to be unattested in Ug) appears to cover the ideas of "be fat, unclean, stupid." (The Syriac meaning "lean flesh" would appear to be a special development in that dialect.)

After examining the picture as whole, we see a quadraliteral formation attested outside BHeb but sufficiently different not to think of borrowing. The semantic range of these plus that of the assumed triliteral base combine to support a retention of the MT. The question of the exact meaning still has to be answered. Something like "his flesh grew plumper than that of a youth" would probably be quite literal, with the context indicating that the comparison was favorable. It is well known that in the pre-cholesterol days of the ancient Near East, being "plump" or "fat" was considered a sign of good health. See, e.g., Deut 31:20 and Prov 11:25; 13:4; 28:25 (Heb *DŠN*). The various words for physical lipids were also often used metaphorically to symbolize richness, prosperity, and health. Of course, the exact connotation to a native speaker of the time is no longer discernible.

The versions seem to give little help. They appear to be translating from the contextual reference to flesh and childhood (with the exception of Vg which, while probably also translating from context alone, seems to have connected *minnōᶜar* with *NᶜR* "to shake"; cf. Dhorme).

§ 35. 35:10

And he did not say, Where is God my maker,
The one giving זמרות in the night?

While widely translated by the normal meaning "songs," a number of commentators take it as "strength" (e.g., Pope and

Tur-Sinai). This is done by connecting it with a PS root *<u>d</u>mr* instead of the PS root **zmr* from which comes "sing."

LXX: ὁ κατατάσσων φυλακὰς νυκτερινάς "the one appointing nightly watches."

Aq: . . . μελῳδίας "songs."

Sym/Th: ὁ διδοὺς αἰνέσεις ἐν τῇ νυκτί "the one giving praises in the night."

Vg: *qui dedit carmina in nocte* "who gave songs in the night."

Tg: דמסדרין אנגלי מרומא קדמוי תושבחן בליליא "before whom high angels set in order praises in the night."

Syr: דיהב מחשבתא בלליא "who gives reasoning in the night."

11QtgJob: ודי חלק לנא לׄ[ ]רׄ לנצבתנא בלילא "and apportioned to us [ ] for our plant in the night." The word *LNṢBTN'* is read "plantation" by the original editors. Pope suggests the word means "strength," comparing *niṣbᵉtā'* in Dan 2:41. Sokoloff also thinks this the most likely meaning of the Qumran reading and translates, "for our firmness (?) in the night." However, there are several objections to be made to this interpretation. First, there seems to be a question as to whether *niṣbᵉtā'* means "strength" in biblical Aram. Granted, KB gives the definition "firmness, hardness." Yet elsewhere in Aram the root seems to have more to do with planting. Thus, Vogt (114) takes Dan 2:41 as a reference to "inborn qualities." One of these "native" qualities may be strength, yet this does not mean that "strength" is the specific definition of the word. The data are probably too skimpy to solve this aspect of the problem. But, secondly, it seems most likely that the translator of 11QtgJob read *ZMRWT* as being from *zāmîr* or *zᵉmôrāh* "tendril, shoot" (cf. Kaufman's review on this passage). While not Aram, these words were still undoubtedly well-known in the translator's environment. To assume that this was his understanding seems much sounder than to postulate that he recognized a rare word *ZMR* with the meaning "strength." (One might also note in this connection that the Qumran community referred to itself as a *MṬᶜT* "plantation" in such passages as 1QS 8:5; 9:8; CD 1:7. However, J. A. Fitzmyer states that "there is not the slightest hint of Essene authorship" in the Qumran Job targum, "Methodology in the Study of . . . Jesus' Sayings," 86.)

The existence of a root **ḏmr* in Semitic is well-attested. The major cognates are listed under *ZMR* III in HAL. That lexicon considers the root a source of *zimrāh* II "strength" and the proper nouns *Z^e^mîrāh* and *Zimrî*. Job 35:10, though, is listed under *zāmir* "song." Pope does not say whether he intends to revocalize the MT form to gain his translation "strength." One would think some explanation of the plural form should have been given. Of course, one could explain it as a plural of abstraction or intensification (GKC § 124).

It is not my intent to examine whether *ZMR* "strength" is indeed certain for BHeb. For present purposes, the basic question is whether "strength" really gives any better sense than "songs" for Job 35:15. The standard explanation of the line is that the one trusting in God will be able to praise him with songs even in the "night"--times of trial and trouble --because he knows God will soon bring the "morning." This explanation still finds a place in Fohrer. The words of the verse are certainly meaningful in themselves even though the exact reference of the metaphor may be unclear. Does "strength" make the metaphor any clearer? One still has to interpret it. This seems to be an example of what is so often found with comparative philological treatments. The suggested meaning multiplies occurrences of what is already a hypothetical root or meaning while not really producing any profound new understanding of the passage in question. If compelling reasons for abandoning "songs" or translating "strength" can be found, the root **ḏmr* seems to have cogent arguments for its existence in Heb as well as elsewhere. But one wonders whether Pope and others have really given such reasons.

§ 36. 35:15

Guillaume. A. "The Unity of the Book of Job," *Annual of the Leeds University Oriental Society* 4 (1962-3), 33.

And, now, for he does not send his anger,
And he does not heed בפש exceedingly.

This *hapax* is usually emended to something like *peša*^{c}. A meaning such as "folly" would be appropriate (cf. BDB), but there is no tri-radical root in Heb which helps us: No root *PŠŠ* is attested in BHeb while *PWŠ* does not give too much help. Guillaume cites Ar *fasīsī* "weak-minded" and translates, "Neither does he give heed to stupidity." Delitzsch compared Ar *fašša* "overflow" to translate "arrogance" or "sulliness."

LXX (Hexaplaric addition): καὶ οὐκ ἔγνω παραπτώματι σφόδρα "and he did not know transgression very much."

Sym: μηδὲ γνωρίζων παραπτώματα σφόδρα "nor making known transgression very much."

Vg: *nunc enim non infert furorem suum nec ulciscitur scelus valde* "now therefore he has not sent his wrath nor avenged evil greatly."

Tg: ולא ידע לאפושי לחדא "and he does not know (how) to increase very much."

Syr: ולא מכא לנפשא "and does not harm a soul."

The form *paš* suggests derivation from the root *PŠŠ* (GKC, p. 229c). However, as has been found in other passages (§§ 4, 8, 23), the cognates seem to fluctuate between *PŠŠ* and *PWŠ*: MHeb--*PWŠ* "breathe, rest oneself"; Old Aram *PŠŠ*--"abolish (?)" (see KAI 215:8; Gibson, II, 83); JAram--*PWŠ* "expand, increase"; Syr--*PWŠ* "remain, stay behind" and *PŠŠ* "be relaxed, dissolve"; Mandaic--*PUŠ* and *PŠŠ* "remain; relax; smash, squeeze"; Akk--*pašǎsu* "salve, rub in"; Amharic and Geez--*fäwwäsä* "nurse, heal, cure"; Tigre--*fässä* "to become plentiful, swell, spread" and in the tD stem "to rejoice"; Ar--*fašša* "cause a swelling to go down, press air out by squeezing." *PWŠ* also occurs four times in the OT (Jer 50:11; Hab 1:8; Mal 3:20; Nah 3:18). Two of these have to do with calves and one with horsemen. They are usually translated by something like "to spring" (if not emended). However, the other cognates listed here suggest some idea connected with expand or overflow, such as "snort," "rejoice (= overflowing with spirit)," or "cavort," would be the meaning or at least included as a part of its meaning. The Nahum usage seems to mean "scatter." There may be question about some of the words given above being cognates. Most are listed by Brockelmann under the Syriac root. As has been pointed out (for example, by Driver on this passage in opposition to Delitzsch' suggestion), the Ar word does not follow the normal sound correspondences. But when the whole system is analyzed, it seems evident that the Ar word is cognate and that we have an example of sporadic variation. Thus, it would seem that Delitzsch' comparison has some probability after all, though he hardly gave much of an argument himself. However, Guillaume's suggestion does not seem to have much philological evidence to support it.

If there is a common denominator to the cognates, it seems to be the idea of overflowing, sometimes with the idea of pressing or squeezing. The context of Job 35:15 would allow a number of rather diverse ideas to fit. V 16 with its mention of "increasing words without knowledge" and Job's opening his mouth "in vain" or "emptily" is suggestive in this light. One might also compare Elihu's being so full of words he is ready to burst (32:18-9). When the cognate evidence is considered, v 15b seems also to have reference to words. One could think of "multitudes (of words)," "gaseous (empty) talk," "excess (of words)," "unrestrained talk" or the like. The semantic range of the cognates allows several possibilities and the context does not limit the choice. The versions give no help, either. Nonetheless, the root *PŠŠ/PWŠ* seems common to the major branches of Semitic, and any emendation of this word would appear to be misplaced.

§ 37. 36:27

Dahood, M. "Ugaritic and the Old Testament," *De Mari à Qumrân*, 27-8.
Ellenbogen, M. *Foreign Words in the Old Testament*, 13.
Speiser, E. A. "'*Ed* in the Story of Creation," BASOR 140 (Dec., 1955), 9-11.
______. *Genesis*, 16.

For he draws up drops of water,
And they distill rain לאדו.

This word occurs only here and in Gen 2:6. While "mist" was a widely used translation in the past (e.g. AV "vapour"), it is now generally accepted that the word comes from Sumerian, via Akk, and means "flood" or something similar. Dahood, however, claimed to find the word "hand" in the form and repointed it to *lᵉʾādô*, translating, "from his hand."

LXX (Hexaplaric addition): καὶ ἐπιχυθήσονται ὑετῷ εἰς νεφέλην "and they are poured out for rain into a cloud."

Vg: *et effundit imbres ad instar gurgitum* "and he pours out heavy rains like floods."

Tg: יזלפון מטרא לעננֵיה "they fall (as) the rain of his clouds."

Syr: ונצור נוטפי מטרא בלחודוהי דמחתין שמיא בזבנא "and he alone forms drops of rain which the heavens send down at the (right) time.

11QtgJob: וזיקי מטר יהכן "and storms of rain he prepares." *YHKN* is taken as a *hafel* of *KWN* by both the editors and Kaufmann though they recognize this form as unusual. Sokoloff thinks this unlikely and reads it as a form of *HWK* ("to go"), translating, "and rainstorms go forth."

Speiser's article summarizes the previous research. When a connection was first made with Akk, there were two possible sources: *edû* "flood" and *id* from Sumerian *ÍD* "river." The equation with *id* gained wide acceptance after Albright published an argument on it. However, Speiser's article pointed out some problems with that comparison and gave strong arguments for Heb *ʾēd* being a borrowing of Akk *edû* (from Sumerian A.DÉ.A). Speiser's conclusions seem to be widely accepted now (cf. Ellenbogen).

Any questions one would have in regard to Job 36:27 do not concern the origin of the Heb word since that seems well established. Also the Akk background of the word fits well in Gen 2 where other Mesopotamian elements occur. The question is whether the author of Job understood the original sense of the Akk or whether the word had undergone a semantic shift during the time separating the two texts. For example, Gray notes, "in any case *flood* (so Assyr. *ʾedu*), preferred by many in Gn. 2^6 . . . is unsuitable here." Speiser similarly writes in his Genesis commentary, "Job xxxvi 27, 'mist' or the like, need signify no more than the eventual literary application of this rare word." Whether Gray and Speiser are right or not would depend upon how one understands the syntax of the sentence. Pope, for example, takes *l*^{e}- as "from" and translates, "That distill rain from the flood."

Dahood quite typically gives no real arguments for his reading but simply claims to identify an unrecognized form and repoints accordingly. He states the Hebrew author had a remarkable knowledge about the formation of clouds by evaporation. Even though Pope opposed this concept in the first edition of his commentary, Dahood later cited Isa 55:10 in support, translating, "Just as the rain and the snow come down from heaven and do not return there without watering the earth." However, this rendering is itself problematic. The NAB and NEB indeed have a reading similar to Dahood's version, but the RSV translates, "and return not thither but water the earth." Since the *kî 'îm* of Isa 55:10 is subject to more than one interpretation, it can hardly serve as proof for Dahood's rendering. (Pope keeps his same arguments in the second edition of his commentary but makes no reference to Dahood's discussion.) Since the word *'ēdô* is now well understood from Gen 2 and Akk documents and since Dahood gives no substantial reasons for accepting his rendering over the normal one, there seems no point in arguing the question further. (The question of taking the preposition *l*^{e} as "from" is also a factor but will not be discussed until Chapter 3.)

I would agree with Speiser (against Pope) that *'ēdô* in Job has likely undergone a semantic shift and does not mean the same as it did in Gen 2. The versions certainly support this notion of an evolution of meaning. It seems a strong possibility that the word means "mist" in Job 36:27 rather than its original Akk reference to natural flooding. This definitely illustrates that the etymology of a word does not always tell us what its meaning is in a particular context.

§ 38. 37:11

Also ברי יטריח the cloud;
The cloud scatters its light(ning).

A number of emendations have been suggested for the problematic *b*^{e}*rî*. One of the more generally accepted is the change to *bārāq* "lightning." However, this requires taking *ṬRḤ* in other than its more accepted "be burdened, toil." To do so, an equation is usually made with Ar *ṭaraḥa* "hurl, throw." This is a clear example of how the textual treatment and the comparative philological treatment are combined. The versions seem generally to have read or understood a text different from the MT (see discussion in Dhorme):

LXX (Hexaplaric addition): καὶ ἐκλεκτὸν καταπλάσσει νεφέλη "and a cloud covers over the chosen one." A variant reads καταπλήσσει "astound" instead of "cover over."

Aq (Syro-Hexapla): καίπερ ἐκλεκτὸν ἐνοχλήσει (s. παρενοχλήσει) πάχος "albeit, the thick (cloud) will trouble the chosen one."

Sym: ἀλλὰ καὶ καρπῷ ἐπιβρίσει νεφέλη "but also the cloud will be heavy with fruit."

Vg: *frumentum desiderat nubes* "the grain longs for the clouds."

Tg: ברם בברירותא מטרח עיבא "also in/with clearness/purity he loads the cloud."

Syr: ורכיכאית מתמתחן עננא "and gently the clouds are spread out."

11QtgJob: אף בהון ימרק עננין "also with them he rubs the cloud."

As most commentaries point out, b^e*rî* is to be analyzed as the preposition b^e plus a noun formation from *RWH*. Some emend because the noun *rî* is unique in this passage. Yet there are analogous noun formations from roots with medial *waw* and final *yod*. Examples are *kî*, ᶜ*î*, and *ṣî*. Furthermore, Ar has the noun *riyy* from *rawaya* (cf. also the Soqoṭri and Šḫauri form given in the next sentence.) The root *rwy* with the meaning "be wet, satiated (with drink)" is common Semitic, occurring in MHeb, JAram, Syriac, Imperial Aram, Mandaic, Ar, Geez, Tigre (*räwā*), Soqoṭri and Šḫauri (*re*). Tigrinya also possesses the root according to the etymologies in the Littmann-Höfner *Wörterbuch*. It therefore seems that the rejection of the word "moisture" in this passage is due to considerations of context and fitness of the imagery here rather than to any dearth of linguistic data.

Defining *ṭāraḥ* as "hurl" seems entirely motivated by the

emendation of *b*^{e}*rî* to *bārāq*. "Throw, hurl" seems the primary sense of the Ar *ṭaraḥa* (both modern written and classical). Tigre also has *ṭärḥa* "cast anchor" (this Tigre word should probably be added to the etymologies given in HAL). But the semantic area of the root in MHeb and JAram is somewhat different. In MHeb the semantic area covered includes "be busy, troubled, work painstakingly" and (in the *hifil*) "to load, put a burden on." JAram covers a similar area of meaning. The variety of meaning and frequency of usage argues against any literary borrowing from Job 37:11. That the root in BHeb is not unique to this passage is evidenced by the noun *ṭōraḥ* "load, burden" in Isa 1:14 and Deut 1:12. A meaning related to "burden, load" is not unknown in Ar, either. One meaning of classical Ar is "to place, set upon" (followed by ^{c}*alā* or accusative). Modern written Ar can mean "dump" (followed by the preposition *b*- or the accusative). In the dialects, Syrian Ar means "remove, take away." Denizeau cites the expression *ṭarḥat id-dinya* "a good rain fell." Landberg (*Glossaire Daṯinoîs*) lists the meanings "give, place, set" among the definitions of the root in that dialect. Cf. also Dozy II, especially 31b on the root.

The question thus is not whether the MT construction has meaning in and of itself, since there is ample comparative as well as intra-Hebrew evidence for the attested words; the question is one of context. Yet the metaphor of leading a cloud with moisture is also quite compatible with the general context. The "light" of v 11b is often interpreted as "lightning." This seems reasonable, especially when v 15, "light of his cloud," is compared. Burdening a cloud with moisture, which in turn scatters its electrical display, makes perfect sense as graphically descriptive language for a thunderstorm. Rather than being meaningless or absurd, the traditional text seems quite intelligible if one takes the trouble to consider it. The various emendations naturally make sense as well, but they hardly do justice to the attested Heb evidence.

§ 39. 37:13

Dahood, M. "Northwest Semitic Philology and Job," *The Bible in Current Catholic Thought*, 72.

> Whether for a staff, whether לארצו,
> Whether for mercy, he will make it happen.

Because "for his land" seems out of place between "staff" (= correction) and "mercy," Dahood suggested the word was not the normal root *'RṢ* but *RṢH* "favor" with prosthetic *alef*. This produces a meaning in the text as it stands which previous commentators had obtained only by emendation. Dahood is followed by Pope here.

The versions all seem to understand the normal meaning "land," though there might be some doubt about the Semitic versions: LXX (Syro-Hexapla)--γῆν; Vg--*terra*; Syr--לארעא; 11QtgJob--לארעא (on this see the editors and Sokoloff). The Tg is practically a midrash at this point, referring to three different types of rain: "whether rain of his recompense upon the seas and deserts, whether the violent rain for the trees of the mountains and hills, whether the gentle rain of mercy for the fruitful fields and vineyards, he furnishes it." One would suppose, even from his rather paraphrastic rendering, that the targumist probably understood "land" as did the other versions.

The cognates of Heb *RṢH* seem to have a proclivity for forming nouns with prosthetic *alef*. Syr has the formation *'arᶜe'*, a passive participle of *Rᶜ'* "be content, pleased, willing." Similarly, modern written Ar *raḍiya* "be satisfied, content" has the noun form *irḍā'* "gratification, satisfaction." Note should be taken of the Palmyrene deity *'rṣw*. This name appears in Thamudic and Safaitic inscriptions as *rḍw* and *rḍy*, indicating the name of the deity originated in this root (G. Ryckmans, *Les noms propres sudsémitiques*, I, 32). KAI 214.11 has the divine name *'RQRŠP*. This is usually analyzed into the name of the god Rešef plus *'RQ*. The first element has been compared with the Heb *RṢH*. (See, e.g., Gibson, II, 71. But cf. the commentary in KAI which notes that it "has escaped all attempts at explanation up to now," pp. 218-19.)

In this case comparative evidence puts what otherwise might be a purely hypothetical suggestion into the realm of real possibility. How the absolute form of the noun was vocalized is uncertain (cf. examples in BL, 487). But the construct form may not have differed from that of *'ereṣ*. It is possible, of course, that the form in Job 37:13 became assimilated to that of *'ereṣ*, especially if knowledge of the form was later lost. In either case the structure of the verse combined with the philological data presents a reasonable argument for seeing "his pleasure" or "his grace" here rather than "his land."

§ 40. 38:30

Like stone the waters יתחבאו,
And the face of the deep contracts.

The root *ḤB'* generally means "hide" or the like. Dhorme, following a predecessor, suggested the word here is related to *ḤM'* and means "congeal, coagulate." Pope gives the same suggestion, presumably taking it from Dhorme, considering that one is "a dialectical form" of the other.

LXX: ἣ καταβαίνει ὥσπερ ὕδωρ ῥέον; "which comes down like flowing water?"

Vg: *in similitudinem lapidis aquae durantur* "the waters are hardened in the likeness of stone."

Tg: היך אבנא מוי קרישן ומיטמרן "the waters freeze like stone and hide themselves."

Syr: איך כאפא מתקשין מיא "the waters congeal like stones."

11QtgJob: כא[בן] מין התקרמו מנה "the waters form a crust from it like stone."

The suggestion of Dhorme is very intriguing and would express the thought of this verse in a meaningful way to modern readers. Unfortunately, there are a number of problems with his solution. A sporadic change of *M* to *B* or vice versa is not difficult to imagine but is only hypothetical. HAL lists most of the cognates of *ḤB'* (add Mandaic *HBA* "hide, cover" and Amharic *abba* "hide"). None of these has *M* in place of the normal *B*. When we turn to *ḤM'*, another problem immediately presents itself: is there even a verbal form of this root? Noun forms are found throughout the major Semitic languages, all meaning "butter" or some other solidified milk product (see HAL, 312, under *ḥem'āh*). There is no free verb form in Heb. For the root only the Ar words *ḥami'a* and *ḫamā* are suggested as cognates. It is very uncertain, though, that these really have any relationship to the noun forms. *Ḥami'a* "be muddy" might have some conceivable semantic connection but the verb should have *ḫ* instead of *ḥ* to fit the nouns. *Ḫamā* "be thick" has the correct laryngal but ends in a *w* instead of an *alif*. This is not an insurmountable difficulty, but no noun form of *ḫamā* is used for "butter" in Ar. These data add one more argument against the existence of a verb form parallel to the noun formations of *ḤM'* in Semitic. It seems most likely from the evidence thus far seen that the noun is the original form of the root. It is well known that a number of common nouns in Semitic have no attested verb forms. A final argument against a dialectic form is that *ḥem'āh* occurs with *M* and not *B* in Job 20:17. What seems to be a variant or corrupted form of the same word (*ḥēmāh*) is found in 29:6 with *M* instead of *B*. Yet *ḤB'* occurs in 5:21; 24:4; 29:8, 10 all with its usual meaning "hide."

Dhorme's proposal must be rejected for lack of evidence, but no other comparative solutions suggest themselves. The meaning "hide, conceal" seems central to the root **ḫb'* throughout Semitic. This throws us back to trying to explain the MT form. The *hitpael* form of the verb occurs in several other passages as well, all with the meaning "hide oneself." This verse evidently refers to the freezing of water. How can this be connected with "hiding"? Since the composer of this passage is no longer around nor are any native informants, it is possible *hitḥabbē'* carried a very specific connotation in regard to water which we can no longer ascertain. But if we work with the meaning "hide," the key to the problem seems to be the preposition k^e (as first pointed out to me by Professor Brownlee). Sometimes its translation requires an English rendering with a double preposition, in this case "as with" (cf. GKC, pp. 375-6). Such a rendering has already been given in the AV, NAB, and Tur-Sinai's commentary (cf. also the NEB).

The idea seems to be that the waters are "hidden"--i.e., covered over--by ice as if it were stone. This would seem to remove much of the vexation from the verse without any need to appeal to linguistic data outside BHeb itself.

The versions all appear to understand the verse as a reference to water freezing and translate accordingly. But the lack of a consistent rendering of *hitḥabbē'* indicates they were not necessarily more sure of its meaning than modern scholars.

§ 41. 39:14

Dahood, M. "The Root עזב II in Job," JBL 78 (1959), 303-9.
Goldie, Fay. *Ostrich Country.*
Martin, Annie. *Home Life on an Ostrich Farm.*

For תעזב upon the earth her eggs,
And upon the dust she warms them.

On the basis of Ug ^{c}*db* and other cognates, Dahood proposed a new root ^{c}*ZB* meaning "set, place." He applied it to this passage since he says the ostrich does not abandon her egg for the sun to heat. Pope accepted this suggestion.

LXX (Hexaplaric addition): ὅτι ἀφήσει εἰς γῆν τὰ ᾠὰ αὐτῆς "for she will leave in the earth her eggs."

Vg: *quando derelinquit in terra ova sua tu forsitan in pulvere calefacis ea* "when she leaves her eggs behind on the earth, perhaps you will warm them in the dust."

Tg: ארום תשבוק לארעא ביעהא "for she leaves her eggs behind on the earth."

Syr: ושבקא על ארעא בנתה "and she leaves her young upon the earth."

The question of whether a root ^{c}*ZB* with the meaning "to set, place" exists in Heb is one too lengthy for us to take up here. This meaning seems clear for Ug ^{c}*db* in certain contexts. Assuming such a homonym in Heb would *prima facie* also explain certain OT passages. For Job 39:14, however, there is serious question of whether the sense "place, lay" is necessary or even plausible in the context. The primary rationale for seeking a different meaning is the supposed knowledge of natural history of the author of the Yahweh speeches. Dahood notes,

"The assertion that the ostrich shows no concern for her eggs, but leaves them to be hatched by the sun, is without foundation and is not found among the classical authors" (307). Rather, the "parents display great solicitude for their young." Thus, it is only through an incorrect rendering that "commentators have been led to cast doubt upon the knowledgeability of the biblical writer who otherwise shows a remarkable understanding of the natural world."

Unquestionably, the writer of Job might possibly have a good knowledge of the habits of ostriches. On the other hand we cannot eliminate the other possibility that the verse is influenced by popular but inaccurate folklore. While some of the natural historians of classical times are quite accurate on the whole, they also perpetuate some rather strange notions. Yet a careful reading of the verse in its present context requires neither a change from the normal meaning of the MT nor the assumption of ignorance on the part of the writer.

Although Fohrer takes v 15 (and 17) as a secondary gloss, v 15 in the present text forms a continuation of the thought of v 14. It emphasizes the dangers to the eggs of the ostrich. Such reference to danger would appear out of place if the nest is carefully watched. As a number of commentaries note, though, there are periods when the female is not on the nest (see especially Delitzsch). During the time when eggs are being laid (one every other day), "they are often left unprotected and then hyenas, jackals, bush pigs and the like often wreak wholesale destruction" (J. Stevenson-Hamilton, late Warden of the Kruger National Park, as quoted by Goldie, 26). Also during the incubation period the eggs are allowed to cool for 15 minutes once a day. The hen ostrich often leaves the nest at this time. Even during such a brief period a crow or other egg fancier may break and devour one (Martin, 123-4). Females have also reportedly been known not to sit on the nest at all, letting the sun do the job by day and the male at night. But this has probably correctly been denied since the temperature of the incubating eggs must be kept at a very specific grade (Martin, 130-1).

Without assuming either a homonym or an error of fact, the text still makes logical sense. A meaningful translation might be, "For she leaves her eggs upon the earth and warms them in the dust." The emphasis is on the location of the eggs, namely, their insecure and relatively unprotected position on the ground; but one cannot rule out the passing on of a popular misconception. The versions also support the normal meaning of [c]*ZB* in this passage.

§ 42. 39:16

Dahood, M. "Northwest Semitic Philology and Job," *The Bible in Current Catholic Thought*, 74.

______. "Ugaritic and Phoenician or Qumran and the Versions," *Orient and Occident*, 54.

Hillers, D. R. "Paḥad Yiṣḥāq," JBL 91 (1972), 90-2.

Tigay, J. "Toward the Recovery of **Poḥar*, 'Company,' in Biblical Hebrew," JBL 92 (1973), 517-22.

She is cruel to her children (as if) not hers,
In vain is her labor without פחד-.

Here and in a number of other places, Dahood argues that *paḥad* means "flock" on the basis of Ug *pḫd*. (A more complete list of references to Dahood's identification on the subject can be found in the Hillers article.) This differs from the traditional understanding of "fear."

LXX (Hexaplaric addition): εἰς κενὸν ἐκοπίασεν ἄνευ φόβου "in vain she labors without fear."

Vg: *frustra laboravit nullo timore cogente* "in vain she worked without thinking of fear."

Tg: לסריקותא ליעותה מדלית דלוחא "in vain is her labor without fear."

Syr: וסריקאית לאית דלא דחלתא "in vain she works without fear."

Hillers examines the linguistic basis for the identification of a root *PḤD* meaning "kinsman" or "group of animals" in Heb. The evidence can be summarized as follows: JAram, *PḤDYN* "testes"; Syriac, *PWḤD'* "thigh, buttock"; Palmyrene, *PḤZ* "clan, tribe" (but this is probably a borrowing from Ar; so DISO and Hillers); Heb, *paḥad* "thigh, testicle" (only in Job 40:17); classical and modern written Ar, *faḫiḏ* "thigh, subdivision of a tribe." As Hillers points out, there seems to be no internal Aram evidence for a meaning "tribe"; only in Ar is this found. (Even there we find no justification for the meaning "kinsman.")

The major cognate which would point to a *PḪD* "flock, herd" is Ug *pḫd*. However, this occurs only in the phrase *imr.bpḫd* (UT 2 Aqht = CTA 17.5.17,23-3). This has been translated "lamb from the flock" by Gordon and Dahood. Hillers argues that this is unproved. He would connect it with Akk *puḫādu* "lamb" and translate "a lamb from among the lambs." He also notes one does not usually use divisions of the human social group for animal groupings, and one should not assume such until he has solid data for doing so. Hillers rejects Dahood's identification as "in every case unnecessary and unjustified."

In his article in the Gordon *Festschrift* (*Orient and Occident*) Dahood made a brief footnoted reference to the Hillers article though attempting no full refutation. Dahood states that evidence for using a term for both a human social group and an assembly of animals is found in the use of *ḥebel* for "band of prophets" (I Sam 10:5, 10) and "herd of deer" (Job 39:3). I feel two strictures can be leveled at Dahood's arguments at this point. First, it is rather doubtful that *ḥēbel* refers to a "herd" of deer in Job 39:3. The generally accepted translation "young" is much more appropriate to the verse. It also seems the word in Job is a form of *ḥēbel* rather than *ḥebel* which occurs in I Sam 10 (Dahood typically does not discuss this point). So the particular example used to refute Hillers is itself extremely weak. Secondly, I feel Dahood has not correctly represented Hillers' comments. Hillers does not deny that a term might be used both for human and animal groupings. He only states that it is unusual and "*unless the usage is specifically attested*, we have no right to assume that the word for a clan would also mean a herd, flock, pack, pride, or gaggle" (92, emphasis mine). For the specific term *paḥad* no such usage has as yet been proved. Until it is, we should not assume it. (Tigay recognizes the problems with trying to find a *paḥad* "company." He attempts to identify a root **paḥar* with that meaning. However, his identification requires emendation and is otherwise irrelevant for the present discussion.)

Part of the problem with the material given earlier is whether we are dealing with one PS root or more than one. If there is one root *$p\underline{h}\underline{d}$*, the Akk and Heb do not fit since they should read a *Z* for the third radical in each case. One could explain this on the basis of borrowing or sporadic sound shifts. Hillers concludes there must be at least two roots--that there is no common denominator. If so, the Akk and Ug would be put into another category and only the Heb would cause any problem. Borrowing from Aram would easily explain it. One could, though, assume a PS *$p\underline{h}d$*. In that case only the Ar would present any problem (including the Ar loan into Palmyrene). This would also mean that the original root had become rather semantically diversified in the course of history.

Regardless of how one reconstructs this part of the philology, the normal connotation "fear" is still the meaning supported by the context and linguistic data now available, as well as by the versions.

§ 43. 39:21

Driver, G. R. "Difficult Words in the Hebrew Prophets," *Studies in Old Testament Prophecy*, 61.

> (His hooves) paw בעמק and he rejoices in
> strength,
> He goes out to meet the weaponry.

The word here has been associated with ^{c}*mq* II "strength" in Ug, and the passage translated "with vigor." Driver cites Gordon's *Ugaritic Grammar* for this explanation of Job 39:21. (This information has been deleted from subsequent editions of the grammar. Whether this represents a change of opinion on Gordon's part is uncertain.) For a list of other scholars who apparently also accept the equation, see Blommerde on this passage.

LXX: ἀνορύσσων ἐν πεδίῳ γαυριᾷ "he prances, pawing in the plain."

Aq/Th: ἐν κοιλάδι "in the deep valley."

Vg: *terram ungula fodit exultat audacter* "he digs the ground with (his) hoof, he rejoices courageously."

Tg: מחפשין בגלימא וייחדי בחילא "(they) paw in the vall valley, and he rejoices in strength."

Syr: חפר בעומקא ודאץ בנחלא "he paws in the valley and exults in the wadi."

11QtgJob: וחפר בבקע ורוט ויחדׄאׄ "and he paws in the valley and runs and rejoices."

The basis of an ^{c}*mq* II "strength" in Ug is generally accepted among Ug scholars. However, it is important to note this is based primarily on only one passage. This is UT 2 Aqht (= CTA 17).6. 45. In this passage Anat describes Aqht's abilities, calling him an ^{c}*mq.nšm*. Sample translations include "strongest of men" (UT § 19. 1874), "great big he-man" (Ginsberg, ANET, 152), "O hero Aqhat (Driver, *Canaanite Myths*, 55). It would seem something like "wisest of men" would be equally plausible. Two other passages must be translated "valley" (UT 62 = CTA 6.1.5 and UT 67 = CTA 5.6.21). Four other passages may possibly go either way. They all refer to Anat's fighting *b*^{c}*mq* (e.g., UT Anat = CTA 3.2.6). In these passages the next phrase in each case speaks of her slaughtering *bn.qr(y)tm* "between the cities." This makes it more likely that *b*^{c}*mq* means "in the valley" rather than "with vigor" since fortified cities stood on hills. This brings us back to the fact that the definition "strength" depends primarily on one passage in Ug, even though this conclusion is bolstered by appeal to cognates.

Elsewhere in Semitic the meaning for ^{c}*mq* is generally something to with being deep. This includes the various Aram dialects, Ar, and the Southeast Semitic cognates (see Leslau for these). These all fit with the normal meaning of ^{c}-*emẹq* in Heb and ^{c}*mq* in Ug. According to the older lexica, Akk *emēqu* means "be strong" as well as "be wise, clever." However, this is not noted by AHW which defines the word simply as "*weise sein*." *Emūqu* definitely means "strength, power," but AHW indicates uncertainty over which particular *alef* the initial *e* represents. CAD does not list the verb *emēqu*, evidently leaving it for the entry *šutēmuqu*. However, it does note that two separate roots with separate senses seem to exist (even though they may have had a common origin). Under *emūqu* (p. 161) it states:

> The fact that the basic meaning "arm" was still felt, as is shown by the frequent use of the dual form where the reference is to physical strength, and the use of the Sum[erian] á, necessitates the separation of *emūqu* (also *emūqa* and *emūqattam*) from *emqu* (also *ēmiqu*, *emiqtu*, *emuqtu*, *emqiš*, *imqu* s., *ummuqu*, *šutēmuqu* v. and *tēmiqu*), because the meanings of the latter group are in the realm of skill, experience, etc., and those of the former in that of strength, violence, etc. Ultimately, of course, both families of words may go back to a common base.

This indicates Akk does not give as sure a help toward defining Ug ^{c}*mq* as might be hoped for. If there is some doubt about this meaning for the Ug, it would also seem to make any such meaning for Heb more uncertain.

In the absence of solid evidence, any identification of ^{c}*MQ* "be strong" in Heb must be abandoned, certainly in this specific passage. Of course, the common meaning "in the valley" makes perfect sense. As Fohrer notes, the plain or bottom of the valley was the usual place for doing battle (cf. Gen 14:8; Judg 7:1). The versions all appear to understand the normal Heb meaning "valley."

§ 44. 39:27

Dahood, M. "Four Ugaritic Personal Names and Job 39$_{5.26-27}$," ZAW 87 (1975), 220.

Driver, G. R. "Job 39:27-8: The *Ky*-Bird," PEQ 104 (1972), 64-6.

Gordis, R. "Studies in the Relationship of Biblical and Rabbinic Hebrew," *Louis Ginzberg Jubilee Volume*, 178-9.

Reider, J. "Etymological Studies in Biblical Hebrew," VT 4 (1954), 294.

> Is it at your word that the falcon mounts up,
> וכי raises high his nest?

The presence of *kî* has presented a problem similar to *kōl* in 24:24--it seems out of place. It has often been emended to some sort of bird's name because of the LXX reading. Reider suggested that no emendation was needed. He compared the Ar *kui* "pelican" and argued *kî* was actually itself the name of a bird. Driver followed Reider in this and went on to try to identify the bird more precisely.

LXX: γὺψ δὲ ἐπὶ νοσσιᾶς αὐτοῦ καθεσθεὶς αὐλίζεται "or the vulture sits ensconced upon its nest?"

Vg: *et in arduis ponet nidum suum* "and places its nest in the heights?"

Tg: וארום ירים שרכפיה "and so it lifts up its nest?"

Syr: מרים קנה לשקיפא "lifting up on a crag its nest?"

11QtgJob: ועוזא̊ י̊ר̊ים̊ קנ]ה "and the hawk lifts up its nest?"

Finding cognate evidence for *kî* outside Ar is difficult. The initial identification came from Dozy (II, 503). The name does not appear in modern written Ar. Payne Smith cites a Syriac-Arabic listing which explains the Ar *kui* as a type of ibis (*Thesaurus syriacus*, 1538). The Ar words show that the root is **kwy* which would appear in Heb as *KWH*. A number of roots with second and third radicals *-WH* form nouns with the first radical plus *-Y* (see §§ 31, 38). It is easy to see why knowledge of the bird's name was lost if it was rare and like the particle *kî* in form.

While the parallels just listed occur only in Ar, Dahood has recently suggested there may be supporting evidence in Ug. A number of personal names in Ug, as in other ancient Semitic cultures, are derived from names of animals (cf. Gröndahl, *Personennamen*, 27-8). Among the animal names is *bn.nṣ* ("son of hawk"--UT 155.1). The Heb cognate *nēṣ* is found in Job 39:26, just preceding the verse with the puzzling *kî*. Dahood points out that *bn.ky* also occurs (UT 146.6) and suggests it is an animal name as well--the counterpart of the *kî* already postulated on other grounds. If so, the argument for Job 39:27 is considerably strengthened.

The cognate evidence, the internal considerations, plus 11QtgJob and the LXX all make out a reasonable case for a rare name for a type of bird here. However Gordis pointed out that the particle *kî* can sometimes be used with interrogative force as is *'im*, especially when a negative answer is expected. It is commonly so used in MHeb. This possibility cannot be ruled out even though the case for a previously unrecognized bird's name seems a rather strong one.

§ 45. 39:30

And his young ones -יעלעו blood,
And wherever the slain are, he is (also) there.

This is a very unusual form since Semitic roots seldom have identical first and third radicals. In the words of Pope, "efforts to explain it without emendation have not been convincing." Most explanations combine the two approaches of first emending the form to something more usual and then relating it to a known cognate. Pope suggests comparing it with the Ar ^{c}*lḍ* "shake a thing (in order) to pull it out." This requires viewing it as an Aramaism since Ar *ḍ* usually corresponds to Heb *ṣ* and Aram ^{c}.

LXX: νεοσσοὶ δὲ αὐτοῦ φύρονται ἐν αἵματι "And his young ones wallow in blood."

Aq: ἐστομισμένοι "taking with the mouth."

Sym: καταρροφῶσιν αἷμα "gulp down blood."

Vg: *pulli eius lambent sanguinem* "his young ones lick/lap up blood."

Tg: ואפרחוי גמען אידמא "and his young ones swallow blood."

Syr: ופרוגוהי דמא לעין "and his young ones lick up blood."

There are several possibilities open to us in regard to this unusual form. The first is the one usually taken by commentators from Gesenius on: to assume a textual error which is then corrected to something like $y^{e}la^{c}l^{ec}\hat{u}$ (from L^{cc} "swallow, lick, lap"). This involves only a slight change in the form, gives a good explanation of the origin of the textual error, and makes good sense in the context. The only problem is that one may be destroying a valuable piece of linguistic evidence which has been preserved only here.

Delitzsch would explain the form as a secondary derivation from ${}^{c}il^{c}\bar{e}l$, which itself comes from ${}^{c}\hat{u}l$ "to suck." This has some plausibility though involving several steps. Certain words with identical first and third radicals seem to owe their origin to geminate verbs. For example, *ŠRŠ* apparently derived from *ŠRR* with a stage *ŠRŠR* in between. (A couple of other identical first and third radical roots, though of uncertain origin, are *ŠLŠ* and *KRK*.) ^{c}*ûl* is not a geminate verb though sometimes weak verbs seem to vacillate between a geminate and a medial *waw* form. For examples of haplography in verbal forms, compare Brockelmann, *Grundriss*, I, pp. 259-67. Forms with the same syllable or even letter twice in the same word may sometimes lose the repeated element. Although Brockelmann seems to include no exact parallels to the form we are trying to explain, he does illustrate a certain tendency.

I can add another possibility similar to that of Delitzsch but with some differences. The root **ǧll* "enter, penetrate, plunge into" is common to Heb, Aram, Ar, and Ug. One would still have to assume an intermediate form $^cL^cL$ between it and our $^cL^c$. This would give a slightly different connotation--though one still suited to the context--that of the young falcons wading or plunging in blood. One could compare the bloody picture of Anat wading in the blood of soldiers, dousing her knees and other bodily parts in the gore (UT Anat = CTA 3.2.13-15,27-8).

Another possibility would assume a root with originally compatible radicals which has altered through phonetic change to produce identical first and third radicals. A recently noticed example of this is $^cB^c$ in 1QapGen 20:9 and 11QtgJob 3:7 which goes back to an assumed PS *^{c}*bḏ* (see Fitzmyer's comment on the *Gen. Apoc.* passage). This particular possibility is the one suggested by Pope who compares with Ar ^{c}*lḍ*. The Ar word means "shake something for the purpose of tearing it." This is very suggestive; the meaning would fit Job 39:30. Unfortunately, I was unable to find any clear cognates of the word. In fact it seems somewhat rare in Ar. It is not found in Dozy nor in any of the Ar dialects for which I have information. This lack of confirmation plus the fact that we must assume a borrowing from Aram as well would seem to require us to abandon this as a possibility unless more data are forthcoming.

Another suggestion, also assuming an Aram borrowing, presents itself. The word $^cL^c$ meaning "rib, side" occurs in

JAram (Syr *'L*^{c}). Other cognates are Heb *ṣēlā*^{c}, Ar *ḍila*^{c}, and Akk *ṣēlu*. Perhaps some sort of denominative verb from that word is used in Job 39:30 (note the *piel* form). Such is even suggested in a later rabbinic reference to this passage (*b. Ḥullin* 22b), but coming up with a convincing denominative verb from "rib, side" is rather difficult.

The most likely comparative suggestion to my way of thinking is to take the form from ^{c}*LL*, the second suggestion mentioned above, but the cogency of any of these proposals must still be weighed against the possibility of a textual corruption. As we have noticed in other examples, the versions here are difficult to assess. They practically all translate with some idea of eating or consuming. This consistency may be pure coincidence since the context allows for little else. If they had ^{c}*L*^{c} in their *Vorlage*, it seems rather unlikely they had any better knowledge of the word than we do today.

CHAPTER III

SYNTHESIS

The purpose of this chapter is to consider the results of the study in Chapter II, catalogue and synthesize them, and compare them with the research of others. The reader will frequently be referred to passages analyzed in the previous chapter for examples or specific data (cited by § number).

Phonetic Considerations

One of the major emphases in modern linguistic work concerns the systems of language.[1] Sounds are not looked at as a loose collection of individual productions of the human speech mechanism but as units in a highly structured system. Historical linguistics entered the realm of scientific study only when it was realized that sound changes follow certain regular patterns. Even though it is also true that each word has its own history, a concentration on this instead of on the place of the individual word within the language system seldom avoids a distortion of the linguistic evidence.

The importance of considering the whole picture--the broader system--of cognate information was forcefully brought home in this study. One of the major problems with the past practice of comparative philology was the myopic tendency of looking only for "a serviceable cognate" to the Heb word in question. Often no attempt was made to find out the whole picture of cognate information throughout Semitic. Certainly the impact of a comparative suggestion on the whole structure of the Heb grammar or lexicon was often overlooked. The single most important result of my study is this: *OT comparative*

---

[1]Standard works on the subject of historical linguistics include Anthony Arlotto, *Introduction to Historical Linguistics* (1972); W. P. Lehmann, *Historical Linguistics: An Introduction* (1970); Robert King, *Historical Linguistics and Generative Grammar* (1969); R. Anttila, *An Introduction to Historical and Comparative Linguistics* (1972); Mary Haas, *The Prehistory of Languages* (1969).

philology must be carried out not simply by comparing the Heb word in question with a cognate but by trying to find out how the Heb root fits within the whole system of cognates throughout the family of Semitic languages.

When various comparative suggestions were considered in Chapter II, a number were judged unacceptable. This was for a variety of reasons. Nevertheless, a good portion of those rejected fell into the category of comparing only with a word in one other language such as Ar (§§ 1, 4, 5, 8, 9, 12, 19, 25, 27, 33, 36, 38). In some cases cognates in other languages also existed, but in a number there appeared to be no other cognates. Thus, the whole picture argued for a special development in the language used for comparison. This does not deny the fact that a root may survive only in two widely separated languages.[2] Yet in testing a hypothesis (the Heb root in question is genuine or means such and such) we cannot resort to another hypothesis (the suggested word is a true cognate despite lack of confirmation due to an anomalous form). The question of probability and plausibility will be further discussed later.

When one is constructing a system of cognate information, how rigidly should the Neogrammarian dictum, "Laws of sound change admit no exceptions," be followed? It is a known linguistic fact that "The Neogrammarian *absolute* regularity (100 per cent) of sound change is untenable and this has always been recognized by most practioners."[3] However, does

---

[2]Examples are given by E. Ullendorff, "The Contribution of South Semitics to Hebrew Lexicography," VT 6 (1956), 190-98.

[3]Antilla, *Introduction*, 85. Barr has been charged with propounding the Neogrammarian idea, e.g., by F. I. Anderson, review of CPTOT, JBL 88 (1969), 345-6. Barr answers as follows: "Andersen must be willing to use his terms very loosely if he classes the linguists cited on p. 83 n. of *Comparative Philology* as 'neo-grammarians'. I make it entirely clear in the book, pp. 83f., that there is a difference between accepting the existence of such abnormalities and taking them as a *basis* for identification where *ex hypothesi* the semantic component is the quantity to be discovered" ("Philology and Exegesis," *Questions disputées d'Ancien Testament*, 44, n. 15). For a discussion of how sound change fits into the prevailing theory of generative grammar, see King, *Historical Linguistics*, 119-39. He shows that sound change may be conditioned by

this mean we can act as Guillaume would apparently have us do and assume that if certain consonants are known to be interchangeable (?) in one language (Ar in his case), they can also be legitimately used to provide a parallel from the other language to Heb?[4] This introduces the question of sporadic sound change.

Sporadic sound change is a known fact. It may operate because of a number of factors, especially analogy. But it is sporadic sound change simply because it cannot be reduced to consistent rules. An example is metathesis. Methathesis may take place under certain conditions, but universal rules for predicting metathesis cannot be formulated. A number of suggestions assume metathesis for their solution. The interchange of certain sounds and even phonemes is also known. Some suggestions have begun with the premise that certain sounds, *B* and *P* for example, are often interchangeable in Semitic (§§ 29, 40). Under what conditions can sporadic sound change be admitted into the argument?

The answer lies in consideration of the whole picture of cognate data. A very useful discussion of the question by a linguist is that of R. Anttila in *An Introduction to Historical and Comparative Linguistics*. He devotes an entire chapter to the relationship of "Philology and Etymology" to historical linguistics. In determining whether two words are etymologically related, there are a number of factors which must be taken into account.[5] Yet he emphasizes that these are guidelines and that chance and intuition still play their roles. My study has also confirmed these guidelines:

1. If the apparent connection between two words contains phonetic difficulties, the linguist should look elsewhere for a better solution.

2. The well-known rules of word formation have to be satisfied. If not, another solution should be sought.

---

things other than phonetic environment. For example, morphology may facilitate or impede a sound shift.

[4] "Hebrew and Arabic Lexicography," *Abr-Nahrain* 1 (1959-60), 4.

[5] Anttila, *op. cit.* (see n. 1 above), 331-2.

3. If one has to assume an unusual semantic development in seeing a connection, he should go back to points 1 and 2 and may find the real solution there.

4. If investigation indicates a particular root had a place in the proto-language (proto-Semitic in our case), its apparent absence in any of the daughter languages requires an explanation. A search often finds the reason or the missing root itself.

5. Various kinds of tests can be performed using a dialect map. For example, if a word seems to go back to the proto-language, adjacent dialects should show the greatest resemblance. (Of course, this is not necessarily the case where migration has taken place. Nomadism is a further complicating factor.)

These five points are just a brief summary and require examples to illustrate them. The major point is that the most parsimonious solution is generally the best. One should look for regular phonetic correspondence first. If the example one has shows irregularities, a search should be made for roots with regular correspondences. Examples in this study are discussed in §§ 7, 9, 10, 27, 29, 40. It was also found that some roots appeared only in Northwest Semitic (§§ 1, 7, 29), but most appeared scattered throughout the various divisions of Semitic languages, suggesting the root was a part of PS. On a few occasions this was useful in trying to decide whether the Heb root in question--which did not conform to normal phonetic correspondences--was actually a cognate of the suggested comparison (§§ 2, 10, 13, 15, 27, 34, 36, 40). Consequently, the pattern presented by the cognates in different languages helped to decide whether another proposed cognate should actually be accepted or not. Undoubtedly, a more diligent search of the various languages and dialects would have produced further cognates in many cases.

A major problem arises in applying Anttila's guideline no. 3. In developing a system of cognates it is necessary and useful. But when the semantic content of the Heb word in question is the information being sought, this adds an unknown quantity to the study. This is where the greater number of cognates adds significantly to the cogency of the argument. If all the cognates fall into a narrow semantic field which also fits the Heb context, the amount of uncertainty is greatly reduced. Unfortunately, this is not always the case. Some of the proposals had to be rejected simply because they required very unusual semantic developments or depended on developments which seemed unique to one language (§§ 4, 5, 14, 19, 25, 29, 31, 38).

In considering phonetic correspondence two things need always to be kept in mind. One of these is the question of the system of correspondence itself. While charts on the major Semitic languages are well known,[6] the pattern for the various lesser known languages and dialects is often overlooked or ignored. Leslau gives charts on the various Southeast Semitic languages in certain of his writings.[7] Yet I have yet to see a thorough chart on the different Ar dialects. This can be very important, especially when considering borrowings. The so-called "free interchange" of certain letters is often the result of comparing words from various dialects without noting the differences in the phonological systems of each. The system of phonetic correspondence between dialect and dialect and between dialect and major language is just as regular and just as important as that between major languages. (A "major" language is that, after all, only because of historical vicissitude rather than any inherent linguistic superiority.) The other problem concerns conditioned sound shifts. Again, it was noted that most of the alleged interchanges between certain sounds are actually conditioned by the phonetic (or even grammatical) environment and do not operate freely (§ 29, 40). Unconditioned interchange is the result of sporadic change and cannot be taken as any sort of general rule.

The question of a biliteral theory of Semitic roots needs a good deal of further study.[8] The aspect which seems of more

---

[6]For example, S. Moscati, *Introduction to the Comparative Grammar of the Semitic Languages*, 43-4; UT, p. 30.

[7]*Lexique Soqoṭri*, 14-5; *Etymological Dictionary of Harari*, 3-8.

[8]A study summarizing previous work on the subject is G. J. Botterweck, *Der Triliteralismus im Semitischen* (1952).

value for comparative philological work in the OT is the relationship of certain weak roots. The particular examples examined in Chapter II (§§ 12, 16, 19, 23, 36) suggested a high degree of correspondence between geminate and middle *waw* or *yod* verbs. That is, if the two stable consonants correspond in a regular way, the words are likely to be cognate even if one is geminate and the other hollow. This may also apply to final *waw* and *yod* roots as well (§§ 16, 23) and exceptionally to roots with *alef* (§§ 8, 18). No examples of initial *nun* verbs were examined, though one would say intuitively that these would be less likely to produce usable information. In any case, the whole question needs systematic study in its own right (apart from comparative philological suggestions) before anything but tentative statements can be made.

Homonyms

Barr devoted a considerable amount of space to the discussion of questions of homonymy and polysemy.[9] My study has generally supported the belief that conflict of homonyms is relatively infrequent and not likely to lie at the base of many textual difficulties. A useful study of homonyms which draws conclusions for language generally is that of E. R. Williams.[10] As she shows, homonyms which conflict must be carefully distinguished from those which do not:

> Only when the words concerned are alike in sound, when they are in common use in the same social and intellectual circles, and when they perform the same syntactical functions in the language, within a common sphere of ideas, do they become, in general, subject to mutual confusion and to conflict.[11]

When such homonymic conflict occurs, one or both of the words is generally dropped from the language. Linguistic studies before and after that of Williams continue to bear this

---

[9] CPTOT, chap. VI.

[10] *The Conflict of Homonyms in English* (1944). I thank Professor Macauley for bringing this to my attention.

[11] *ibid.*, 5.

fact out. This is important for Heb because the phonetic changes which brought about the merging of certain consonants and thus the production of homonyms seem to have taken place quite some time before the period when much of the OT was shaped.[12] During the intervening time most conflicting homonyms would probably have been dropped out of use. They were likely to be preserved in only two situations:

1. Literature produced in a dialect or area which did not have the conflict may have preserved a homonym lost elsewhere. Thus, if a particular writing such as Job should represent a dialect or usage different from other parts of the OT, it is possible that a homonymic form may occur there with a sense different from the normally expected one. One should be able to discover this, however, if the word in question is used with any frequency, by a study of its characteristic meaning in the language of an individual writing. §§ 25 and 42 investigated examples of alleged homonyms (*ᶜŚH* and *PḤD* respectively). In both instances the roots were used frequently throughout the book with the sense normal in other parts of the OT. (*PḤD* as a genuine homonym also occurs in Job 40:17 but causes no conflict because the contexts would normally differentiate the two as they do here.) In a third example (§ 43),

---

[12] There are several reasons for believing this. One is the use of the paleo-Heb (Phoen) script which has no special signs for marking sounds once distinguished. Some of the earliest Aram inscriptions indicate that some of these consonants were still separately pronounced in Aram in the late 2nd millennium. Yet there is no evidence for such in our earliest Phoen and Heb inscriptions. It was also once thought that the LXX showed ᶜ and *ğ* still existed as separate sounds into the post-exilic period. However, that belief has now generally been rejected by Semitists (Moscati, *Introduction*, § 8.49; T. Muraoka, VT 21 [1971], 612-18). While the Ug alphabet has separate symbols for sounds which are merged in the Heb alphabet, the mirror-written texts from northern Palestine apparently have only 22 letters (UT § 3.6). One of the texts seems dated at the latest in the early 12th century (D. R. Hillers, BASOR 173 [Feb., 1964], 45-50; F. M. Cross, BASOR 190 [April, 1968], 41-6). This indicates the phonemes *ḏ*, *ṯ*, *ẓ*, *ḫ*, *ğ* had already merged with *z*, *š*, *ṣ*, *ḥ*, ᶜ respectively. This merging was also indicated by other data known before the discovery of these tablets (Z. S. Harris, *Development of the Canaanite Dialects*, especially 40f and 62-4).

the root (^{c}MQ) appeared only twice, but both occurrences were in the same context and one definitely had its usual meaning ("valley"). Therefore, a consideration of the conflict of homonyms argued against the alleged homonymy even before other factors were taken up. (See also §§ 9, 14, 29, 35, 40, 41 for other examples.)

2. Homonyms may be preserved in set idioms or fossilized expressions even when they are lost in common usage. Such an occurrence might be harder to discover than that given above. If the set phrase had not otherwise survived in our literature, the lack of a parallel might make the identification difficult. Other Semitic literature could be helpful since stylized expressions may occur in several languages. Ug has provided a great deal of assistance in this regard.

This subject can be only briefly touched upon here. A thorough study of the question of homonyms needs to be made in BHeb as has already been done for many modern European languages.

Semantics and Lexical Meaning

An observation which soon emerges in any comparative work is the problem of semantic relationship between cognate roots. Ths use of comparative philology to elucidate OT passages necessarily puts great stress on semantics. Yet it soon becomes apparent that words in one language often mean something rather different from their cognates in other languages. The meaning may be related but perhaps only distantly so. Thus, comparative philology deals primarily in *gross semantics*.[13]

At times the semantic range of cognates throughout is very narrow (examples include §§ 10, 18, 24, 38; cf. also §§ 19, 20). At other times the meanings covered a somewhat broader range (§§ 22, 36). A few examples occurred in which there was a question of whether the words were cognate at all. The phonetic forms corresponded exactly but the senses seemed

---

[13] See J. Barr, "Etymology and the Old Testament," OTS 19 (1974), 16, who uses the term specifically in reference to OT comparative philology.

totally unrelated (see an example in §§ 15, 34). This should not surprise any English speaker who is learning German or French. Some words are so similar that they seem to leap out at the student. At other times the relationship of words he is learning to cognates in his own language may appear rather puzzling even when pointed out to him. Just finding a root which conforms to the phonetic requirements may not be enough. The scholar may also have to try to bridge the semantic gap between apparent cognates in different languages or between them and the Heb word in question. However, when the semantic content of the Heb word is what is to be ascertained in the first place, there may be some insurmountable barriers.

This is where the important matter of context comes in. Even though the Heb word in question may have an unknown meaning, the context may itself indicate the meaning or at least limit the possibilities. Examples in which the context left little leeway for variation include §§ 5, 6, 10, 12, 18, 22, 23, 24, 34, 45. Yet at other times the context may not actually limit the field all that much or perhaps only deceptively so. This is where the semantic field of cognates may be very important. If all cognates but one fall into a rather restricted range of meaning and the one falls outside that, it may be rather high-handed treatment to draw on the meaning of the lone cognate even if it best fits the Heb context. Various factors have to be considered. The greater the agreement between OT context and the best-attested semantic field of the cognates, the more likely the proposed solution is correct.

Considerations of context and structure are very important for another reason. Our knowledge of ancient Heb and a number of the other languages used for comparative purposes is derived entirely from written records. In the case of Ug, Phoen, and to a lesser degree ancient Heb, records are rather limited. We have no native informants. The emotional connotations of words, the subtle plays on similarity of sound, the sly jabs at contemporary figures or events, the proverbial sayings--in short many of the nuances and fine shades of the language--often elude us. This consideration may make us hesitate to emend the text, but it may also mean that comparative philology is too crude to refine our understanding. This argues for a greater effort to be paid to the intra-Hebrew considerations of context and parallel uses elsewhere in the OT. In a number of instances comparative philology had been called upon to elucidate a problem or give a new interpretation when a more careful appraisal of the passage in its specific context and within Heb literature generally rendered the new interpretation unnecessary (§§ 1, 2, 3, 4, 9, 11, 14, 17, 25, 27, 35, 40, 41, 42, 43). J. Sawyer summarizes the point in these words:

> Overtones and associations must be sought within the language itself by research into semantic fields and within each context. Contexts can be collected and classified according to the criteria at our disposal (date, context of situation, *Sitz im Leben*, idioms, recurring collocations), and some conclusions drawn about words which consistently appear in certain contexts. . . . Such conclusions are far more valuable than doubtful (or even irrefutable) etymologies which may have no relevance to a particular context.[14]

<u>Lexical Meaning</u>

The major concern of comparative philology for OT purposes is lexical meaning. Rare words which are not otherwise defined by context are the problem and comparative philology a means toward a solution. The weakness is often not in the principle involved--though certain inadequacies are inherent in the method as already noted--but in its practice. The question of lexical meaning may be too inadequately dealt with in the language(s) being used to throw certain light on the Heb. A number of examples were noted in this regard (§§ 4, 9, 11, 14, 17, 40, 42, 43). The construction of lexica or the determination of meaning by the individual scholars may have ignored certain fundamental linguistic principles. These principles are laid out in considerable detail in the definitive *Manual of Lexicography* (1971) by L. Zgusta. His thorough

---

[14] "Root-Meanings in Hebrew," JSS 12 (1967), 49. Cf. also E. Nida's statement, "Concern for language as a part of the total culture has also resulted in a greater emphasis upon the context of a word. The individual word is thus largely meaningless apart from context and it is only within the various contexts that the semantic structure of any word or semantic unit can and must be defined" (JBL 91 [1972], 77).

analysis of the subject cannot be summarized in any detail, but certain important points should be noted as they have impact on the study of specific examples in the previous chapter.

Zgusta notes the generally accepted concept that lexical meaning is composed of three elements:[15] (1) The *designation* has reference to the relationship between the lexical symbol (word or phrase) and the part of the extra-linguistic world being referred to (called the *denotatum*). A person calls a particular object a "door." The lexical symbol is the English word "door." The denotatum is a particular object--a specific door in this case. The relationship between the two is the designation. The relationship is not a simple one since it entails all the criteria by which one judges that an object falls into the overall category which goes under the lexical item "door." (A somewhat commonly used equivalent for designation is "concept." The relationship between the word and the specific item is the concept of a class of objects which goes by the name "door.")

(2) The *connotation* includes all the other features outside of the designation (except for no. 3 given below). It generally includes the emotional and judgmental qualities of the word. An example already given are the expressions "marry," "tie the knot," and "get hitched." All three express the same designation or concept, but they all have different connotations. The first is rather neutral and would be acceptable in any situation. The second is more colloquial with a hint of levity. The third is rather vulgar and would be out of place except in a narrow humorous situation.

(3) The *range of application* has to do with the specific range of usage of a word. Take the example of the terms "thesis" and "dissertation" in the academic degree program. Both refer to a research report; both carry much the same connotation. But whereas "thesis" may apply to more than one level of graduate studies, the "dissertation" is usually used in the narrow range of doctoral level research. Another example concerns the prepositions "between" and "among." Both

---

[15] Pp. 27-47. See also Eugene Nida, *Componential Analysis of Meaning* (1975), 25-30.

show the same designation; both have a neutral connotation; but "between" is applied only to two things while "among" covers the range of three or more.

The concept of what is covered by lexical meaning is important. Zgusta gives the necessary analysis even if one wishes to use other terminology (the terminology is not in fact completely unified even among linguists). For comparative philology the important thing is the fact that it may be difficult to determine these three requirements for some words because of our limited corpus of literature. One might be able to determine the basic designation of a word without knowing the connotation or range of application. An example already discussed is Ar *šbm* (§ 11). Even if the word were certain, could we use it to refer to a lion as well as a lamb? In other words, is its range of application narrow or wide?

In § 17 of Chapter II the question of semantic range of a word was discussed at some length with a reference to a recent article by Nida.[16] Now that we have discussed the components of lexical meaning, it becomes even clearer that the range of application of a word is very important. A word with a very broad range of application depends heavily on the context for specification. Zgusta states, "One of the outstanding properties of lexical meaning is its generality. . . . whereas lexical meaning is general, signification is concrete. This concretization results from the context (verbal or situational) which either connects the word used with the concrete 'thing' referred to by it, or eliminates any other possible senses of the word than that in which it is applied . . . ."[17] This is important in regard to words which are near-synonyms.[18] Near-synonyms are not interchangeable in every context. For example, even though *māqôm* can refer to a tomb, one cannot freely

---

[16]"Semantic Structure and Translating," BT 26 (1975), 120-132. His book on the subject (see previous note) discusses the subject in much more detail.

[17]*Manual*, 47-8.

[18]Zgusta distinguishes two types of synonyms. *Absolute* synonyms, in which the three components of lexical meaning are identical, are rare. *Near*-synonyms are those in which at least one of the lexical components differs. See *Manual*, 89-90.

take it to mean "tomb" unless absolutely specified by the context. Similarly with *'ereṣ* which is at times supposed to be used for the netherworld. This particular usage was not investigated, but considering the wide use of the term, it would be a mistake to apply the meaning "netherworld" in a loose manner to suit one's subjective desires unless the context is rather specific.[19]

This illustrates why consideration of the *hierarchy of meaning* among certain words must be taken into account. Nida discusses this at length in some of his writings on translating.[20] Many words have a hierarchial structure in which a number of specific words are broadly covered by a few general words. These more general words may in turn be summarized by a fewer number of words. Depending on the specific area of vocabulary being considered, there may be anywhere from two to three or four or more levels. For example, one may name a great number of individual things which are covered by categorical words such as "plant," "animal," "person." These may be covered at another level by a broader category such as "living thing." In a translation one may use a general word such as "plant" for a specific object such as a "rose." This interchange does not require one to think the two terms are synonymous or on the same plane of meaning.

Understanding the complexity of determining the range of lexical meaning is also a caution against another common error: confusing meaning with translation. Lexical meaning covers what a word means in its own language, including all the shades of connotation and range of application. Translation is how one renders a particular word or lexical unit in a particular context. To repeat an example, one may occasionally translate *māqôm* by "tomb" because of the specific context of a specific passage. That does not give one the right to define *māqôm* as "tomb." The same applies to the use of certain prepositions.

---

[19] On the occasional use of general words instead of specific ones, cf. Zgusta, 93.

[20] *Toward a Science of Translating* (1964), 73-82; *Componential Analysis*, 84-98. See also A. Lehrer, *Semantic Fields and Lexical Structure* (1974), chap. 2.

The complexity of their use requires much more detailed study.[21] Even though one may translate a particular Heb preposition by a certain English word in a particular grammatical and literary context, that does not necessarily make the two equivalent or even permit defining one by the other.

Parallelism

The question of parallelism is another extremely important point in comparative philology. A great many treatments appeal to parallelism as evidence of the meaning of a particular word or phrase or to show that the commonly accepted understanding of the Heb text is at fault. My impression is that there has been a disproportionate amount of attention devoted to synonymous parallelism.[22] Synonymous parallelism assumes the second stich of a verse is equivalent--or contains words equivalent--to the first. There are many instances of synonymous parallelism. If one can be sure of it, it is a valuable aid to textual work. But many times it is assumed and the text reconstructed on the basis of it with little or no other justification (§§ 4, 11, 12, 14, 20, 25, 27, 42, 43).

---

[21] Recent articles examining the usage of the prepositions in a rigorous way are C. Brekelmans, "Some Considerations on the Translation of the Psalms by M. Dahood," UF 1 (1969), 5-14, and Ziony Zevet, "The So-called Interchangeability of the Prepositions *b*, *l*, and *m(n)* in Northwest Semitic," JANESCU 7 (1975), 103-12. Dennis Pardee's thorough dissertation study on the subject is now being published serially in UF ("The Preposition in Ugaritic," UF 7- [1975-]).

[22] It is well known that Lowth's classic work divided parallelism into three categories: synonymous, antithetic, and synthetic. Yet it seems that much treatment is overly concerned with finding only synonymous parallelism. As has already been noted in CPTOT, 277-82, one may not be certain that any kind of parallelism exists in the verse in question. Thus, the parallelism may itself be an assumption which adds one more hypothetical factor to the discussion. For a useful review of the major writings on Hebrew poetic form from Lowth to about 1953, see Theodore H. Robinson, "Basic Principles of Hebrew Poetic Form," *Festschrift Alfred Bertholet*, 438-50; "Hebrew Poetic Form: The English Tradition," VTS 1 (1953), 128-49. More recently, see D. N. Freedman's "Prolegomenon" to the reprint of G. B. Gray, *The Forms of Hebrew Poetry* (1972). Freedman gives an annotated bibliography of work since 1915 when Gray's work first appeared.

The fact is that synonymous parallelism is only one of several different types. These other types do not allow us to draw any conclusions of meaning when one component is an unknown quantity. The so-called "synthetic" type of parallelism, in which the second stich advances the thought of the first, is widely used. A good example of this is climactic parallelism.[23] So any textual treatment based on parallelism needs to justify the reason for assuming synonymous parallelism. Yet even proved synonymous parallelism does not always give simple answers to linguistic questions as has been demonstrated by M. Z. Kaddari.[24] Kaddari expressly acknowledges the fact that Heb lexicography can benefit from parallelism,[25] but even synonymous parallelism is a complex thing and requires certain considerations to be kept in mind:[26]

1. Some parallelism is between semantic units larger than words, where the individual parts of the unit are not parallel. Two cola can be parallel as units, expressing the same thought, yet without any real synonymity between any of the individual words within the cola.

2. Even where word pairs, as opposed to pairs of larger units, are clearly attested, they may be implicit parts of larger units. Kaddari cites the example of *'ĕmûnāh* "faith" in the Psalms. One cannot merely list the words with which it is parallel because these differ according to whether it is faith of man or of God. Thus, one has to think of the qualifying phrases "of God" or "of man" whenever the term is encountered. Both this and no. 1 are cautions against a simplistic listing

---

[23] See especially S. E. Loewenstamm, "The Expanded Colon in Ugaritic and Biblical Verse," JSS 14 (1969), 176-96 (supplemented by Y. Avishur, UF 4 [1972], 1-10), and "The Expanded Colon, Reconsidered," UF 7 (1975), 261-4.

[24] "A Semantic Approach to Biblical Parallelism," JJS 24 (1973), 167-75.

[25] P. 174.

[26] The numeration is mine, since Kaddari gives no such explicit breakdown, but it follows his divisions of the article.

of word pairs without further qualifications.[27]

3. In considering semantics of individual words no attention should be paid to any parallel cola which do not have the same syntactic structure. If the syntactic structure is different, the grammatical meaning--and thus the meaning of the word--is going to be different.

4. Even when the conditions of nos. 1-3 are properly met, this is still only a case of parallels in a common semantic field. In other words the parallels may not be absolute synonyms or even near-synonyms. They may share neighboring sections of the semantic field without overlapping (e.g., "hand" and "foot"). Or they may be units which are normally associated together but divided at this point for the sake of the poetry. For example, a hendiadys or merismus may be split and its component parts used in separate stichs.

Keddari concludes his study with a note of caution which would be well taken by all who work in comparative philology: "This study has shown that Biblical poetry does not necessarily presuppose semantic parallelism. Poetical units even if they display metrical 'parallelism', are often deprived of all semantic parallelism." While parallelism may be helpful in elucidating doubtful words or phrases, as he states, only rigorous methodology can avoid a purely subjective (and often unacceptable) judgment in the matter.

Languages

One conclusion definitely arising from this study is that no Semitic language can be overlooked in attempting to find relevant comparative material. There is obviously a practical limit to the number of languages and dialects which can be con-

---

[27] One would need to keep this in mind in making use of Dahood's lengthy lists of word pairs common to both Ug and Heb in *Ras Shamra Parallels*. One extensive review of vol. I of this work (BO 31 [1974], 3-26) contains a judgment that 20 percent of Dahood's word pairs are invalid, and another 25 percent questionable (p. 6). Vol. II lists fewer word pairs, but the additional ones are subject to much the same criticism as those of vol. I. See Dietrich-Loretz-Sanmartín in UF 7 (1975), 597-8.

sulted. Some languages are also more likely to contain cognates than others. There is, however, no way to predict in any specific situation which languages may actually bring forth the desired information. Instances in which often-ignored languages may provide the necessary linguistic information are discussed in §§ 5, 6, 7, 13, 22, 33, 34, 38, 39. Thus, Barr's statement, "In principle all Semitic material is likely to be relevant,"[28] seems borne out.

Of course, some languages are statistically more likely to yield usable information than others. The reasons are rather complex. Under normal circumstances one would expect the languages more closely related to Heb to have more cognate roots. In actual practice that is not so. *Phoenician* is indisputedly the language most closely related to Heb. While the exact position of *Ugaritic* in Northwest Semitic is still debated,[29] there is no doubt that it is fairly closely related in certain features. Yet both Phoen and Ug produced surprisingly few cognates. The major reason seems to be the small corpus of Phoen and Ug literature which has come down to us. The literature that is available also tends to fall into certain rather specific categories. Phoen comes primarily from epigraphic sources. Much of Ug is best known through the epic and mythological poetic texts. It is understandable that these specialized types of literature are unlikely to provide the full range of vocabulary contained in the original languages. Broken and damaged texts are a major problem since this may eliminate the help which context gives toward understanding a Ug or Phoen root.

---

[28] CPTOT, 112.

[29] See most recently M. Sekine, "The Subdivisions of the North-West Semitic Languages," JSS 18 (1973), 205-21. Other discussions are UT, pp. 144ff; A. F. Rainey, "Observations on Ugaritic Grammar," UF 3 (1971), 152-3; J. C. Greenfield, "Amurrite, Ugaritic and Canaanite," *Proceedings of the Intern. Conf. on Sem. Studies in 1965*, 92-101; A. Goetze, "Is Ugaritic a Canaanite Dialect?" *Language* 17 (1941), 127-38. Cf. also E. Ullendorff, "Comparative Semitics," *Linguistica Semitica*, 29-30, and J. Blau, "On Problems of Polyphony and Archaism in Ugaritic Spelling," JAOS 88 (1968), 523-6.

Let me emphasize--lest my point here be misunderstood--that I in no way intend to denegate or denigrate the value of either Phoen or Ug. They have produced valuable material for a better understanding of the culture and religion of ancient Israel. Ug has greatly improved our knowledge of Heb poetry, its grammar, construction, and formulaic language. Yet this usually involves linguistic data other than that of lexicography. My study simply found Ug and Phoen far down the list of languages providing helpful cognate roots. New discoveries of material could conceivably change that, but the situation is not likely to be drastically altered without finds of new texts.

The *Southeast Semitic* languages turned out to be surprisingly helpful, surprising perhaps only because of the neglect of these languages (examples include §§ 8, 15, 21, 38, 39; cf. §§ 23, 34). Scholars of that branch of Semitic have already tried to bring this fact to the attention of OT scholars generally.[30] The major difficulty with using the Southeast Semitic languages other than the fact they are just not generally studied is the lack of good accessible editions of texts and lexica. W. Leslau has done a great deal toward alleviating the situation.[31] Unfortunately, he seldom suggests cognates for rare words in his *Contributions* and *Hebrew Cognates in Amharic* even though such often exist. One suspects the reason was partly a practical one--that he felt these rare words may only be the result of textual corruption and thus unproductive for research. My study naturally included only that information available to me as a non-specialist. A working scholar in the area could undoubtedly find a higher percentage of cognates among the multiplicity of South Arabic and Ethiopic languages and dialects.

Along with MHeb and Aram the language providing the most cognate data was *Arabic*. This demonstrates why Ar has so often been used: it has so often provided information. While a scientific lexicon of the classical language is still very much

[30] E.g., Ullendorff (see n. 2 above).

[31] See the appropriate section of Chapter I.

needed, we are well supplied with studies on the modern written language and many of the modern dialects. If use of the language is carefully controlled, it can be a valuable tool in comparative philological work. The major drawback is the lateness of the linguistic information available to us in relation to BHeb. Another complicating factor is the fact that Ar is not so closely related to Heb as some of the other languages. Any suggestion which depends on Ar alone is likely to be rather tenuous. On the other hand, Ar can be very valuable in confirming a suggestion already supported by intra-Heb arguments or cognate information from languages more directly related to Heb (§§ 6, 19, 22, 26, 28, 33, 39, 44).

The value of *Mishnaic Hebrew* and *Aramaic* (including the DSS) cannot easily be over-emphasized (see §§ 6, 7, 8, 13, 22, 26, 33, 34). The neglect of these is hard to explain. A certain amount of prejudice probably plays a part.[32] Perhaps more justified is the possibility of borrowing from BHeb. However, the examples investigated in my study drew basically negative results on this; rare biblical words which also occurred in MHeb generally seemed genuine survivals and not borrowings. From the historical situation alone, one would expect to obtain the greatest help from MHeb and JAram. Heb never ceased to be spoken in Palestine; MHeb is the natural development of the Heb used in OT times. JAram was used so closely in conjunction with MHeb that the two languages influenced one another to a large degree. One must also consider the fact that the Hebrew Bible was preserved by the community which used and perpetuated MHeb and JAram. If one wishes to understand the developing tradition, he can do so only with consideration of these later languages. (See below for a discussion of the importance of evaluating the whole tradition and not just the earliest form of it.) All of the Aram dialects were helpful as well. The number of usable works on Aram make the entire gamut of the language and its various dialects readily accessible.

Akkadian was probably the least helpful language, primarily because of the phonetic problems in relation to the

---

[32] R. Gordis, "On Methodology in Biblical Exegesis," JQR 61 (1970-1), 104-5.

other Semitic languages and the fact that a sizable portion of the lexicographical stock seems to have no clear parallel elsewhere in Semitic.[33] However, it gave major help in a few instances (§§ 26, 37; cf. 28, 32). It is also likely to be of help where the OT may have borrowed from or have been influenced by Mesopotamian literature.

Versions

Our examination of the versions has only one purpose: their assessment in relation to comparative philology. (Their normal usage in textual criticism has already received considerable attention and is outside the purposes of this study.) Any analysis is difficult, however, because of the unavoidable subjectivity involved. Two points must be kept in mind: (1) the particular nature of the versions for Job make extrapolation of the results to other parts of the Bible somewhat hazardous; (2) the versions can be evaluated only relatively to each other because of the complexity of the question.

An overall view of the value of the versions for comparative philology, as indicated by this particular study, is somewhat negative. If one expects the versional translators to have understood rare words which trouble scholars today, he will be disappointed. With some exceptions the ancient translators seem to have had the same difficulties as modern scholars when it came to rare words and forms. The *singular value* of the versions is the following: *where they unitedly support the MT, this gives reason to think that the use of comparative philology to elucidate a rare word or form at this point is legitimate. Such united support would also caution against a comparative suggestion which requires a deviation from the MT (revocalization, word redivision, etc.).*

The individual versions can be evaluated as follows:

The *Septuagint* is problematic because of its abridged

---

[33]Akk has, however, borrowed less and been more resistant to external penetration than is often thought. See J. Bottéro in *Studies on Semitic Lexicography*, 57-60.

character in relation to the MT. At times its rendering accords well with the MT, but it so often diverges that it is very hard to evaluate. Surprisingly, it supported several comparative suggestions which took the MT in other than its traditional sense (§§ 26, 44; cf. §§ 7, 13, 30). Its value was thus very sporadic. One would have to do study on sections of the OT in which the LXX *Vorlage* was certainly close to the MT in order to gain a clearer picture of its value for comparative philology.

The *Minor Versions* occasionally seemed to give support to a comparative suggestion (§ 13). But their fragmentary nature detracts greatly from their potential value. It will be interesting to see how much Field's assembly of MV material will be improved upon by the Göttingen edition of the LXX of Job.

The *Vulgate* gave no outstanding help. However, it must be remembered that Job was translated relatively early in Jerome's translating career. It would be of interest to see whether the Vg might be of more value in books translated after Jerome had more experience and knowledge.

The *Rabbinic Targum* was probably the most helpful outside the 11QtgJob (§§ 13, 24, 28; cf. §§ 7, 12, 30, 34). Its value seems to have been reduced because of the lateness and midrashic character of some of the material. Earlier targums such as exist for other sections of the Bible might prove to be of more use in comparative work. (The Pentateuch would probably be the best place to test the true value of the rabbinic targums.)

The *Syriac* version was not overly useful, often seemingly a bad translation (but cf. §§ 8, 12, 34). However, this would probably not apply to many other sections of the OT (see the comments on the Peshitta in Chapter I).

The most useful version was the *11QtgJob*. Although extant for only a few of the passages studied, it gave a disproportionate amount of support for comparative suggestions (§§ 26, 44; cf. § 28).

I have not been able to test the value of the versions in the vigorous way ultimately required for comparative philology. However, Barr's suggestion that the Semitic versions are more likely to preserve knowledge of rare words and forms seems borne out by my study, especially in relation to our earliest Semitic version--the 11QtgJob. Although we have no copies of the rabbinic targums anywhere near the age of the Qumran targum, some of their material seems to be early (though exactly how early is still a major question). Further study is required for a full evaluation.

Comparative Philology Versus Other Considerations

Comparative philology is only one of a number of disciplines to be used in the attempt better to understand the OT text. Since it basically falls in the general category of textual criticism, it can be said to lie in the "basement" of OT research. It attempts to provide an understanding of the words and phrases of the text before broader questions of theology and literature can be asked. This tendency toward an atomistic approach can also be its undoing. It is true that one bases literary conclusions and theology on an exegesis of small units of the text; but sometimes this narrow focusing on a small unit of text can produce a distortion of understanding if broader questions are not also asked and answered.

One might take the example of theology. No one is advocating a return to reading individual passages only in the light of preconceived dogmatic theology. Yet the individual units of text may be misinterpreted if some broader aspects of the theology of the OT are not considered. An example to illustrate this concerns the question of afterlife in earlier sections of the Hebrew Bible. Dahood has translated a number of passages in the Psalms as if referring to an afterlife, a concept generally felt to be a later development in Hebrew thought. Bruce Vawter has taken exception to Dahood's translations at these points.[34] Without going into the arguments for either position, this example illustrates the point that considerations of theology should at least caution one about finding hints of an afterlife in earlier portions of the OT.

---

[34]"Intimations of Immortality and the Old Testament," JBL 91 (1972), 158-71. But cf. J. F. A. Sawyer, "Hebrew Words for the Resurrection of the Dead," VT 23 (1973), 218-34.

Most scholars would agree that Dahood has read more in the individual passages than is there.

Another major consideration is that of form criticism. As presently being practiced, form criticism is a broad term encompassing the structure, sources, themes, different textual units, and the relationship between these units and their matrix in ancient society. It goes beyond the old usage in which form criticism dealt only with the preliterary stage of the tradition.[35] In several passages considerations of form criticism seemed to support the traditional interpretation of the text against attempts to find a new meaning by comparative philology (§§ 3, 14, 24, 43; cf. §§ 2, 18, 35, 41).

The particular age of the composition of a book or the influence by other literature can be very important. In the case of Job the dating is a rather moot question. It is generally assigned to some time around the 6th century or even later. If that is correct, the alleged frequence of Aramaisms may have some plausibility and may play a factor in evaluating comparative philological suggestions. Yet the study by David Robertson suggests a date some centuries earlier.[36] If the indication of Robertson's study is correct, the treatments involving the assumption of wholesale Aramaizing are more tenuous.

The important thing is to place no artificial limits on methods used to elucidate the text. Different methods give different types of information. Each is a valid discipline in its own right. The total meaning of the text will emerge only through the combined efforts of all disciplines. Some problems are simply insoluble without contributions from different areas

---

[35] See Klaus Koch, *Growth of the Biblical Tradition*, chap. 6, esp. p. 77. An important recent discussion of the question is R. Knierim, "Old Testament Form Criticism Reconsidered," *Interpretation* 27 (1973), 435-68. A convenient handbook on the subject is J. H. Hayes, *Old Testament Form Criticism*. See also note 39 below.

[36] *Linguistic Evidence in Dating Early Hebrew Poetry*, especially 155. He emphasizes this dating is only a working hypothesis and nothing more.

of scholarship. Ar may give information which simply does not exist in Ug. The sole use of one method to the exclusion of others must be avoided. Yet one of Dahood's recent articles seems to indicate just such an extreme approach.[37] Certainly the title suggests it is a completely "either-or" situation. Granted, as he says, it is not generally possible to master both Ugaritic studies and also Qumran studies and the use of other versions. But the implication that it has to be one or the other is misleading. The Ug texts give only a certain amount of information. Try as one might, no one can solve all textual problems by Ug alone. Any attempt to do so creates a caricature of scholarship. If one intends to do textual work, he should have a working knowledge of both areas. Naturally, the requirements of specialization make scholarly cooperation necessary. It may not be humanly possible to take account of all the implications of the whole field of scholarship. Nevertheless, the cogency of any research done in any but the most narrow limits is directly proportional to the account taken of the impact of research in the field as a whole.

History and Witnesses of the Tradition

One question which seems seldom asked by comparative philologists--or by many scholars of other disciplines as well --is this: what point in the history of the tradition(s) is one trying to elucidate? That this question is often not asked seems clear from the fact that so many discussions never attempt to provide an answer to it. The reason for this is probably the dominance of the scholarly tradition (!) of getting back to the most original meaning of the text. This is certainly *a* legitimate inquiry, so long as it is realized this is not the *only* legitimate study.

Recent years have seen the revival of an interest in the meaning of the tradition for different communities at different

---

[37] "Ugaritic and Phoenician or Qumran and the Versions," *Orient and Occident*, 53-8.

times.[38] Accompanying this has been the recognition of the contributions of later editors and their important function of collecting, shaping, reinterpreting, and making meaningful the traditions for their contemporary community.[39] Research on the Qumran scrolls and other MS discoveries from the Judaean Desert have added new concepts on the development of the OT text. This research first of all recognized the antiquity of the (consonantal) Masoretic text-type, demonstrating this was not just the creation of a medieval Jewish community.[40] But it also showed that castigation of the LXX as only a poor or corrupted translation of the Heb was equally ill-founded.[41] The Qumran documents demonstrated that several different recensions (using "recension" only in the sense of text-type) of various parts of the Hebrew Bible were in existence and use. The problem of sorting out these recensions is not an easy task and no one theory has had the last word as yet.[42]

Theoretically, therefore, one could take any particular recension and work from it. However, whatever we might think of it otherwise, we must recognize that of all the various Heb versions known the MT is the most nearly complete and carries

---

[38] Note especially B. Childs, *Isaiah and the Assyrian Crisis*, 121-7; *Biblical Theology in Crisis*. See below for discussion of his commentary on Exodus in the Old Testament Library.

[39] On the Old Testament, a useful summary of the major contributors and research can be found in D. Knight, *Rediscovering the Traditions of Israel*. See also B. Childs, *Memory and Tradition in Israel*. On the Evangelists cf., e.g., G. Bornkamm, *Tradition and Interpretation in Matthew*.

[40] E.g., F. M. Cross, *The Ancient Library of Qumran*, 168-9.

[41] *ibid.*, 180.

[42] Cross proposed a theory of textual development in two influential articles: "The Contribution of the Qumran Discoveries to the Study of the Biblical Text," IEJ 16 (1966), 81-95; "The History of the Biblical Text in the Light of Discoveries in the Judaean Desert," HTR 56 (1964), 281-99. But his theories were challenged by George Howard, "Frank Cross and Recensional Criticism," VT 21 (1971), 440-50, and S. Talmon in *The Cambridge History of the Bible*, vol. 1, 193-9. The debate has been carried on in scholarly meetings and literature (see a further discussion in the Appendix). Many important articles on the subject have been collected in Cross/Talmon, *Qumran and the History of the Biblical Text* (1975).

the most detailed amount of textual information. Whatever the antiquity of the Heb text underlying the various parts of the LXX, that text with a very few exceptions no longer survives.[43] The Samaritan Pentateuch covers only that section of the OT. None of these carry the very important indication of voweling and accentuation found in the MT. One writer recently to argue for the MT as *a* valid stage of the text for research is John F. A. Sawyer.[44] His is not a reversion to some sort of neo-fundamentalism since he recognizes this is not the only stage or level of the text of which one can make valid inquiries. He recognizes that the selection of any particular point of the tradition is somewhat arbitrary and subjective. Nonetheless, there are several reasons why he chooses the MT:

1. The final form of the text is still neglected even in recent research.

2. The finished text as it now stands is quite intelligible for the most part and remarkably consistent.

3. The MT has been the generally accepted canon of scripture for religious communities for centuries and has been accepted, understood, and used by them as a rule of life. In a comment significant for our purposes here he notes, "The expertise of textual critics and comparative philologists has on occasion blinded us to the plain sense of the text as it stands. Passages which are quite intelligible and which made perfectly good sense to masoretic scholars are described as difficult or impossible or meaningless as they stand."[45]

---

[43]The LXX was used as the OT of at least certain segments of the early church. Yet it was generally realized the LXX was a translation even when regarded in some sense as an "inspired" translation. Despite the resistance received by Jerome from his contemporaries, it was probably nothing compared to what would have ensued if the Heb basis of the LXX were in existence alongside the (consonantal) MT. Thus, I am not ruling out the use of the LXX as a valid stage of the tradition for inquiry, but we can never forget the LXX Greek text is not the same as having hard Heb evidence. Cf. M. Goshen-Gottstein, "The Theory and Practice of Textual Criticism," *Textus* 3 (1963), 130-58.

[44]*Semantics in Biblical Research*, 10-16. See also his more recent article, "The 'Original Meaning of the Text' and Other Legitimate Subjects for Semantic Description," *Questions disputées d'Ancien Testament* (1974), 63-70.

[45]*ibid.*, 14.

4. Unlike certain other documents of the ancient Near East, the OT was not left in its specific original context. Rather, as a religious writing it was disassociated from its particular situation and recontextualized in an infinite number of historical situations in synagogue and church.

In his new Exodus commentary Brevard Childs has tried to demonstrate how a commentator can take all stages of the text into account. He begins with form and literary criticism but does not stop there, taking into account--if briefly--the meaning of the text to rabbinic, patristic, medieval, and even later theologians. One hopes to see his example followed.

Recent research has tended to confirm the antiquity even of the traditional vowel-pointing and accentuation of the Masoretes despite the very late date of recording this in writing. This is too large a subject to take up here. A survey of the more recent literature and research indicating the MT was not a late, artificial creation of Jewish scholars in the Middle Ages is given in the Appendix. But disregarding the vowel points and accent marks which were given graphic form only about the 6th-8th centuries A.D., is it true that such things as word division and vowel letters can also be rejected as late?

Older works on textual criticism generally discussed the problem of *scriptio continua* in the earlier stages of the Heb text. It was thought that graphic word division was a product of the Masoretes or other late editors and that many problems in the text were the result of wrong word division. The Dead Sea Scrolls discoveries caused some revision of that common assumption since material from as far back as about 200 B.C. showed word division.[46] There are always questions about word division at certain points in any MS. This was also true of the Qumran documents, but divisions between words are clearly indicated for the most part. More recently A. R. Millard did a detailed study of the question.[47] After considering all the

---

[46] F. M. Cross, "Contribution" (see n. 42 above), 82.

[47] "*Scriptio Continua* in Early Hebrew," JSS 15 (1970), 2-15.

textual evidence available (MSS, ostraca, inscriptions, clay tablets), he concluded that "word-division was normal amongst the majority of West-Semitic scribes."[48] While pointing out that biblical MSS earlier than the Qumran scrolls are unknown, the weight of the evidence is "heavily in favour" of the conclusion that biblical writers used word division.[49] He notes this conclusion is not new but was already accepted by a number of eminent predecessors (including S. R. Driver, F. Buhl, and M. Noth).

Another consideration is that of *matres lectionis*, especially internal ones. The standard work on the subject concludes that final long vowels were not indicated before about 900 B.C. but were used consistently from about 850 B.C. on.[50] Internal *matres lectionis* begin to appear sporadically in the 6th century but do not reach full usage until the post-exilic period. This scheme has been criticized,[51] which criticism was followed by a rebuttal.[52] Regardless of the fact that some of Goodwin's claims seem incorrect, modification on a few points is indicated by other researchers.[53] This is due to the Sefire inscriptions, stelas II and III of which were undiscovered when Cross and Freedman did their original work while stela I was inadequately studied.[54] The Sefire inscriptions, of course, support the general conclusions of Cross and Freedman. Yet there may be some evidence of the use of medial vowel letters a little earlier than they thought in their study. But

---

[48]*ibid.*, 12.

[49]*ibid.*, 14.

[50]F. M. Cross and D. N. Freedman, *Early Hebrew Orthography*, 56-7.

[51]Donald Goodwin, *Text-Restoration Methods in Contemporary U.S.A. Biblical Scholarship*, chap. 3.

[52]Cross and Freedman, "Some Observations on Early Hebrew," *Biblica* 53 (1972), 413-20.

[53]See, e.g., M. Tsevat, "A Chapter on Old West Semitic Orthography," *Joshua Bloch Memorial Volume*, 82-91.

[54]J. Fitzmyer, *The Aramaic Inscriptions of Sefîre*, 141-9; Cross and Freedman (see note 50 above), 27-9.

even if the later dates are adhered to, this requires one to consider the time of editing and revision of earlier traditions. For Job specifically the date one gives it is important for any textual reconstruction done. The presence of diphthongs instead of long vowels would also have to be taken into account since these were indicated in the consonantal text.

To consider just two examples (§§ 3, 20), how one attempted to evaluate the *matres lectionis* now in the MT would also indicate the antiquity of the present vocalization. *Yôm* (§ 3) has *plene* spelling. If this is to be taken as "sea" instead of "day," some explanation needs to be given for the *waw* which presumably goes back centuries before the vowel pointing. Dahood (§ 20) revocalizes the MT phrase *ᶜālêmô bilᵉḥûmô*. More than that, though, he also redivides the words and eliminates certain vowel letters. Regardless of Dahood's feeling for the vowel points, the *matres lectionis* were definitely recorded in graphic form in the post-exilic period--long before the time of the Masoretes. Also original diphthongs were shown in the consonantal text, even before vowel letters were used. If he regards the MT consonantal text as "eminently sound," he should explain this contradiction in terms. The vowel letters may indeed be explained as a graphic error, but this would require emending the consonantal text rather than considering it "sound."

There seems no question that Dahood's defense of the MT consonantal text is a correct tempering of the extreme views of some textual critics in the past. Recognition of the fact that peculiarities of the Heb text may represent actual historical linguistic features rather than scribal corruption was already noted by other scholars.[55] But Dahood's consideration for the pointing, word division, etc., seems inversely proportional to the homage paid to the consonantal text (however that may be defined). A statement which seems to summarize the nature of his work is this: "where the Masoretic punctuation cannot be

---

[55] E.g., C. H. Gordon, "Azitawadd's Phoenician Inscription," JNES 8 (1949), 112-14; G. D. Young, "The Significance of the Karatepe Inscriptions for Near Eastern Textual Criticism," OTS 8 (1950), 298-9.

coaxed into yielding sense, the textual critic should cut free and chart a course on the linguistic map of Northwest Semitic."[56] The voweling is neither so late nor the consonantal text so original as Dahood appears to believe.[57] Even though certain features of the MT were preserved orally, that does not negate their value, nor does the fact that the consonantal text was written down early require a return to bibliolatry.[58] All features require a respectful but rigorous inquiry and any emendation--whether of vowel pointing, word division, or consonants--should be plainly recognized for what it is.[59]

---

[56] *Psalms* II, p. XVII. Dahood does indeed state on the next page, "While I try in each instance to give respectful consideration to Masoretic vocalization . . . ." The actual textual work completely belies this statement!

[57] For a discussion of the history and preservation of both, see the Appendix. One is reminded of a statement of Cyrus Gordon in another context, "Oral literature is not so fickle (nor is written literature so stable) as one might suppose," *The Ancient Near East*, 300. On oral literature in general, see note 6 in Chapter IV below.

[58] Morton Smith discusses the question of "pseudorthodoxy" in a delightfully humorous yet penetrating article in JBL 88 (1969), 19-35. In regard to comparative philology he remarks: "Of course, it is necessary, because of the poverty of the remains of ancient Hebrew, to rely on comparative linguistics for the elucidation of many difficult passages, but we must never forget that this is a *pis aller*. The best guide to the meaning of words in a given language is the tradition of that language, including the translations made from it. Considerations of historical proximity must always be taken into account in evaluating analogies from other languages; and in a vowelless text, which has undergone both transcription from one alphabet to another and several centuries of uncontrolled copying, corruption is far more likely than the occurrence of a root meaning otherwise unattested in the language" (24).

[59] Note Barr's conclusions, CPTOT, 221-2. Two recent criticisms of the incongruous way in which Dahood and his students often deal with the MT are by O. Loretz, "Textologie des Zephanja-Buches," UF 5 (1973), 219-28, and A. F. Rainey (note 29 above), 152-3. Cf. also the review article by de Moor and van der Lugt (note 27 above). An arm's-length view of the situation might provide a satirist with a commentary on the perversities of human nature (even among scholars): The lack of clear vocalization in early texts is constantly bemoaned by those working in the area. But the OT scholar, who has a very detailed system of vowel points, seems always wanting to ignore them and work from the consonantal text alone!

Weighing the Possibilities

Textual criticism is a statistical method rather than an exact science. No one has yet perfected a way of testing text critical suggestions under laboratory conditions. The nearest thing to experimental verification is the discovery of new MS evidence. Such good fortune seldom smiles on textual work. Thus, we must fall back into the use of statistics. Suggestions must be considered, evidence weighed, alternatives explored, methods investigated. Finally, the scholar makes a judgment. He may feel he has adequately demonstrated the veracity of his conclusions. Conversely, a colleague may wonder how one could operate on such flimsy evidence. Proof, like beauty, is so often in the eye of the beholder.[60]

Subjectivity can never be eliminated from biblical research. But the more data one has and the more directly one's theory explains all the known evidence, the more likely it is to be convincing (i.e., the principle of parsimony). There may be dozens of possible explanations but not all have equal probability. This applies to judging between comparative philological suggestions, as well as to judging between a comparative treatment and the use of some other method for solving the problem. Comparative philologists sometimes forget that there are form critics or even that there are other textual critics who use a different method. This tendency toward isolationism is not limited to those who use comparative philology. A number of the best-known scholars using ancient Near Eastern languages and literatures on the OT seem to know little of the work being done in form criticism. The form critical commentaries, on the other hand, mainly still deal with textual problems by the old version-and-emendation method.

This is one of the negative results of specialization and is unavoidable to some extent. More unfortunate is the occasional dogmatism and even truculence with which the advantages of one particular method are touted. It is not necessary to repeat the discussion given earlier on the subject, but what

---

[60] For a penetrating discussion on this question, one should consult R. Gordis (note 32 above), 115-8.

one would think was an elementary principle in scholarship seems all too often to be forgotten. Only by cooperation can the biblical tradition be understood in all its complexity. The best solution to any textual difficulty is the one which not only explains the textual evidence and the immediate context but also conforms to known linguistic, form critical, literary, and theological considerations.

This is not meant as a negation of suggestions for the sake of suggestion. Many textual problems have never been solved and any new suggestions should be welcomed. Even an unlikely suggestion may spark a thought in the mind of another researcher and result in the eventual solution of the problem. On the other hand, poorly supported or unsupported suggestions should be set forth as such. For example, Gordon commented, "The bearing of Ugaritic on Old Testament Studies has presumably been evident since the decipherment in 1930; and yet Dahood's outstanding service in bringing Ugaritic philology to bear comprehensively on the text of a Hebrew book is not always understood, let alone appreciated, by professional reviewers."[61] Part of the problem may be the way Dahood's ideas are set forth. If he means most of his treatments to be only suggestions, one could only applaud the quantity and ingenuity of output. But when Heb grammar is entirely rewritten and whole sections of the Bible completely reinterpreted, it is not surprising that most scholars are somewhat reluctant to throw out all other considerations just for those which Dahood brings up. (Dahood's manner of putting forth his new interpretations also does not usually imply that he thinks of them only as tenuous possibilities.)

The same applies to any comparative philological suggestion. Finding an Ar cognate may be suggestive but only so. Further evidence is needed to demonstrate probability as opposed to just a possibility. J. A. Emerton in a review

---

[61]UT *Supplement*, p. 549. One might note that some of the "unappreciative" are hardly ignorant of Ugaritic studies or their value, and this charge does not sit well with such qualified critics of Dahood as listed in note 59 above and elsewhere in this study.

briefly outlined what seemed to him to constitute the elements of probability in a proposed comparative solution.[62] His comments so closely parallel the general conclusions of my own study, I feel they are worth quoting at length:

> First, the correspondence of consonants should be exact, although some allowance should be made for the possibility of, for example, metathesis, or the interchange between a voiced consonant and its unvoiced counterpart. Secondly, the meaning should be well-attested in the cognate language, and there should be no reason to suppose that it represents a development peculiar to that language . . . . Thirdly, it is an advantage if the meaning is found in several languages, and if it is attested in a time and a place not too far removed from the Hebrew word to be explained. Fourthly, the needs of the context are of decisive importance . . . . it is not enough to show that a new meaning fits a particular context if the word can be explained satisfactorily from a meaning that is already well-attested in Hebrew . . . . What is wanted is a new explanation of what is otherwise inexplicable or, at least, an explanation that can be shown to fit the context better than other explanations. Further, it is an advantage to a theory if it sheds light, not just on one passage, but on several.

Sometimes an individual treatment may be possible and plausible but the overall picture created, if carried to its logical extremes, is ludicrous. Perhaps we could consider the example of the enclitic *mem*. It is not generally doubted that such exists in BHeb, so any textual treatment which assumes an enclitic *mem* is not of itself unlikely because of that. Yet if all the passages for which the enclitic *mem* has been proposed are considered as a whole, the result is complete absurdity. Similarly with the multiplication of homonyms. All languages have homonyms; Heb has a good many homonymous roots. The concept itself is not unusual. However, if all the suggested homonyms were actually entered into the lexicon, the resulting chaos might see the end of Hebraic studies. Therefore, any treatment which requires the invoking of a new homonym or some rare feature of grammar or morphology will demand greater confirmation of evidence to establish probability than one which

[62] Review of HAL, VT 22 (1972), 505.

does not. The final test is the strength of the data and the simplicity of the explanation which accounts for all of them. Joshua Blau stated the whole question of probability succinctly even though writing in a slightly different context: "Yet what we have claimed for the general difficulties of reconstruction, applies to our solutions as well: one only tries to offer the simplest theory that is in accordance with the facts known, without being at all sure that the actual development was not quite different."[63]

A final consideration concerns the question of textual corruption. Here is where comparative philology can perform a valuable function even if it does not solve the problem. In a number of examples (§§ 5, 6, 16, 21, 22, 31, 33, 36, 45) I expressed the judgment that the comparative evidence was strong enough at least to caution against thinking of a textual corruption, even though it did not give a full solution. This can sometimes be a very useful aid to the textual critic in knowing where to concentrate his work. If little confirmation of a textual or lexical abnormality is found, one would probably be best advised to look for a corruption and work from there. But if a check shows what seems to be a cognate--or more especially *cognates*--in other branches of Semitic with a semantic area appropriate to the Heb context, perhaps one should work from

---

[63]"Some Difficulties in the Reconstruction of >>Proto-Hebrew<< and >>Proto-Canaanite<<," BZAW 103 (1968), 43. One might mention here Rainey's comments in reference to a statement of Dahood: "Dahood goes on to claim that scholars now 'enjoy greater maneuverability before formidable texts' . . . . Such 'greater maneuverability' is the absolute antithesis of sound scholarship. What is really needed is a *stricter discipline* in sticking to the solid facts discernable in any given context" (note 29 above), 152. While the two statements were in regard to a particular point, both seem to have application to a wider context. Some seem to act as if they had the "great maneuverability" to make the text say anything they want through ample use of the enclitic *mem*, "flexible" prepositions, 3rd singular *yod*, repointing, and new word division. This is indeed the antithesis of sound scholarship, and the probability of such treatments seems inversely proportional to their maneuverability. (On prepositions, see note 21 above. On the 3rd singular *yod*, see Ziony Zevit, "The Linguistic and Contextual Arguments in Support of a Hebrew 3 m.s. Suffix -*Y*," forthcoming in UF 9. I thank Professor Zevit for allowing me to read the article in MS form.)

the assumption that the text is correct even if the comparative data do not immediately elucidate the passage further.

CHAPTER IV
SUMMARY AND CONCLUSIONS

The task remaining before us is to summarize the study in a way meaningful for the actual practice of comparative philology in textual work. Many considerations, both positive and negative, have arisen from the previous analysis and synthesis. Some are more important than others. Some are only tentative and require further study. These various needs for further study will be indicated at the end of this chapter.

While the methodology of comparative philology should be consistent enough--as well as broad enough--to cover all anticipated textual problems, the scholar is likely to embark on comparative philological work for one of two separate reasons. The first one is the desire to test out a suggestion already given by another scholar. This is listed first because it is likely to be the more frequent reason for most scholars to take up the subject. Someone brings out a suggestion in a commentary or other publication. It may appear to have some plausibility or even be rather convincing, but there is need for independent checking and investigation even if it seems rather solid on the surface. The second reason for using comparative philology is to generate new suggestions. A new proposal may be brought forward from a variety of possible causes. One may be the identification of a previously unrecognized textual problem. Another may be an attempt to solve an old crux, one in which the various offered solutions seem unconvincing or inadequate. Another purpose which has dominated the field since the first Ras Shamra discoveries is the recognition of a particular feature in a cognate language and the attempt to find the same or a similar feature in Heb--the heuristic approach.

The basic steps taken should be the same in either of the two approaches. However, there are certain potential dangers which are more likely to be encountered in the heuristic approach. One tends to be more cautious and critical in evaluating the work of a colleague than his own. The fever of discovery may make the researcher more tolerant of inexactitude in his own work than in that of others. Or one may become so preoccupied with his own particular discipline or method that he ignores or slights the contributions of others. When infatuation with the individual specialty blinds a scholar to the absolute necessity of interacting with other methods of research, a travesty of scholarship is the likely outcome. The potential benefits of heuristic research need not be extolled since they are obvious, but the potential evils must always be kept in mind and guarded aginst.

It should be noted that the following points assume the discussion in Chapter III and are only concise summaries here. If they seem to state the obvious at times, it is only because the obvious seems too often ignored!

1. Collecting the Cognates

Normal phonetic considerations should always come first. Care must be taken that these are also observed for dialects and other languages within a group since they may not be the same as for the dominant language of the group. Once a reasonable number of cognates with regular correspondences are gathered and form some sort of pattern, it can be asked whether the root is likely for PS. If so, a search needs to be made in the other areas of Semitic where it is not otherwise known. Naturally, there are practical limits to this, mainly the matter of time and the lack of proper lexica and studies for portions of Semitic. But there are also useful collections of cognate information in Brockelmann's lexicon, in the various works of Leslau, Gordon's UT (supplemented by Leslau), AHW, and especially in HAL. Cohen's dictionary should be extremely useful as well when completed.[1]

Yet the listings presently available are only aids and cannot take the place of independent investigation. My studies found that even HAL occasionally missed fairly accessible material. In any event no dictionary can give the semantic range of, and complete lexical information on, each individual

---

[1]David Cohen (ed.), *Dictionnaire des racines sémitiques ou attestées dans les langues sémitiques*. Fascicles now available are into the letter *g* (Heb order).

cognate. These are best learned within the individual language. Nothing yet available does this necessary collection and analysis for the researcher, so he must still do it for himself.

The question of any unusual phonetic correspondences must be carefully weighed. Where the lexical meaning of the various cognates is well known, this may be a large help in determining whether a particular root is a cognate or not. But a check should always be made that a root with regular correspondence has not been overlooked. An interchange of certain letters or metathesis or other sporadic irregularities may actually be attested in several languages. The important thing is the system of unquestionable cognate evidence and the place of the non-conforming cognate within that system. This is especially true where the Heb root is thought to show an unusual phonetic makeup. If determining cognates is difficult, the comparative suggestion is not as likely to be persuasive. One problem in comparing Semitic cognates is that of roots with weak letters. These also need to be considered. A one-to-one phonetic correspondence for the unstable radical seems less obligatory, and lack of such correspondence more tolerable, in identifying the cognates. But this can be determined for sure only after careful study.

2. Semantic Analysis

This analysis follows after as complete a collection of cognate evidence as is possible. The narrower the semantic domain within which the cognates fall, the more likely they are to give convincing information for the Heb text in question. That is, since we are dealing only in gross semantics, the more a common semantic field is attested by the cognates the more likely the Heb root in question will also fall in that same semantic field. Conversely, the less a common semantic range is attested by the cognates, the more difficult to decide which, if any, of the cognates will throw light on the Heb root.

One exception needs to be made to this last statement: the closer the language is to Heb, the more likely it will have a cognate with the same general meaning. By the law of averages MHeb is more likely to retain the meaning of the BHeb word. After that comes Phoen. Then follow Ug and the Aram dialects. However, the proximity of usage of JAram and MHeb for many centuries caused a great deal of influence and intermingling. This means a JAram root is often semantically closer to Heb than the other Northwest Semitic cognates. Yet it can also work the other way so that the JAram influence actually caused the MHeb root to diverge from its earlier usage. Also the Northwest Semitic cognates may for some reason be further removed from the Heb sense than the cognate in a more distantly related language. This would more likely result from direct borrowing but could also come about through other causes, such as literary influence from non-Heb speaking areas at certain points in history. For example, Mesopotamian literature was very influential at times. Formulae and stereotyped phrases may have come over directly or as calques even though Akk as a whole differs considerably from Heb.

Next, the semantics of the Heb word itself need to be analyzed. This may be difficult if it is a *hapax legomenon*, but even words used only once have the one particular context within which they occur. If genuine synonymous parallelism is present, identification may be simplified. Yet the cautions of Kaddari must be kept in mind.[2] In determining the context, questions of form criticism may need to be answered here rather than later. They must be taken up later in any event. The result of the Heb analysis is in turn compared with that of the cognate semantic investigation. The more specifically these point to a particular sense, the more likely a probable solution. Unfortunately, the results may be rather ambiguous because of lack of specific context or a clearly defined common semantic area.

Special attention needs to be paid to such features of the Heb context as mythological elements or other unusual features which may cause more weight to be given to one particular cognate (cf. §§ 30, 37). The OT text may be affected by a very specific type of literature such as Mesopotamian creation

---

[2]See the summary and discussion in Chapter III, pp. 144-6.

mythology in the case of Gen 2:6. Cognates from other languages or even later stages of the same language may not be of any assistance. Another example which may fit here concerns the strange word *šaddûn* (*Qere*) in Job 19:29. Loren R. Fisher compared the ending *-yn* on names from Ugarit (texts in both Ug and Akk), specifically the names *ša-du-ya* and *šadû-ia-nu* and especially *šdyn*. He concluded the word in Job was a variant form of the divine name Shaddai.[3] This type of information may carry much more weight than normal cognates.

3. Versional Information

The versions should always be examined. Even if they give no help for comparative purposes (cf. the generally negative conclusions mentioned in Chapter III), they will eventually have to be reckoned with as potential sources for remedying a possible textual corruption. The questions of intraversional corruptions, retroversion, free translation, etc., are too lengthy to deal with here.[4] Nevertheless, one can never predict when the version may preserve genuine knowledge of a rare Heb word or expression even if the probability is not exceptionally high. (An early targum may improve the likelihood considerably.) Or if all the versions agree with the MT, this may indicate the proposed new understanding (assuming the MT is completely understandable in its own right at this point) should be abandoned as unlikely. In heuristic study the version may also serve as the spark for a possible new understanding of a particular passage.

4. Intra-Hebrew Considerations

Sometimes this step may come before the collection of cognates if the Heb form is such that the exact root is uncertain. One of the intra-Heb considerations is the morphology of the word in question. But even when a triliteral root seems certain, the particular form of the word may suggest a solution which has nothing to do with comparative philology (for illu-

---

[3]"*ŠDYN* in Job XIX 29," VT 11 (1961), 342-3.

[4]See the bibliographies and discussion in Chapter I.

strative examples, see §§ 1 and 5).

Even if the form is no problem, the Heb construction and usage may actually be the solution. Care should be taken not to reject the Heb text as "meaningless" when it actually makes sense in and of itself. The temptation to present something original has led many a scholar to ignore the plain sense of the text and seek to find a "new understanding" never before recognized. Perhaps one of the major faults of heuristic treatments is failure to take account of the full Heb information. Included in this is the information of the MT. Is the cognate information also consistent with the vocalization as well as the consonantal root? If the vocalized form seems unacceptable, how does one account for the fact that the Masoretes recorded it? If they knew of an easier reading, were they not as likely to prefer it as the modern critic? A comparative suggestion making full use of all the cognate information may be consistent and otherwise convincing yet still unacceptable if one based on intra-Heb considerations is more suited to the context.

5. Other Methods of Scholarship

If the comparative suggestion has survived the previous steps, it may be a rather cogent one. Yet it still has to meet the tests of broader disciplines such as form criticism and OT theology. These may have had to be considered earlier in the research for various reasons. For example, comparative literature could serve to evaluate various cognates as already mentioned in relation to Gen 2:6. Archaeology may have produced evidence which forces a complete re-evaluation of all other considerations. A newly found text might reveal a simple textual corruption.

One could list many other disciplines without being in the least exhaustive. For example, "history of religions" research has shown how the mythology and psychology of religions in the ancient Near East and even the world over can give us a better understanding of the religious writings of Israel.[5]

---

[5]An overview of the history of research and a summary of

While recent study on the development and composition of oral tradition and literature is really a branch of form criticism, it is very important in its own right. Contemporary oral poetry in various parts of the world as well as epic poetry from the classical and ancient Near Eastern world have opened up many new avenues for a better understanding of ancient Heb literature.[6]

Under this category can also be placed the more traditional methods of textual criticism. A very ingenious comparative argument may collapse when a simple emendation takes care of the problem. The versions may not support a comparative suggestion because they support a superior reading lost from the present MT. If the text has been corrupted, no amount of comparative work by itself is likely to solve the difficulty.

The step being taken here is perhaps one of the most complex in the process since the types of methods of value for any particular passage may vary greatly. When these are also outside the researcher's major specialty, a further roadblock is encountered (even if he is unaware of it). Information is sometimes conveniently available in good commentaries, but this is not always the case. Sometimes tremendous advances take place over a considerable period of time before being set down in a commentary or other encyclopaedic form. No one can keep up with all the periodical literature--no matter how hard he

---

the major literature on the subject up to about 1963 is found in H. Hahn, *The Old Testament in Modern Research*, 83-118, 277-80. As stated in the survey of literature, it is really not possible to separate history of religions from archaeology and form criticism. Much of the advance in the field has come from the finds of archaeology and the analysis of literature from Mesopotamia and Ugarit. On the phenomonology and psychology of religion, groundbreaking work has been done by M. Eliade, especially his *Cosmos and History: The Myth of the Eternal Return*. See also T. Gaster, *Myth, Legend, and Custom in the Old Testament*, 2 vols.

[6]R. Culley, *Oral Formulaic Language in the Biblical Psalms* (1967), gives an introduction to the field as well as applying the method to a specific portion of Heb literature. An appendix surveys research and relevant literature to the time of his writing. Most recently, see Burke Long, "Recent Field Studies in Oral Literature and their Bearing on OT Criticism," VT 26 (1976), 187-98.

might try. Scholarly cooperation is the only answer to this problem.

6. Which Stage of the Text?

One might ask this question at the beginning of his research and work toward elucidating only one particular stage of the text. But it seems generally better to work with all information available first since new ideas on the history of a particular tradition may emerge in the study. Even if one is most interested in the earliest level of the tradition, it seems wise to consider the final form as well. After all, the particular unit in question may have been so well integrated into its context in the final stage of the text that it no longer has more than a semblance of its original function or meaning.

7. Judging the Evidence

At every stage of the research various facts, methods, and considerations have to be weighed. No level is free from this judgmental requirement. It is, however, most important at the conclusion of the research, especially in considering the force of a comparative philological argument in relation to arguments produced by other methods. This evaluation may end in the complete rejection of the comparative suggestion, or it may end in the rejection of one of the other solutions. Occasionally no other discipline bears on the textual question, though generally some sort of a synthesis is probable. The more harmonious a comparative suggestion is with all other related disciplines, the more convincing it is likely to be.

* * * *

The foregoing points on using comparative philology in OT work are only guidelines. They are in no way an attempt to substitute some sort of mechanical procedure for insight, ingenuity, and flashes of sheer genius; but we have seen too many examples of genius without guidelines which turned into madness bereft of method. Inspiration is no substitute for discipline. The guidelines given above should be broad enough to take in all conceivable examples of textual difficulty. The details may need to be varied according to the particulars of each case (more work certainly needs to be done toward working out details for particular types of problems). Yet if any of the basic steps are omitted, the result is likely to be an unproven, if not unacceptable, proposal.

Although these guidelines are specifically tailored to OT work, they also apply to the use of comparative philology for other literatures. Such methods are very necessary for the advancement of the knowledge of Ug philology which depends so highly on comparative evidence for its decipherment. The secondary literature on Ug abounds with comparative discussions (cf. § 11). Hopefully, most words will not be so difficult as to require lengthy study, but some do require it and will not be correctly understood until the proper study is done.

Desiderata

My research has confirmed the conclusions of CPTOT for the most part. In some cases further evidence was added to that given by Barr or evidence was given where he gave little. A number of proposals advanced by him were not touched on by my research one way or the other. In a few areas I feel I have been able to advance the state of the inquiry. However, a great number of needs still exist. These include study in certain problem areas as well as scholarly tools which will enable proper study to be done. Both are included in the following list:

1. Scholars should be aware of the need to make their research known not only to their colleagues but also to those in neighboring areas of scholarship. Specialization makes it impossible to delve too deeply into areas outside one's own. The more conveniently those other areas are summarized and the information made accessible to other scholars, the further biblical studies as a whole can advance. An example of a scholar who has assiduously applied himself to this is W. Leslau. He has compiled Southeast Semitic etymological lists for the OT, Ug, and Akk as well as producing other convenient lexica not difficult for biblical scholars to use. Another

example of the type of thing which needs to be done is the form critical project sponsored by Abingdon Press which will be producing a form critical handbook on the OT. Another is the *Ras Shamra Parallels* project. Work by the Society of Biblical Literature and other learned societies in establishing research centers and clearing houses for various areas of study is greatly welcomed. Yet more is still needed.

2. A great number of the Semitic languages and dialects are still inadequately studied. Even so plowed a field as classical Ar still lacks a good, scientifically constructed lexicon (WKAS should supply this). Comparative philology can advance no faster than a rate strictly governed by the existence or production of proper editions, grammars, and lexica.

3. Much more linguistic analysis is needed of Heb and especially Heb poetry. The Semitic languages as a whole are only now beginning to receive proper modern linguistic--as opposed to the old philological--study.[7] On the other hand, many of the studies by trained linguists are written in such a way as to be practically unintelligible to the average OT scholar. Any writer applying linguistic methods should consider the fact that some introduction to the method may be necessary for his readers.

4. More study needs to be done on the relationship of roots with one or more weak radicals. Some modified biliteral theory applicable to these roots in particular might help explain many idiosyncracies of form in comparison to the semantic relationship.

5. Further study needs to be done on the various versions in relation to comparative philology. Most study of the versions has not been oriented to this question.

6. A thorough study of the conflict of homonyms in BHeb is very much needed. Much comparative work has multiplied

---

[7]An example for BHeb is Gene Schramm, *The Graphemes of Tiberian Hebrew*. See also J. Barr, "The Ancient Semitic Languages--the Conflict between Philology and Linguistics," *Transactions of the Philological Society* (1968), 37-55.

homonymic roots or morphemes (such as the enclitic *mem*) without considering what the results would produce in an actual linguistic community.

Some of these represent rather large requests and are unlikely to be satisfied in the immediate future. Each one of the major needs can be subdivided into a myriad of specific requirements. Despite a somewhat lengthy history, OT comparative philology as a discipline in itself is surprisingly still in its infancy--as evidenced by the appearance of CPTOT as the first full treatment of the subject. Only as it is applied with definite criteria in mind can the methodology be refined to the point characteristic of many other specialities.

Edward Ullendorff recently expressed the need for the "general Semitist" alongside the Hebraist, Arabist, and Ugaritic expert.[8] Perhaps now is the time to draw on this concept and suggest the need for the interdiscipline specialty of comparative philology. If one wishes to take up a new and challenging field, he need look no further.

---

[8] "Comparative Semitics," *Linguistica Semitica*, 26.

APPENDIX

SURVEY OF LITERATURE ON THE AUTHENTICITY OF MASORETIC VOCALIZATION

The climax of what one might call "the Great Vowel Point Debate" of the 17th century was the general recognition that the vowel points were not recorded in writing until about the 6th-8th centuries A.D.[1] Since that time, though, the treatment of the value of the MT vowel pointing has wavered between practically blind conservatism and almost complete disregard, with all stages in between taken by someone. Paul Kahle has been the most influential figure in this century to regard the work of the Masoretes as the creation of an artificial book language which often differed from the actual spoken language.[2] His student Alexander Sperber has carried on this basic hypothesis, though with modifications.[3]

Kahle's ideas still have a great deal of influence, though that influence is presently on the wane. More and more studies are being published which show a trend toward seeing the MT as authentic tradition with a long history behind it. This present literature survey is primarily concerned with showing that there is indeed a movement toward a more conservative view of the MT and the reasons for it. While some earlier literature is mentioned, most is within this present century

---

[1] An interesting summary of the debate is found in D. C. Allen, *The Legend of Noah*, 49-55. In CPTOT, 66-7, Barr seems to feel the conclusion of the 17th century debate may be one of the causes of the rather cavalier handling of the MT vowels by some. Since those who had greatest respect for the MT (such as the Buxtorfs) were proved wrong, this may have suggested their respect for the tradition in general was also misplaced.

[2] His most mature work on the subject was the second edition of *The Cairo Geniza* (1959). His collected articles were published in his *Opera Minora* (1956).

[3] Much of Sperber's work is included in his *Historical Grammar of Biblical Hebrew* (1966), a great deal of which is a composite of earlier publications. See also his *Grammar of Masoretic Hebrew* (1959). S. Talmon has argued that Sperber's theories actually invalidate Kahle's to a considerable degree (*Cambridge History of the Bible*, I, 180-81).

and much within the last two decades. All publications before 1947 were outdated in detail by the DSS even if their general conclusions survived.

Variation Within the Masoretic Tradition

The MT preserves within itself a considerable amount of variation in textual reading, minute though it is in comparison to the whole. Perhaps one of the most easily noted features is the *Ketiv-Qere* system which has received considerable treatment by Robert Gordis whose monograph has recently been reissued.[4] The collections of variants within the medieval MSS by Kennicott and de Rossi are widely known.[5] However, the quantity of those variants is somewhat of an illusion since they are primarily the result of normal scribal activity rather than genuine variants.[6] This does not include the many variants found in the Talmudim, Midrashim, and other rabbinic literature; the *piyyut*; and between the various Masoretic schools such as the Babylonian versus the Palestinian, or Ben Asher versus Ben Naphtali. This led Harry Orlinsky to write:

> We are now ready to deal with the crux of the whole matter, something that the numerous editors of "masoretic" editions of the Bible have overlooked, namely: There never was, and there never can be, a single fixed masoretic text of the Bible! It is utter futility and pursuit of a mirage to go seeking to recover what never was.[7]

---

[4] *The Biblical Text in the Making: A Study of the Kethib-Qere* (1937), reprinted by Ktav Publishing House in The Library of Biblical Studies series. The original publication was reviewed by W. F. Albright (JBL 57 [1938], 223-4). Gordis replied (*ibid.*, 329-31) and Albright gave an answer to the reply (*ibid.*, 332-3). A thorough but critical review by H. M. Orlinsky appeared soon thereafter ("Problems of Kethib-Qere," JAOS 60 [1940], 30-45).

[5] B. Kennicott, *Vetus Testamentum Hebraicum cum variis lectionibus*, (1776-80). Johannis de Rossi, *Variae lectiones Veteris Testamenti librorum* (1784-8).

[6] See especially M. Goshen-Gottstein, "Hebrew Biblical Manuscripts," *Biblica* 48 (1967), 243-90.

[7] "The Masoretic Text: A Critical Evaluation," Prolegomenon to the KTAV reissue of C. D. Ginsburg, *Introduction to the Massoretico-Critical Edition of the Hebrew Bible*, p. XVIII. (A

Orlinksy's argument that one can refer only to *a* Masoretic text is well taken. Norman H. Snaith agrees with this but also notes that we can use the term "the Masorah" in reference to "the whole corpus of masoretic notes found in the various manuscripts with all the contradictions and discrepancies."[8] (As noted in my table of abbreviations, I use MT to stand for "Masoretic tradition" as well as for "Masoretic text." In this Appendix it usually stands for the former--advisedly!)

C. D. Ginsburg catalogued many of the differences between the Eastern and Western Masoretic traditions.[9] The major study of the differences between the two traditions has been made since then, however, by Paul Kahle.[10] There are only a few consonantal differences; differences in vowel pointing and accentuation are more substantial. The Tiberian Masoretic activity was not the sum of Palestinian work since other Palestinian codices are known with both a different graphic notation and a different pronunciation.[11]

Yet when the field is surveyed, all the variants noted, and divergencies taken account of, two points stand out:

1. The variants and divergencies represent multiple but authentic traditions. That is, the divergencies are not primarily the result of innovating, archaizing, or imaginary creating of the Masoretes, even though there may have existed different "schools" among the Masoretes.[12] Some of the variety

---

number of other significant articles as well as this on Masoretic studies are conveniently collected in *The Canon and Masorah of the Hebrew Bible*, edited by Sid Z. Leiman.) See also Goshen-Gottstein, *ibid.*, 245, n. 4.

[8]"Prolegomenon" to the Ktav reissue of Jacob ben Chayim's *Introduction to the Rabbinic Bible*, pp. XIV-XV.

[9]*Introduction* (see n.7 above), pp. 197-240.

[10]These include a section in BL (pp. 71-162); *Der masoretische Text des Alten Testaments; Masoreten des Westens* I, II; *Masoreten des Ostens*; *The Cairo Geniza*; also the Prolegomena to the *Biblia Hebraica*³.

[11]See *infra*.

[12]M. H. Goshen-Gottstein has written extensively on the subject. See especially his "The Rise of the Tiberian Bible Text," *Biblical and Other Studies*, 79-122. In regard to the well-known "schools" (families) of Ben Asher and Ben Naphtali, Goshen-Gottstein argues that Ben Naphtali was in general agree-

is undoubtedly the result of normal scribal activity which includes copying errors as well as assimilation, etc.[13] But much is also due to real variation within the tradition.[14]

2. The variety consists mainly of minutiae, and the overall unity of the tradition is remarkable when compared with other text-types. Despite the heterogeneity the MT is only one recension. The variation within the tradition must be recognized but not exaggerated.

It is also clear that some of the differences in various sources are neither the result of artificial linguistic creation nor of real textual variation. A number are simply the result of dialect differences, both synchronic and diachronic. This seems to be the case with most of the differences between the Babylonian Masorah and the Tiberian.[15]

---

ment with the Ben Asher text and disagreed only on a few specific points (*ibid.*, 104, n. 88). He points out there is no known MS claiming to be Ben Naphtali's. Moses Ben Asher the father and Aaron the son also differed. But the differences were all within the family: "The tiny differences between Aaron Ben Asher and Moses Ben Asher were not their inventions. They handed on, each in his own slightly different way, some earlier tradition. What finally became crystallized and connected to the name Ben Naftali was essentially the tradition of his predecessors, among them Moses Ben Asher . . . . But for the fact that history made that subsystem finally stick to the name of Ben Naftali . . . it would not be too far from the truth to speak of the two subsystems inside the Ben Asher family" (*ibid.*, 107).

[13]This is discussed especially by Goshen-Gottstein, "Hebrew Biblical Manuscripts" (note 6 above). This article deals with the question of variants within the many medieval MT MSS. (The general conclusion is that only a minute number of significant variants are likely to be found there.) Part of this variety is undoubtedly due to different types and qualities of codices. Goshen-Gottstein, "Biblical Manuscripts in the United States," *Textus* 2 (1962), 28-59, also discusses the difference between mass-produced study MSS, model codices, and listener copies.

[14]Much more study needs to be done on the biblical quotations within rabbinic literature. See Goshen-Gottstein, *The Book of Isaiah: Sample Edition with Introduction*, p. 35 and notes. There is, however, no doubt that many genuine variants--and even superior readings--exist in them. Cf. *ibid.*, p. 17. A pioneer work on the subject is V. Aptowitzer, *Das Schriftwort in der rabbinischen Literatur.*

[15]In addition to Ginsburg's *Introduction* (note 7 above) and Kahle's works listed in note 10, see such studies as

This is definitely the case with the Palestinian (non-Tiberian) text as shown by a number of recent studies by E. J. Revell.[16] It had been assumed (e.g., by Kahle) that the MSS with Palestinian vocalization represented a tradition earlier than the Tiberian. Revell's studies have shown the need to alter that assumption because of the following conclusions arising from his research:

1. The Tiberian system represents an older (more conservative) form of the language. The Palestinian biblical MSS are more conservative than the non-biblical, but both show a later development of the language with more "modern" features than the Tiberian. Thus, they clearly represent the colloquial pronunciation of Palestine and neighboring areas used in normal life except for the formal reading of the Bible.[17]

2. The Palestinian texts show a clear division into two groups, one more conservative and the other with considerable change. These may represent two different geographical areas, such as Egypt and Palestine proper.[18]

3. The graphic notation for both vowels and accentuation was less exact than that of the Tiberian system.[19]

4. The reading tradition was not so carefully preserved as the Tiberian tradition.[20]

Points 3 and 4 apparently account for most of the difference between the Palestinian and Tiberian traditions.[21] All in

---

Shelomo Morag, *The Hebrew Language Tradition of the Yemenite Jews* (in Hebrew; reviewed by E. Y. Kutscher, "Yemenite Hebrew and Ancient Pronunciation," JSS 11 [1966], 217-25) and I. Yeivin, *The Babylonian Vocalization and the Linguistic Tradition it Reflects* (1968 dissertation at the Hebrew University, in Heb with English summary).

[16] These are listed in the following notes 17-22. Cf. also M. Dietrich, *Neue palästinisch punktierte Bibelfragmente* (1968).

[17] "Studies in the Palestinian Vocalization of Hebrew," *Essays on the Ancient Semitic World*, 51-100 (especially 77-82).

[18] *Hebrew Texts with Palestinian Vocalization*, especially 120-1.

[19] "The Relation of the Palestinian to the Tiberian Massora," *Masoretic Studies* 1 (1974), 87-97 (especially 94-5).

[20] *ibid.*, 94-5.

[21] "A New Biblical Fragment with Palestinian Vocalization," *Textus* 7 (1969), 61-75 (especially 74-5).

all, Revell sums up the general situation as follows:

> It seems to me correct to conclude from this information on the various facets of the Palestinian tradition that the basic difference between the Palestinian and Tiberian traditions is graphic. They are simply different methods of representing in writing what was basically the same reading tradition. . . . This, then, is how I would see the relationship of the Palestinian to the Tiberian Massora: They originated in the same stream of tradition, and came to differ mainly because the Palestinian tradition became isolated and lacked any leading scholarly body, so that its reading tradition changed faster than the Tiberian, while its pointing system developed more slowly.[22]

A somewhat similar case is the famed Codex Reuchlinianus which Sperber took as "pre-Masoretic."[23] Shelomo Morag investigated the question and concluded that the Reuchlinianus vocalization, far from being pre-Masoretic, actually represented a later development in the history of Masoretic activity:[24]

> Professor Sperber's assumption that the vocalization of C[odex] R[euchlinianus] represents a "pre-Masoretic" school appears, therefore, incompatible with the actual findings. As we observed, there is good reason to believe that the aforementioned tendency towards a fuller phonetic notation, so conspicuous in CR, is typical of a later stage in the development of the vocalization systems. We have here to do with a school, a Palestinian school . . ., which is distinctly *post-Masoretic*.

Morag feels that the fuller representation of the phonology is characteristic of a later stage of activity when the previous living oral tradition was declining and readers were becoming more dependent on the written tradition.

---

[22] *op. cit.* (note 19 above), 96-7.

[23] See *A Grammar of Masoretic Hebrew*. Sperber published a facsimile edition of the Codex Reuchlinianus along with two other codices in *The Pre-Masoretic Bible*. For a review, see R. Meyer, VT 11 (1961), 474-86.

[24] "The Vocalization of Codex Reuchlinianus: Is the 'Pre-Masoretic' Bible Pre-Masoretic?" JSS 4 (1959), 216-37 (quotation from 229).

Greek Transliteration

The major source for the transliteration of Hebrew is the Second Column of Origen's *Hexapla*. The exact origin of this transliteration is uncertain. Kahle concluded that Origen simply used Jewish transliterations produced quite some time before he lived, perhaps from the 1st or 2nd centuries A.D.[25] But others have argued that Origen himself made the transliteration of the Second Column.[26] Regardless of the exact source, scholarship is generally agreed that it represents the actual reading of the Heb text less than two centuries after the destruction of the Second Temple.

It has often been assumed that the Hexaplaric transliteration showed the artificiality of the MT since it was supposed to represent a different voweling. Kahle also claimed it proved the non-pronunciation of the laryngeals, thus allegedly showing the Masoretes revived their pronunciation as part of an idealized Heb.[27] Several studies on the Column II material came to contrary conclusions. The first major study was that of E. A. Speiser.[28] Speiser discussed the very important question of trying to use the orthography suited to the phonology of one language (Greek) for the rather different phonology of another (Heb).[29] The transliterations evidently attempt to show actual pronunciation and thus did not always carry a consistent representation. This problem of

---

[25] *The Cairo Geniza*, 158-9.

[26] This idea has been developed most recently by J. A. Emerton, JTS 7 (1956), 79-87; 21 (1970), 17-31; 22 (1971), 15-28. See also S. Jellicoe, *The Septuagint and Modern Study*, 104-11.

[27] *Cairo Geniza*, 164-7.

[28] "The Pronunciation of Hebrew according to the Transliterations in the Hexapla," JQR 16 (1925-6), 343-82; 23 (1932-3), 233-65; 24 (1933-4), 9-46; unfortunately, the rest of the study did not appear. Speiser was following up an earlier article by M. L. Margolis, "Pronunciation of the שוא according to New Hexaplaric Material," AJSL 26 (1909), 62-70. Margolis had concluded the Hexaplaric pronunciation of Heb was in some respects more modern and in others more archaic than the MT (70).

[29] JQR 16 (1925-6), 360-3.

graphic notation and the phonological systems of the different transcribing languages has often been somewhat blithely passed over. Speiser unfortunately published only about half of his proposed study and never completed the rest. He did however investigate the question of the *bgdkpt* letters, the sibilants, and the laryngeals. He concludes that from Origen's work alone, their existence would be difficult to prove conclusively. But when the Hexaplaric transliterations are considered in the light of other evidence, it becomes clear that Hexaplaric material presupposes much the same distinction as that found in the later MT. Even the laryngeals, which had already begun a process of weakening in the local speech of some areas in the Second Temple period, were still fully preserved in the reading of the Bible.[30]

A more thorough study which had the benefit of Speiser's work was that of Einar Brønno.[31] Although I will not attempt to discuss his work in detail, Brønno's basic conclusion in regard to the relationship between Column II and the later MT is worth quoting:[32]

---

[30] JQR 23 (1932-3), 233-41, especially 238. The loss of the laryngeals in the Galilean pronunciation is proverbial and such passages as *b. Erubin* 53b are often quoted in support of this fact. However, the classic study by E. Y. Kutscher, *Studies in Galilean Aramaic* (now available in English), shows the situation was by no means so simple. He demonstrates that the Jews of Palestine could still pronounce the laryngeals even up to the time of the Arabic conquest (contrary to Kahle). However, the use of laryngeals varied according to place in the country and stratum of society (English edition, pp. 67-96, esp. p. 89).

[31] *Studien über hebräische Morphologie und Vokalismus* (1943). See also his later articles cited in notes 35 and 36 below and "The Isaiah Scroll DSIa and the Greek Transliterations of Hebrew," ZDMG 106 (1956), 252-8.

[32] *Studien*, 462-3: "Die grosse Bedeutung der SEC für die hebräische Sprachwissenschaft liegt u. a. darin, dass diese alte Überlieferung deutlich zeigt, dass das tiberische Formensystem in seinen wesentlichen Hauptzügen eine alte Tradition hinter sich hat . . . . Die SEC zeugt deutlich davon, dass die tib. Überlieferung rücksichtlich des Aufbaus des Formensystems viel zuverlässiger ist, als einige Forscher nach der Entdeckung der bab. und der pal. Vokalisationssysteme zu glauben geneigt waren. Dass zwischen der Entstehungszeit des Textes der SEC und der des MT eine Entwicklung stattgefunden hat, ist ja kein Wunder."

> The great significance of the SEC [Column II] for Hebrew linguistic study lies, among other things, in that this old tradition clearly shows that the Tiberian system in its essential features has an old tradition behind it . . . . The SEC plainly witnesses that the Tiberian tradition is much more reliable in regard to the structure of the linguistic system than some investigators, after the discovery of Babylonian and Palestinian vocalization systems, were inclined to believe. That a development occurred between the origin of the text of the SEC and that of the MT is indeed no surprise.

Brønno had already finished his study when Sperber published a monograph on the evidence of Greek and Latin transliterations.[33] Therefore, Brønno included an appendixed critique of Sperber's work, naturally concentrating on the Greek evidence. (The Latin evidence will be discussed in the following section.) Kahle gave a brief criticism of Brønno but simply referred to Sperber's work for refutation.[34] It is interesting that Kahle made no attempt to give an objective review of Brønno's analysis. Brønno replied to this in a lengthy review of the first edition of *The Cairo Geniza*.[35] In a later article Brønno also criticized Kahle's attempt to relate the material of the *Hexapla* to Samaritan Heb.[36] He concluded that such an attempt at comparison is illegitimate because "Samaritan Hebrew and the Secunda represent quite different grammatical traditions." In fact, Column II "is much more closely related to the MT and has, because of its great antiquity, much greater value for the history of the Hebrew language than the Samaritan tradition."

Other Greek material is scanty and will not be discussed

---

[33] "Hebrew Based upon Greek and Latin Transliterations," HUCA 12-13 (1937-8), 103-274. Reprinted with some changes in *A Historical Grammar of Biblical Hebrew*, 105-214.

[34] *Cairo Geniza*, 1st edition, 232-4. This material is omitted from the 2nd edition, with only a brief footnote dismissing Brønno's work (160, n. 3).

[35] ZDMG 100 (1950), 521-65.

[36] "Samaritan Hebrew and Origen's Secunda," JSS 13 (1968), 192-201.

except for a recent article on Masoretic accentuation.[37] E. J. Revell found that the Greek papyrus John Rylands 458 (Göttingen 957), the oldest known LXX papyrus (2nd century B.C.), contained information on accentuation.[38] The spaces within the Greek text correspond to the major disjunctive accents of the MT, with a few exceptions which "can readily be recognized as the variants to be expected in texts a thousand years apart."[39] The correlation between these spaces and the underlying Heb text is made even clearer by the fact that the spacing "occasionally ran counter to the word division normal for Greek." The conclusion is very important: "For the Hebrew Bible, it shows clearly that the basis of the system of cantillation represented by the later accents was already firmly established in the second century B.C., and was so much a part of the formal reading of the Torah, that it was also used for the Septuagint."[40]

Jerome's Transliterations

The importance of Jerome's writings cannot be exaggerated since they form one of the few sources of information in the linguistically sterile period between Bar Kokhba and the Masoretes. His transliterations of Heb words were thoroughly tabu-

---

[37] Some study has been done on the proper names in the LXX, but much more needs doing. Earlier works include a section in Z. Frankel, *Vorstudien zu der Septuaginta* (1841), 90ff, and C. Könnecke, *Die Behandlung der hebräischen Namen in der Septuaginta* (1885), neither of which were available to me. However, Speiser noted that both these studies were rather careless in their treatment of phonetic problems (JQR 16 [1925-6], 347). A more recent study is W. E. Staples, "The Hebrew of the Septuagint," AJSL 44 (1927-8), 6-30. Any such study must keep in mind that proper names have their own particular idiosyncracies and may give a distorted picture if not handled very carefully.

[38] "The Oldest Evidence for the Hebrew Accent System," BJRL 54 (1971-2), 214-22.

[39] *ibid.*, 219.

[40] *ibid.*, 222.

alted by Carl Siegfried in the last century.[41] His study has been criticized for its indiscriminate use of material from various sources as well as its failure to take account of certain phonetic problems in transcribing Hebrew into Latin. More recent is Sperber's treatise which attempts to prove the artificiality of the Masoretic system.[42] E. F. Sutcliffe made a start at analysis but recognized that the lack of a good critical edition made his work provisional.[43] He showed awareness of the transcriptional problems and noted that not all the transliterations were Jerome's own.

The most definitive recent discussion of the subject is that of James Barr.[44] Barr devotes most of the space to the consonants but also has a section on vowels. Against Sperber, Barr concludes the reading tradition which Jerome received from his teachers differs little from the later Masoretic structure. Barr notes that previous studies have generally failed to consider the fact that a person learning a foreign language will usually classify the new sounds according to the phonemic (not just phonetic) system of his own language. That is, even when Jerome was aware of differences between Heb and Latin pronunciation, this would not prevent his classifying the Heb according to the Latin phonemic structure wherever possible. Other points also to be aware of include (a) the influence of the conventional spelling of Latin, (b) the method of transliteration (mainly Greek) already used by his predecessors, (c) the lack of a conscious Heb grammar, and (d) the fact that Heb is usually cited as an adjunct to a particular exegetical question rather than as a linguistic point in its own right.

He concludes that Jerome did not show a distinction in the *bgdkpt* letters simply because they were allophones without

---

[41] "Die Aussprache des Hebräischen bei Hieronymous," ZAW 4 (1884), 34-83.

[42] *op. cit.* (note 33).

[43] "St. Jerome's Pronunciation of Hebrew," *Biblica* 29 (1948), 112-25 (specifically 116).

[44] "St. Jerome and the Sounds of Hebrew," JSS 12 (1967), 1-36. Cf. also his "St. Jerome's Appreciation of Hebrew," BJRL 49 (1966-7), 281-302.

phonemic status and because of the incapacity of the Latin alphabet to express the distinction. A careful examination of Jerome's discussions on the laryngeals shows that he was aware of their being pronounced as well as graphically marked (even though it was not generally possible to indicate them in transliteration). The conclusion of Sperber that *śin* and *šin* were not distinguished again fails to take note of the graphic problem and also involves a careless reading of what Jerome himself says on the subject. On the question of vowels, "Variety and inconsistency do appear in Jerome's vocalic transcriptions; but some examples are to be ascribed to other causes than real differences of vowel phonemes in the Hebrew of his time. . . . Where causes of this kind are not present, most variation in the registration of vowels can plausibly be ascribed to the difficulty of phonemicization and transcription . . . ."[45] Jerome also generally agrees with the MT in his gemination of consonants.

In concluding, Barr observes that "Jerome's material can be interpreted in a sense which keeps it closer to the Masoretic structure of Hebrew than has recently been supposed."[46] Some other arguments which may help confirm this are (a) Jerome is really not far removed in time from the first Masoretic activity, (b) his informants appear to be Palestinian Jews as opposed to groups with a diverse linguistic tradition such as the Samaritans, (c) his translation and commentaries generally agree with the semantic content of the MT even against such versions as the LXX and Aquila. Jerome's interest was not primarily phonetic. Therefore, it should not be surprising he gives only limited information.

Einar Brønno has since produced a more specialized monograph on Jerome's knowledge of the laryngeals.[47] He had the benefit of Barr's study but covered the question much more

---

[45] *ibid.*, 32-3.

[46] *ibid.*, 35.

[47] *Die Aussprache der hebräishen Laryngale nach Zeugnissen des Hieronymus* (1970). J. H. Hospers gives the book a favorable review in BO 30 (1973), 464-6.

thoroughly. He similarly concluded that the laryngeals were still pronounced by Jerome's informants at that time. In view of Brønno's limitation of subject and Barr's admission that his study was not exhaustive, a full treatment of Jerome's discussions of Heb is still needed. But the views of Kahle and Sperber seem in serious question if not disproved, especially when consideration of the Hexaplaric material is added to this evidence.

Dead Sea Scrolls

Any attempt to cover all the possibly relevant material would be futile. Good bibliographies already cover the secondary literature conveniently and almost exhaustively.[48] The discussion here can mention only the literature which appears to me to be the most relevant for the MT.

The Qumran scrolls showed that the consonantal MT was not a late text created by editorial activity of the rabbis. What has been characterized as a "proto-MT" was already well-attested by the time of the Qumran scrolls in the last century or so B.C.[49] One of the earliest MS fragments at Qumran is

---

[48] C. Burchard, *Bibliographie zu den Handschriften vom Toten Meer*. B. Jongeling, *A Classified Bibliography of the Finds in the Desert of Judah 1958-1969*. W. LaSor, *Bibliography of the Dead Sea Scrolls 1948-1957*. A current listing of new literature can also be found in each issue of *Revue de Qumran*. A recent listing of the most important texts and studies is J. A. Fitzmyer, *The Dead Sea Scrolls, Major Publications and Tools for Study* (1975).

[49] Perhaps one of the best general references on the subject is F. M. Cross, *The Ancient Library of Qumran*, chapter IV. General articles on the OT text which make extensive use of the DSS, by S. Talmon and B. J. Roberts, can be found in the *Cambridge History of the Bible*, vols. I and II. In addition to the literature in notes 50-52 which follow, here are other relevant publications (a good deal of it of a survey or summary type): M. Burrows, *The Dead Sea Scrolls* (1955); *More Light on the Dead Sea Scrolls* (1958); H. Orlinsky, "Notes on the Present State of the Textual Criticism of the Judean Biblical Cave Scrolls," *A Stubborn Faith*, 117-31; B. J. Roberts, "The Dead Sea Scrolls and the Old Testament Scriptures," BJRL 36 (1953-4), 75-96; C. Rabin, "The Dead Sea Scrolls and the History of the O.T. Text," JTS 6 (1955), 96-104; B. J. Roberts, "The Second Isaiah Scroll from Qumran (1QIs^b)," BJRL 42 (1959-60), 132-44;

"proto-MT."[50] The most famous and one of the most important of the biblical scrolls, 1QIs[a], is definitely the Masoretic text-type despite a number of differences from our present *textus receptus*.[51] Yet it soon became clear that other text-types were also present, including those which seemed to represent the *Vorlage* of the LXX (where it differed from the MT) and the tradition in the Samaritan Pentateuch. This soon led to theories about the number, geographical provenance, time of appearance of, and relationship between the various recensions.[52] Regardless of the ultimate answers to these ques-

---

J. P. Hyatt, "The Dead Sea Discoveries: Retrospect and Challenge," JBL 76 (1957), 1-12; P. Skehan, "Qumran and the Present State of Old Testament Text Studies: The Masoretic Text," JBL 78 (1959), 21-5; H. Orlinsky, ". . .: The Septuagint Text," *ibid.*, 26-33; M. Mansoor, "The Thanksgiving Hymns and the Massoretic Text," RQ 3 (1961-2), 259-66, 387-94; S. Talmon, "Aspects of the Textual Transmission of the Bible in the Light of Qumran Manuscripts," *Textus* 4 (1964), 259-96; P. Wernberg-Møller, "The Contribution of the *Hodayot* to Biblical Textual Criticism," *ibid.*, 133-75; P. Skehan, "The Biblical Scrolls from Qumran and the Text of the Old Testament," BA 28 (1965), 87-100; M. Goshen-Gottstein, "The Psalms Scroll (11QPs[a])," *Textus* 5 (1966), 22-33; P. Skehan, "The Scrolls and the Old Testament Text," *New Directions in Biblical Archaeology*, 99-112. Most recently, see F. Cross and S. Talmon, *Qumran and the History of the Biblical Text* (1975), which reprints a number of classic articles as well as adding some new discussion.

[50]F. M. Cross, "The Contribution of the Qumran Discoveries to the Study of the Biblical Text," IEJ 16 (1966), 82. The "proto-MT" fragment is 4QJer[a], dated to about 200 B.C. The method of dating is discussed by Cross in "The Oldest Manuscripts from Qumran," JBL 74 (1955), 147-72 (especially 164).

[51]W. H. Brownlee, *The Meaning of the Qumran Scrolls for the Bible*, 155-6. H. Orlinsky even contested some of the accepted identifications of differences in a series of articles, "Studies in the St. Mark's Isaiah Scroll": JBL 69 (1950), 149-66; JNES 11 (1952), 153-6; JJS 2 (1951), 151-4; JQR 43 (1952-3), 329-40; IEJ 4 (1954), 5-8; HUCA 25 (1954), 85-92; *Tarbiz* 24 (1954-5), 4-8 (English summary I-II).

[52]In addition to the literature cited in Chapter III, note 42 above, note W. F. Albright, "New Light on Early Recensions of the Hebrew Bible," BASOR 140 (Dec., 1955), 27-33; M. H. Segal, "The Promulgation of the Authoritative Text of the Hebrew Bible," JBL 72 (1953), 35-47; Moshe Greenberg, "The Stabilization of the Text of the Hebrew Bible, Reviewed in the Light of the Biblical Materials from the Judean Desert," JAOS 76 (1956), 157-67; S. Talmon, "The Textual Study of the Bible--A New Outlook," *Qumran and the History of the Biblical Text*, 321-400.

tions, the important thing is that the MT represents an old tradition.[53]

Documents from other parts of the Judaean desert tend to be slightly later, but they coincide with the consonantal MT in an even more striking fashion.[54] One outstanding representative of these is the scroll of the Minor Prophets from Murabba^{c}at. J. T. Milik who edited it for publication made a list of the variants between it and the *Biblia Hebraica*^{3}. He notes that most of these are matters of defective versus plene spelling or of *Qere* versus *Ketiv*.[55] The other biblical fragments from Masada and the Judaean desert also deviate only minutely from the standard printed editions of today. The variants are usually of the same type as found within the medieval MSS and seldom of significance. This suggests that the consonantal MT was the standard text of at least part of Judaism even before the destruction of the Second Temple.[56]

---

[53] Of course, certain parts of the MT--such as Samuel and Jeremiah--are not usually considered as pristine as other textual traditions. However, Talmon (*ibid*., 327-32) shows that the problem is more complicated than that. Texts which differ to such a degree (e.g., the LXX text of Jer versus the MT) bring up questions which have traditionally been treated under "higher criticism." (This implies that the traditional clear-cut division between "lower" and "higher" criticism cannot necessarily be maintained.) This naturally leads to the question about which stage of the text one is trying to work with. See Chapter III for a further discussion of this issue.

[54] A number of these are published in DJD II. The Israeli expedition under Y. Yadin found many more which have been published only in preliminary form in "Expedition D," IEJ 11 (1961), 36-52; 12 (1962), 227-57. (A phylactery from Expedition B is published in IEJ 11 [1961], 22-3.) See also Yadin's more popular *Bar-Kokhba* (1971) and *Masada* (1966) and "New Discoveries in the Judean Desert," BA 24 (1961), 34-50; "More on the Letters of Bar Kokhba," *ibid*., 86-95; "The Excavation of Masada--1963/1964, Preliminary Report," IEJ 15 (1965), 1-120, esp. 103-5.

[55] DJD II, 183-4.

[56] While some of the biblical material may date only from the decades shortly before the Bar Kokhba revolt, other MSS are evidently earlier than 70 A.D., certainly those from Masada. It has been widely assumed that the text was basically "canonized" at Yavneh about 90 A.D. This assumption is called into question now, both by the scrolls and by a study of the traditions in regard to Yavneh. See J. P. Lewis, "What Do We Mean by Yabneh?" JBR 32 (1964), 125-32.

The same MSS also provide evidence for the antiquity of other textual features such as verse and paragraph division since these are often marked.[57] Again, as with the evidence of accentuation (see above under "Greek Transliteration"), the agreement with the Tiberian text is striking despite some occasional differences. The Greek MS of the so-called *kaige* recension published by Barthélemy indicates verse division by the use of spaces. Divisions within the verse are marked by the use of enlarged letters, these corresponding to several of the major disjunctive accents of the MT.[58] The scrolls from Qumran also sometimes have divisions, though these are less likely to coincide with those of the later MT.[59]

A thorough study of the linguistic tradition represented by the Qumran scrolls as a whole has yet to be made. The best so far available is that of E. Y. Kutscher, but it covers only 1QIs[a].[60] For this particular document Kutscher concluded that the scribe's dialect "was apparently largely similar if not identical with that of Mishnaic Hebr. It does not seem to have been pure Hebrew, but rather a Hebrew-Aramaic patois."[61] The

---

[57]Yadin, *Masada*, 171-2, 179; DJD II, 182-3.

[58]*Les devanciers d'Aquila*, VTS 10 (1963), 165-6. See also the comments of E. J. Revell (note 38 above), 215-6. It is to be noted that the regularity of the system ceases after part of Hab, and the Zech fragments mark word divisions but no others.

[59]Revell (note 38 above), 214-15, discusses the verse and intraverse divisions. The phrase and paragraph divisions of 1QIs[a] are well-known and were recognized from the beginning (M. Burrows, *The Dead Sea Scrolls of St. Mark's Monastery*, vol. I, xxii-xxiii).

[60]*The Language and Linguistic Background of the Isaiah Scroll (1QIsa[a])* (1974). Unfortunately, the English translation was not updated from the 1959 Heb edition nor is it always an accurate rendering of the original. See the lengthy review by J. Barr, JSS 21 (1976), 186-93. Other examples of shorter studies on various aspects of the Qumran scrolls are Z. Ben-Ḥayyim, "Traditions in the Hebrew Lanugage, with Special Reference to the Dead Sea Scrolls," *Scripta Hierosolymitana* 4 (2nd edition, 1965), 200-14; M. Goshen-Gottstein, "Linguistic Structure and Tradition in the Qumran Documents," *ibid.*, 101-37; C. Rabin, "The Historical Background in Qumran Hebrew," *ibid.*, 144-61; M. Mansoor, "Some Linguistic Aspects of the Qumran Texts," JSS 3 (1958), 40-54.

[61]Kutscher, *ibid.*, 61.

language of the writer of the Isaiah scroll, then, appears to be a later form of Heb than that represented by the MT. By "later" is meant the stage of development of the language, not the actual chronological time. The MT was written down much later but generally preserved features of a stage of Heb older than that of 1QIs^{a}. But when this diachronic dialect difference is taken into account, the actual meaning is basically the same in each tradition. That is, in most cases the differences concern features of (diachronic) dialect, not of real content or meaning.

Linguistic Studies on the Masoretic Tradition

Until recently the well-developed science of linguistics had seemed to bypass the Semitic languages, certainly Hebrew, to a large extent even though getting on toward its bicentenary. The field of Semitic studies has been dominated by philology.[62] Fortunately, this is now beginning to change. A number of recent studies apply the principles of both synchronic and diachronic linguistics to the MT.

Probably the most thorough work on the subject of the MT graphic system is that of Gene Schramm.[63] He admits his results need further checking but concludes that the Tiberian graphic structure was a rather loose one, not at all highly regularized as was classical Ar. This and other facts lead Schramm to the following conclusion, provisional though it is:

> In other words, all levels of analysis would seemingly lead to the observation that the Massoretes could not have sat down to their task by deciding which reading made the most sense at a given point. If they had worked this way, then a highly regularized patterning would have been likely. It would seem much more probable, then, that the Massoretes simply reduced to a writing system the pronunciation of biblical Hebrew that

---

[62] Cf. the remarks of James Barr, "The Ancient Semitic Languages--the Conflict between Philology and Linguistics," *Transactions of the Philological Society* (1968), 37-55.

[63] *The Graphemes of Tiberian Hebrew* (1964).

> was traditional for them, i.e., that one generation had learned by rote from the prior generation.[64]

There are also other recent linguistic studies which generally conclude the MT represented a traditional pronunciation (even though that may not have been their main objection of investigation).[65]

The study of traditional reading traditions among Yemenite Jews is a promising one. A good deal of work has already been done, especially by S. Morag.[66] This has potential value for our question though exactly how to relate it is not always certain. It is interesting, though, that the Yemenite reading tradition is quite close to that of texts with Babylonian punctuation and apparently is to be considered an offshoot of the Babylonian dialect.[67] Yet the Yemenites preserve the double pronunciation in all the *bgdkpt* letters. Their tradition of reading the biblical (and targumic) texts differs from that of reading post-biblical texts (such as texts in MHeb and Babylonian Aram).

Morag has also published a very recent article of significant value on the validity of the MT vocalization.[68] He investigated examples of three categories of heterogeneous features in the MT. Different books of the Bible were influenced by three types of "dialect" within their linguistic environment which should have left their mark if the MT vocalization is historical: (1) the later Heb used at the time of such

---

[64] *ibid.*, 64-5.

[65] Cf., e.g., U. Ornan, "The Tiberian Vocalisation System and Principles of Linguistics," JJS 15 (1964), 109-23; A. D. Corré, "Phonemic Problems in the Masora," *Essays presented to Chief Rabbi Israel Brodie*, 59-66.

[66] *The Hebrew Language Tradition of the Yemenite Jews* (1963--in Hebrew). An extensive English review is E. Y. Kutscher, "Yemenite Hebrew and Ancient Pronunciation," JSS 11 (1966), 217-25. See also Morag, "Oral Traditions and Dialects," *Proceedings of the International Conference on Semitic Studies*, 180-89.

[67] Kutscher, *ibid.*, 220.

[68] "On the Historical Validity of the Vocalization of the Hebrew Bible," JAOS 94 (1974), 307-15.

late books as Chronicles and Daniel, (2) isolated dialects which existed alongside the more standard speech in biblical times, and (3) various foreign languages in contact with Heb. The influence of these "dialects" would not have changed the overall pattern of the language but should have left a few discernable marks. Morag finds examples of each and concludes as follows about the MT vocalization:[69]

> To sum up, it appears that the vocalization peculiarities we have attempted to elucidate in the present paper are evidently not to be considered as whims of the Massoretes. The vocalization is definitely of historical value, and even those of its features that look strange should be examined seriously, and must not be labeled as 'errors' of the vocalizers. This point cannot be stressed too far. We do not mean to say, of course, that no errors have crept into the vocalization; it must, however, be borne in mind that the origins of the vocalization go back to a period far earlier than that of the Massoretes, and that, as a source of historical information, the vocalization should be accorded serious consideration.

It would probably not be inappropriate to conclude this survey with mention of James Barr's work which includes a chapter on the MT.[70] Morag refers to this as a "turning point" in the general views about the vocalization.[71] The tendency to dismiss the vocalization as having little value is changing, and Barr's book may indeed be characterized as a significant signpost.

The revival of interest in the MT is evidenced by the founding of the International Organization for Masoretic Study at the First International Congress of Learned Societies in Los Angeles, 1972. The first volume of the proceedings of the IOMS came out in 1974 as *Masoretic Studies 1* and other monographs have appeared since.[72]

---

[69] *ibid.*, 315.

[70] CPTOT, chap. VIII.

[71] *op. cit.* (note 68 above), 307.

[72] For example, J. P. Siegel, *The Severus Scroll and 1QIs[a]* (1975). A useful survey of matters Masoretic is the lengthy article by A. Dotan in the new *Encyclopaedia Judaica* (vol. 16, 1401-82).

BIBLIOGRAPHY

OF WORKS CITED

Abrahams, M. *Aquila's Greek Version of the Hebrew Bible* (London: Spottiswoode, Ballantyne & Co., 1919).

Aharoni, Y. "Expedition B," IEJ 11 (1961), 11-24.

Aistleitner, Joseph. *Wörterbuch der ugaritischen Sprache* (2nd edition; Berlin: Akademie-Verlag, 1965).

Albright, William F. *Archaeology and the Religion of Israel* (5th edition; Baltimore: John Hopkins, 1968).

______. Review of Gordis, *Biblical Text in the Making*, JBL 57 (1938), 223-4.

______. Reply to Robert Gordis, JBL 57 (1938), 332-3.

______. "Northwest-Semitic Names in a List of Egyptian Slaves from the Eighteenth Century B.C.," JAOS 74 (1954), 222-33.

______. "New Light on Early Recensions of the Hebrew Bible," BASOR 140 (Dec., 1955), 27-33.

Allen, Don Cameron. *The Legend of Noah* (Urbana: University of Illinois, 1963).

Ancient Syriac Old Testament (Urmia edition, 1913; reprinted London: Trinitarian Bible Society, 1954).

Anderson, F. I. Review of CPTOT, JBL 88 (1969), 345-6.

Anttila, Raimo. *An Introduction to Historical and Comparative Linguistics* (New York: MacMillan, 1972).

Aptowitzer, Victor. *Das Schriftwort in der rabbinischen Literatur* (1906-15; reprinted New York: Ktav, 1970).

Arlotto, Anthony. *Introduction to Historical Linguistics* (Boston: Houghton Mifflin, 1972).

Armbruster, Carl H. *Initia Amharica* (Part III, Vol. 1; Cambridge: University Press, 1920).

Assyrian Dictionary of the Oriental Institute of Chicago, The (Chicago: University of Chicago, 1956-).

Aufrecht, Walter E., and John C. Hurd. *A Synoptic Concordance of Aramaic Inscriptions* (International Concordance Library, 1; Missoula, MT: Scholars Press, 1975).

Avishur, Y. "Addenda to the Expanded Colon in Ugaritic and Biblical Verse," UF 4 (1972), 1-10.

Bacher, Wilhelm. "Das Targum zu Hiob," MGWJ 20 (1871), 208-23, 283-4.

______. "Targums," *Jewish Encyclopaedia* (New York: 1905).

Baeteman, J. *Dictionnaire amarigna-français* (Dire-Daoua, Ethiopia: Saint Lazare, 1929).

Barr, James. *Comparative Philology and the Text of the Old Testament* (Oxford: Clarendon, 1968).

______. "St. Jerome's Appreciation of Hebrew," BJRL 49 (1966-7), 281-302.

______. "St. Jerome and the Sounds of Hebrew," JSS 12 (1967), 1-36.

______. "The Ancient Semitic Languages--the Conflict between Philology and Linguistics," *Transactions of the Philological Society* (1968), 37-55.

______. "Seeing the Wood for the Trees? An Enigmatic Ancient Translation," JSS 13 (1968), 11-20.

______. "Ugaritic and Hebrew *šbm*?" JSS 18 (1973), 17-39.

______. "Etymology and the Old Testament," *Language and Meaning* (OTS 19; Leiden: Brill, 1974), 1-28.

______. "Philology and Exegesis," *Questions disputées d'Ancien Testament* (Bibliotheca Ephemeridum Theologicarum Lovaniensium, 33; Gembloux: Leuven University, 1974).

______. Review of the English translation of Kutscher, *Language and Linguistic Background of the Isaiah Scroll*, JSS 21 (1976), 186-93.

Barthélemy, A. *Dictionnaire arabe-français: dialectes de Syrie* (Paris: Paul Geuthner, 1935-69).

Barthélemy, Dominique. *Les devanciers d'Aquila* (VTS 10; Leiden: Brill, 1963).

Bauer, H., and P. Leander. *Historische Grammatik der hebräischen Sprache* (Halle: 1922; reprinted Hildesheim: Georg Olms, 1965).

Bauer, Theo. *Die Ostkanaanäer* (Leipzig, 1926).

Baumann, Eberhard. "Die Verwendbarkeit der Pešita zum Buche Ijob für die Textkritik," ZAW 18 (1898), 305-38; 19 (1899), 15-95, 288-309; 20 (1900), 177-201, 264-307.

Baumgartner, Walter, et al. *Hebräisches und aramäisches Lexikon zum Alten Testament* (3rd edition of KB; Leiden: Brill, 1967-).

Beeston, A. F. L. *Sabaean Inscriptions* (Oxford, 1937).

______. *A Descriptive Grammar of Epigraphic South Arabian* (London: Luzac, 1962).

______. "Notes on Old South Arabian Lexicography," *Le Muséon* 63-7 (1950-4); 85 (1972).

Ben-Ḥayyim, Zeev. *The Literary and Oral Tradition of Hebrew and Aramaic amongst the Samaritans* (in Heb; vol. 1- ; Jerusalem: Academy of the Hebrew Language, 1957-).

______. "Traditions in the Hebrew Language, with Special Reference to the Dead Sea Scrolls," *Aspects of the Dead Sea Scrolls* (Scripta Hierosolymitana, 4; ed. C. Rabin and Y. Yadin; 2nd edition; Jerusalem: Magnes, 1965), 200-14.

Benz, Frank L. *Personal Names in the Phoenician and Punic Inscriptions* (Studia Pohl, 8; Rome: Pontifical Biblical Institute, 1972).

Bergsträsser, G. *Hebräische Grammatik* (Wilhelm Gesenius' hebräische Grammatik, 29. Auflage, mit Beiträgen von M. Lidzbarski; Leipzig: F. C. W. Vogel, 1918-29).

Biblia Sacra iuxta Latinam Vulgatam Versionem (Rome: Typis Polyglottis Vaticanis, 1925-).

Bickerman, Elias J. "The Septuagint as a Translation," PAAJR 28 (1959), 1-39.

Blachère, Régis, et al. *Dictionnaire arabe-français-anglais* (Paris: G. -P. Maisonneuve et Larose, 1964-).

Blau, Joshua. *The Emergence and Linguistic Background of Judaeo-Aramaic* (Oxford: Clarendon, 1965).

______. *Grammar of Christian Arabic* (vols. 1-3; CSCO 267, 276, 279; Louvain: Secrétariat du Corpus SCO, 1966-7).

______. *On Pseudo-Corrections in Some Semitic Languages* (Jerusalem: Israel Academy of Sciences and Humanities, 1970).

______. *A Grammar of Biblical Hebrew* (Porta Linguarum Orientalium, Neue Serie, 12; Wiesbaden: Harrassowitz, 1976).

______. "Some Difficulties in the Reconstruction of >>Proto-Hebrew<< and >>Proto-Canaanite<<," *In Memoriam Paul Kahle* (BZAW 103, ed. M. Black and G. Fohrer; Berlin: Töpelmann, 1968), 29-43.

______. "On Problems of Polyphony and Archaism in Ugaritic Spelling," JAOS 88 (1968), 523-6.

______. "Arabic Lexicographical Miscellanies," JSS 17 (1972), 173-90.

Blommerde, Anton C. M. *Northwest Semitic Grammar and Job* (Biblica et Orientalia, 22; Rome: Pontifical Biblical Institute, 1969).

Boris, Gilbert. *Lexique du parler arabe des Marazig* (Paris: Imprimerie nationale, 1958).

Bornkamm, Günther, et al. *Tradition and Interpretation in Matthew* (tr. P. Scott; Philadelphia: Westminster, 1963).

Bottéro, Jean. "La lexicographie accadienne," *Studies on Semitic Lexicography* (ed. P. Fronzaroli; Quaderni di Semitistica, 2; Firenze: University, 1973), 25-60.

Brekelmans, C. "Some Considerations on the Translation of the Psalms by M. Dahood. I," UF 1 (1969), 5-14.

Brock, Sebastian P. "The Phenomenon of the Septuagint," OTS 17 (1972), 11-36.

______. Review of Goodwin, *Text-Restoration Methods*, JSS 17 (1972), 259-60.

______, et al. *A Classified Bibliography of the Septuagint* (Arbeiten zur Literatur und Geschichte des hellenistischen Judentums, VI; Leiden: Brill, 1973).

Brockelmann, Carl. *Grundriss der vergleichenden Grammatik der semitischen Sprachen* (vols. I-II; Berlin: 1908, 1913; reprinted Hildesheim: Georg Olms, 1966).

______. *Lexicon syriacum* (2nd edition; Halle: Max Niemeyer, 1928).

Broek, R. van den. *The Myth of the Phoenix according to Classical and Early Christian Traditions* (Etudes préliminaires aux religions orientales dans l'empire romain, 24; Leiden: Brill, 1972).

Brønno, Einar. *Studien über hebräische Morphologie und Vokalismus* (Abhandlungen für die Kunde des Morgenlandes, XXVIII; Leipzig: Brockhaus, 1943).

______. Review of Kahle, *Cairo Geniza*, ZDMG 100 (1950), 521-65.

______. "The Isaiah Scroll DSIa and the Greek Transliterations of Hebrew," ZDMG 106 (1956), 252-8.

______. "Samaritan Hebrew and Origen's Secunda," JSS 13 (1968), 192-201.

______. *Die Aussprache der hebräischen Laryngale nach Zeugnissen des Hieronymus* (Aarhus: Universitetsforlaget, 1970).

Brown, Francis, et al. *A Hebrew and English Lexicon of the Old Testament* (1907 edition corrected by G. R. Driver; Oxford: Clarendon, 1953).

Brownlee, William H. *The Meaning of the Qumran Scrolls for the Bible* (Oxford: Clarendon, 1964).

Buccellati, Giorgio. *The Amorites of the Ur III Period* (Seminario di Semitistica Ricerche, I; Naples: Istituto Orientale, 1966).

Buhl, Frants. *Wilhelm Gesenius' hebräisches und aramäisches Handwörterbuch über das Alte Testament* (17th edition, 1915; reprinted Berlin: Springer-Verlag, 1949).

Burchard, Christoph. *Bibliographie zu den Handschriften vom Toten Meer* (vols. 1-2; BZAW 76, 89; Berlin: Töpelmann, 1957, 1962).

Burrows, Millar. *The Dead Sea Scrolls* (New York: Viking, 1955).

______. *More Light on the Dead Sea Scrolls* (New York: Viking, 1958).

______, et al. *The Dead Sea Scrolls of St. Mark's Monastery* (vol. I; New Haven, CT: American Schools of Oriental Research, 1950).

Cassuto, Umberto. *The Goddess Anath* (tr. I. Abrahams; Jerusalem: Magnes, 1971).

Childs, Brevard S. *Memory and Tradition in Israel* (Studies in Biblical Theology, 37; London: SCM, 1962).

______. *Isaiah and the Assyrian Crisis* (Studies in Biblical Theology, Second Series, 3; London: SCM, 1967).

______. *Biblical Theology in Crisis* (Philadelphia: Westminster, 1970).

______. *The Book of Exodus* (Old Testament Library; Philadelphia: Westminster, 1974).

Clines, D. J. A. "The Etymology of Hebrew *Ṣelem*," JNSL 3 (1974), 19-25.

Cohen, David (ed.). *Dictionnaire des racines sémitiques ou attestées dans les langues sémitiques* (comprenent un ficher comparatif de J. Cantineau; vol. 1- ; Paris: Mouton, 1970-).

Conti Rossi, Karl. *Chrestomathia Arabica meridionalis epigraphica* (Rome: Istituto per l'Oriente, 1931).

Corre, A. D. "Phonemic Problems in the Masora," *Essays Presented to Chief Rabbi Israel Brodie* (ed. H. Zimmels, et al.; Jews' College Publications, New Series, 3; London: Soncino, 1967), 59-66.

Cowley, Arthur E. *The Samaritan Liturgy* (vols. 1-2; Oxford: Clarendon, 1909).

______. *Gesenius' Hebrew Grammar* (2nd edition revised from the 28th German edition of E. Kautzsch; Oxford: Clarendon, 1910).

Cross, Frank M. *The Ancient Library of Qumran* (revised edition; Garden City: Anchor, 1961).

______. "The Oldest Manuscripts from Qumran," JBL 74 (1955), 147-72.

______. "The History of the Biblical Text in the Light of Discoveries in the Judaean Desert," HTR 57 (1964), 281-99.

______. "The Contribution of the Qumran Discoveries to the Study of the Biblical Text," IEJ 16 (1966), 81-95.

______. "The Canaanite Cuneiform Tablet from Taanach," BASOR 190 (April, 1968), 41-6.

______, and D. N. Freedman. *Early Hebrew Orthography* (American Oriental Series, 36; New Haven, CT: American Oriental Society, 1952).

______, and D. N. Freedman. "Some Observations on Early Hebrew," *Biblica* 53 (1972), 413-20.

______, and S. Talmon (ed.). *Qumran and the History of the Biblical Text* (Cambridge, MA: Harvard, 1975).

Culley, Robert C. *Oral Formulaic Language in the Biblical Psalms* (Near and Middle East Series, 4; Toronto: University, 1967).

Dahood, Mitchell J. *Ugaritic-Hebrew Philology* (Biblica et Orientalia, 17; Rome: Pontifical Biblical Institute, 1965).

______. *Psalms* (vols. 1-3; Anchor Bible; Garden City: Doubleday, 1965-70).

______. "Canaanite-Phoenician Influence in Qoheleth," *Biblica* 33 (1952), 30-52, 191-221.

______. "A New Translation of Genesis 49,6a," *Biblica* 36 (1955), 229.

______. "Some Northwest-Semitic Words in Job," *Biblica* 38 (1957), 306-20.

______. "The Root עזב II in Job," JBL 78 (1959), 303-9.

______. "*mišmār* 'muzzle' in Job 7,12," JBL 80 (1961), 270-1.

______. "Northwest Semitic Philology and Job," *The Bible in Current Catholic Thought* (Gruenthaner Memorial Volume, ed. J. L. McKenzie; New York: Herder and Herder, 1962), 55-74.

______. "Qoheleth and Northwest Semitic Philology," *Biblica* 43 (1962), 349-65.

______. "Hebrew-Ugaritic Lexicography," *Biblica* 44-55 (1963-74).

______. "Ugaritic Lexicography," *Mélanges Eugène Tisserant* (vol. I; Studi e Testi, 231; Vatican: Biblioteca Apostolica, 1964), 81-104.

______. "Nest and Phoenix in Job 29,18," *Biblica* 48 (1967), 542-4.

______. "Ugaritic and the Old Testament," *De Mari à Qumran* (Bibliotheca Ephemeridum Theologicarum Lovaniensium, 24; Gembloux: J. Duculot, 1969), 14-33.

______. "Ugaritic and Phoenician or Qumran and the Versions," *Orient and Occident* (AOAT 22, ed. H. A. Hoffner; Neukirchen-Vluyn: Verlag, 1973), 53-8.

______. "*Ḥôl* 'Phoenix' in Job 29:18 and in Ugaritic," CBQ 36 (1974), 85-8.

______. "Four Ugaritic Personal Names and Job $39_{5.26-27}$," ZAW 87 (1975), 220.

Dalman, Gustav. *Grammatik des jüdisch-palästinischen Aramäisch* and *Aramaïsche Dialektproben* (1905, 1927; reprinted Darmstadt: Wissenschaftliche Buchgesellschaft, 1960).

Déaut, Roger le. *Introduction à la littérature targumique* (premiere partie; Rome: Pontifical Biblical Institute, 1966).

______. "Les études targumique," *De Mari à Qumran* (Bibliotheca Ephemeridum Theologicarum Lovaniensium, 24; Gembloux: J. Duculot, 1969), 302-31.

______. "The Current State of Targumic Studies," *Biblical Theology Bulletin* 4 (1974), 3-32.

Degen, Rainer. *Altaramäische Grammatik der Inscriften des 10.-8. Jh. vor Chr.* (Abhandlungen für die Kunde des Morgenlandes, Bd. 38,3; Wiesbaden: Franz Steiner, 1969).

Delitzsch, Franz. *Job* (Commentary on the Old Testament; tr. F. Bolton; reprinted Grand Rapids, MI: Eerdmans, 1973).

Delitzsch, Friedrich. *Assyrisches Handwörterbuch* (1896; reprinted Leipzig: DDR Zentralantiquariat, 1968).

Denizeau, Claude. *Dictionnaire des parlers arabes de Syrie, Liban et Palestine* (Supplément au Dictionnaire arabe-français de A. Barthélemy; Etudes et Documents, III; Paris: G.-P. Maisonneuve, 1960).

Dhorme, E. *A Commentary on the Book of Job* (tr. H. Knight; London: Thomas Nelson, 1967).

Dietrich, Manfried. *Neue palästinisch punktierte Bibelfragmente* (Leiden: Brill, 1968).

______, and O. Loretz. "Untersuchungen zur Schrift- und Lautlehre des Ugaritischen (I)," WO 4 (1968), 300-15.

______, and O. Loretz. "Das Ugaritische in den Wörterbüchern von L. Köhler und W. Baumgartner," BZ 13 (1969), 187-207.

______, and O. Loretz. "Zur ugaritischen Lexikographie," BO 23, 25 (1966, 1968); OLZ 62 (1967); UF 4 (1972). Continued in conjunction with J. Sanmartín, UF 5- (1973-).

______, O. Loretz, and J. Sanmartín. Review of Fisher, *Ras Shamra Parallels II*, UF 7 (1975), 597-8.

______, et al. *Ugarit-Bibliographie (1928-1966)* (vols. 1-4; AOAT 20; Neukirchen: Verlag, 1973).

Dillmann, August. *Lexicon linguae aethiopicae* (Leipzig: T. O. Weigel, 1865).

______. *Hiob* (3rd edition; Kurzgefasstes exegetisches Handbuch zum Alten Testament; Leipzig; S. Hirzel, 1869).

______. *Ethiopic Grammar* (tr. J. Crichton from the enlarged edition by C. Bezold; London: Williams & Norgate, 1907).

Dion, Paul-Eugène. *La langue de Ya'udi* (Corporation for the Publication of Academic Studies in Religion in Canada, 1974).

Discoveries in the Judaean Desert, The (vols. I- ; Oxford: Clarendon, 1955-).

Donner, H., and W. Röllig. *Kanaanäische und aramäische Inschriften* (2nd edition; vols. 1-3; Wiesbaden: Harrassowitz, 1969).

Dozy, R. *Supplément aux dictionnaires arabes* (vols. 1-2; 1881; reprinted Beruit: Librairie du Liban, 1968).

Driver, G. R. *Canaanite Myths and Legends* (Old Testament Studies, III; Edinburgh: T. & T. Clark, 1956).

______. "Difficult Words in the Hebrew Prophets," *Studies in Old Testament Prophecy* (ed. H. H. Rowley; Edinburgh: T. & T. Clark, 1950), 52-72.

______. "Some Hebrew Medical Expressions," ZAW 65 (1953), 255-62.

______. "Hebrew Poetic Diction," *Congress Volume, Copenhagen* (VTS 1; Leiden: Brill, 1953), 26-39.

______. "Birds in the Old Testament II," PEQ 87 (1955), 129-40.

______. "Job 39:27-8: The *Ky*-Bird," PEQ 104 (1972), 64-6.

Driver, S. R., and G. Gray. *A Critical and Exegetical Commentary on the Book of Job* (International Critical Commentary; Edinburgh: T. & T. Clark, 1921).

Drower, E. S., and R. Macuch. *A Mandaic Dictionary* (Oxford: Clarendon, 1963).

Ecker, Roman. *Die arabische Job-Übersetzung des Gaon Saadja ben Josef al-Fajjûmî* (Studien zum Alten und Neuen Testament, 4; Munich: Kösel-Verlag, 1962).

Ehrlich, Arnold. *Randglossen zur hebräischen Bibel* (Leipzig: Hinrichs, 1908-14).

Eissfeldt, Otto. *The Old Testament, An Introduction* (tr. P. Ackroyd; New York: Harper, 1965).

Eitan, Israel. *A Contribution to Biblical Lexicography* (Contributions to Oriental History and Philology, 10; 1924; reprinted New York: AMS, 1966).

Eliade, Mircea. *Cosmos and History: The Myth of the Eternal Return* (tr. W. R. Trask; Bollingen Series, XLVI; Princeton: University Press, 1954).

Ellenbogen, Maximilian. *Foreign Words in the Old Testament, Their Origin and Etymology* (London: Luzac, 1957).

Emerton, J. A. "The Purpose of the Second Column of the Hexapla," JTS 7 (1956), 79-87.

______. "Were Greek Transliterations of the Hebrew Old Testament Used by Jews before the Time of Origen?" JTS 21 (1970), 17-31.

______. "A Further Consideration of the Purpose of the Second Column of the Hexapla," JTS 22 (1971), 15-28.

______. Review of HAL, VT 22 (1972), 502-11.

Encyclopaedia Judaica (vols. 1-16; New York: Macmillan, 1971).

Field, Fridericus. *Origenis Hexaplorum quae supersunt* (vols. 1-2; 1875; reprinted Hildesheim: Georg Olms, 1964).

Fischer, Boniface, et al. *Biblia Sacra* (vols. 1-2; Stuttgart: Württembergische Bibelanstalt, 1969).

Fishbane, Michael. "Jeremiah IV 23-26 and Job III 3-13: A Recovered Use of the Creation Pattern," VT 21 (1971), 151-67.

Fisher, Loren R. "*ŠDYN* in Job XIX 29," VT 11 (1961), 342-3.

______. "An Ugaritic Ritual and Genesis I,1-5," *Ugaritica VI* (Mission de Ras Shamra, 17; Paris: Paul Geuthner, 1969), 197-205.

______ (ed.). *Ras Shamra Parallels* (vol. 1- ; Analecta Orientalia, 49; Rome: Pontifical Biblical Institute, 1972-).

Fitzmyer, Joseph A. *The Aramaic Instriptions of Sefîre* (Biblica et Orientalia, 19; Rome: Pontifical Biblical Institute, 1967).

______. *The Genesis Apocryphon of Qumran Cave 1* (Biblica et Orientalia, 18a; 2nd edition; Rome: Pontifical Biblical Institute, 1971).

______. *The Dead Sea Scrolls, Major Publications and Tools for Study* (Sources for Biblical Study, 8; Missoula, MT: Scholars Press, 1975).

______. "The Languages of Palestine in the First Century A.D.," CBQ 32 (1970), 501-31.

______. "Some Observations on the Targum of Job from Qumran Cave 11," CBQ 36 (1974), 503-24.

______. "Methodology in the Study of the Aramaic Substratum of Jesus' Sayings in the New Testament," *Jésus aux origines de la christologie* (Bibliotheca Ephemeridum Theologicarum Lovaniensium, 40; Gembloux: Leuven University, 1974), 73-102.

Fohrer, Georg. *Das Buch Hiob* (Kommentar zum Alten Testament, 16; Gütersloh: Gerd Mohn, 1963).

Frankel, Z. *Vorstudien zu der Septuaginta* (Leipzig: F. C. W. Vogel, 1841).

Freedman, David Noel. "Prolegomenon" to George B. Gray, *The Forms of Hebrew Poetry* (1915; reprinted New York: Ktav, 1972), vii-lvi.

Freytag, Georg. *Lexicon arabico-latinum* (vols. 1-4; Halle: Schwetschke, 1830-7).

Friedlaender, Israel. *Arabisch-deutsches Lexikon zum Sprachgebrauch des Maimonides* (Der Sprachgebrauch des Maimonides I. Lexikalischer Teil; Frankfurt: J. Kauffmann, 1902).

Friedrich, Johannes. *Phönizisch-punische Grammatik* (2nd edition, ed. W. Röllig; Analecta Orientalia, 46; Rome: Pontifical Biblical Institute, 1970).

Fronzaroli, Pelio (ed.). *Studies on Semitic Lexicography* (Quaderni di Semitistica, 2; Firenze: Istituto di Linguistica, 1973).

Fück, J. "Zur arabischen Wörterbuchfrage," ZDMG 107 (1957), 340-7.

Gard, Donald H. *The Exegetical Method of the Greek Translator of the Book of Job* (Journal of Biblical Literature Monograph, VIII; Philadelphia: Society of Biblical Literature, 1952).

Gaster, Theodor H. *Myth, Legend, and Custom in the Old Testament* (vols. 1-2; New York: Harper, 1969).

______. "The Canaanite Epic of Keret," JQR 37 (1946-7), 285-93.

Gerleman, Gillis. *Studies in the Septuagint I. Book of Job* (Lunds Universitets Årsskrift, N.F. Avd. 1, Bd.43, Nr. 2; Lund: C. W. K. Gleerup, 1946).

Gevirtz, Stanley. "West-Semitic Curses and the Problem of the Origins of Hebrew Law," VT 11 (1961), 137-58.

Gibson, John C. L. *Textbook of Syrian Semitic Inscriptions* (vol. 1- ; Oxford: Clarendon, 1971-).

Ginsberg, H. L. *The Legend of King Keret, a Canaanite Epic of the Bronze Age* (BASOR Supplementary Studies, 2-3; New Haven, CT: American Schools of Oriental Research, 1946).

______. "A Ugaritic Parallel to 2 Sam 1_{21}," JBL 57 (1938), 209-13.

______. "Lexicographical Notes," *Hebräische Wortforschung* (ed. B. Hartmann, et al.; VTS 16; Leiden: Brill, 1967), 71-82.

Goetze, Albrecht. "Is Ugaritic a Canaanite Dialect?" *Language* 17 (1941), 127-38.

Goldie, Fay. *Ostrich Country* (Cape Town: Books of Africa, 1968).

Goodwin, Donald. *Text-Restoration Methods in Contemporary U.S.A. Biblical Scholarship* (Ricerche V; Naples: Istituto Orientale, 1969).

Gordis, Robert. *The Biblical Text in the Making: A Study of the Kethib-Qere* (1937; reissued New York: Ktav, 1971).

______. Reply to the W. F. Albright review of *Biblical Text in the Making*, JBL 57 (1938), 329-31.

______. "Studies in the Relationship of Biblical and Rabbinic Hebrew," *Louis Ginzberg Jubilee Volume* (New York: American Academy for Jewish Research, 1945), 173-99.

______. "Corporate Personality in Job: A Note on 22:29-30," JNES 4 (1945), 54-5.

______. "On Methodology in Biblical Exegesis," JQR 61 (1970-1), 93-118.

Gordon, Cyrus H. *Ugaritic Textbook* (Analecta Orientalia, 38; Rome: Pontifical Biblical Institute, 1965; Supplement, 1967).

______. *The Ancient Near East* (New York: W. W. Norton, 1965).

______. *Ugarit and Minoan Crete* (New York: W. W. Norton, 1966).

______. "Azitawadd's Phoenician Inscription," JNES 8 (1949), 108-20.

Goshen-Gottstein, Moshe H. *The Book of Isaiah: Sample Edition with Introduction* (Jerusalem: Magnes, 1965).

______. "Linguistic Structure and Tradition in the Qumran Documents," *Aspects of the Dead Sea Scrolls* (Scripta Hierosolymitana, 4; ed. C. Rabin and Y. Yadin; 2nd edition; Jerusalem: Magnes, 1965), 101-37.

______. "Biblical Manuscripts in the United States," *Textus* 2 (1962), 28-59.

______. "Rise of the Tiberian Bible Text," *Biblical and Other Studies* (ed. Alexander Altmann; Philip W. Lown Institute of Advanced Judaic Studies, Studies and Texts, I; Cambridge, MA: Harvard, 1963), 79-122.

______. "The Theory and Practice of Textual Criticism," *Textus* 3 (1963), 130-58.

______. "The Psalms Scroll (11QPs^{a})," *Textus* 5 (1966), 23-33.

______. "Hebrew Biblical Manuscripts," *Biblica* 48 (1967), 243-90.

Gray, John. *The Krt Text in the Literature of Ras Shamra* (Documenta et monumenta orientalis antiqui, 5; 2nd edition; Leiden: Brill, 1964).

______. "The Massoretic Text of the Book of Job, the Targum and the Septuagint Version in the Light of the Qumran Targum," ZAW 86 (1974), 331-50.

Grébaut, Sylvain. *Supplément au Lexicon linguae aethiopicae de August Dillmann* (Paris: Imprimerie nationale, 1952).

Greenberg, Moshe. "The Stabilization of the Text of the Hebrew Bible, Reviewed in the Light of the Biblical Materials from the Judean Desert," JAOS 76 (1956), 157-67.

Greenfield, Jonas C. "Amurrite, Ugaritic and Canaanite," *Proceedings of the International Conference on Semitic Studies, 1965* (Jerusalem: Israel Academy of Sciences and Humanities, 1969), 92-101.

Gröndahl, Frauke. *Die Personennamen der Texte aus Ugarit* (Studia Pohl, 1; Rome: Pontifical Biblical Institute, 1967).

Grossfeld, Bernard. *A Bibliography of Targum Literature* (Cincinnati: Hebrew Union College, 1972).

Guillaume, Alfred. *Studies in the Book of Job* (ed. J. Macdonald; Supplement II to the Annual of the Leeds University Oriental Society; Leiden: Brill, 1968).

______. "Hebrew and Arabic Lexicography, A Comparative Study," *Abr-Nahrain* 1 (1959-60), 3-35; 2 (1960-1), 5-35; 3 (1961-2), 1-10; 4 (1963-4), 1-18.

______. "The Unity of the Book of Job," *Annual of the Leeds University Oriental Society* 4 (1962-3), 26-46.

______. "The Arabic Background of the Book of Job," *Promise and Fulfilment* (ed. F. F. Bruce; Edinburgh: T. & T. Clark, 1963), 106-27.

Gunkel, Hermann. *Schöpfung und Chaos in Urzeit und Endzeit* (Göttingen: Vandenhoeck und Ruprecht, 1895).

Hass, Mary R. *The Prehistory of Languages* (Janua Linguarum, Series Minor, 57; The Hague: Mouton, 1969).

Haefeli, Leo. *Die Peschitta des Alten Testaments* (Münster: Aschendorff, 1927).

Hahn, Herbert F., and Horace Hummel. *The Old Testament in Modern Research* (expanded edition; Philadelphia: Fortress, 1966).

Harding, G. Lankester. *An Index and Concordance of Pre-Islamic Arabian Names and Inscriptions* (Near and Middle East Series, 8; Toronto: University Press, 1971).

Harrell, Richard S. (ed.). *A Dictionary of Moroccan Arabic: Moroccan-English* (Washington, DC: Georgetown University, 1966).

Harris, Zellig S. *A Grammar of the Phoenician Language* (American Oriental Series, 8; New Haven, CT: American Oriental Society, 1936).

______. *The Development of the Canaanite Dialects* (American Oriental Series, 16; New Haven, CT: American Oriental Society, 1939).

Hastings, James (ed.). *A Dictionary of the Bible* (vols. 1-5; Edinburgh: T. & T. Clark, 1898-1904).

Hatch, Edwin, and H. A. Redpath. *A Concordance to the Septuagint* (3 vols. in 2; 1897; reprinted Graz: Akademische Druck- und Verlagsanstalt, 1975).

Hayes, John H. (ed.). *Old Testament Form Criticism* (San Antonio: Trinity University, 1974).

Heras, Henry. "The Standard of Job's Immortality," CBQ 11 (1949), 263-79.

Herdner, Andrée. *Corpus des tablettes en cunéiformes alphabétiques* (Mission de Ras Shamra, 10; vols. 1-2; Paris: Imprimerie nationale, 1963).

Hillers, Delbert R. "An Alphabetic Cuneiform Tablet from Taanach (TT 433)," BASOR 173 (Feb., 1964), 45-50.

______. "A Convention in Hebrew Literature: The Reaction to Bad News," ZAW 77 (1965), 86-90.

______. "Paḥad Yiṣḥāq," JBL 91 (1972), 90-2.

Hirschberg, Harris H. "Some Additional Arabic Etymologies in Old Testament Lexicography," VT 11 (1961), 373-85.

Horst, Friedrich. *Hiob* (Biblischer Kommentar, Altes Testament, 16; Neukirchen: Verlag des Erziehungsvereins, 1968).

Hospers, J. H. Review of Brønno, *Die Aussprache der hebräischen Laryngale*, BO 30 (1973), 464-6.

______ (ed.). *A Basic Bibliography for the Study of the Semitic Languages* (vols. 1-2; Leiden: Brill, 1973-4).

Howard, George. "Frank Cross and Recensional Criticism," VT 21 (1971), 440-50.

Huffmon, Herbert B. *Amorite Personal Names in the Mari Texts: A Structural and Lexical Study* (Baltimore: Johns Hopkins, 1965).

Hyatt, J. Philip. "The Dead Sea Discoveries: Retrospect and Challenge," JBL 76 (1957), 1-12.

Interpreter's Dictionary of the Bible, The (vols. 1-4; Nashville: Abingdon, 1962; supplementary vol., 1976).

Isbell, Charles D. *Corpus of the Aramaic Incantation Bowls* (SBL Dissertation Series, 17; Missoula, MT: Scholars Press, 1975).

Jahn, Alfred. *Die Mehri-Sprache in Südarabien* (Südarabische Expedition, III; Vienna: Alfred Hölder, 1902).

Jamme, Albert. *Sabaean Inscriptions from Maḥram Bilqîs (Mârib)* (Publications of the American Foundation for the Study of Man, III; Baltimore: Johns Hopkins, 1962).

Jastrow, Marcus. *A Dictionary of the Targumim, the Talmud Babli and Yerushalmi, and the Midrashic Literature* (vols. 1-2; 1903; reprinted New York: Pardes, 1950).

Jean, C.-F., and Jacob Hoftijzer. *Dictionnaire des inscriptions sémitiques de l'Ouest* (Leiden: Brill, 1965).

Jellicoe, Sidney. *The Septuagint and Modern Study* (Oxford: Clarendon, 1968).

Jongeling, B. *A Classified Bibliography of the Finds in the Desert of Judah 1958-1969* (Studies on the Texts of the Desert of Judah, 7; Leiden: Brill, 1971).

______. "Contributions of the Qumran Job Targum to the Aramaic Vocabulary," JSS 17 (1972), 191-7.

Kaddari, M. Z. "A Semantic Approach to Biblical Parallelism," JJS 24 (1973), 167-75.

Kahle, Paul E. *Masoreten des Ostens* (Leipzig: J. C. Hinrichs, 1913).

______. *Der masoretische Text des Alten Testaments, nach der Überlieferung der babylonischen Juden* (1902; reprinted Hildesheim: Georg Olms, 1966).

______. *Masoreten des Westens* (I and II; Texte und Untersuchungen zur vormasoretischen Grammatik des Hebräischen, 1 and 4; Stuttgart: W. Kohlhammer, 1927, 1930).

______. *Opera Minora* (Leiden: Brill, 1956).

______. *The Cairo Geniza* (2nd edition; New York: Praeger, 1959).

Katz, Peter. "The Recovery of the Original Septuagint, A Study in the History of Transmission and Textual Criticism," *Actes du premier congrès de la Fédération Internationale des Associations d'Etudes Classique* (Paris: C. Klincksieck, 1951), 165-82.

______. "Septuagintal Studies in the Mid-Century," *The Background of the New Testament and its Eschatology* (ed. W. Davies and D. Daube; Cambridge: University Press, 1956), 176-208.

Kaufmann, Stephen A. "The Job Targum from Qumran," JAOS 93 (1973), 317-27.

Kazimirski, A. de Biberstein. *Dictionnaire arabe-français* (vols. 1-2; 1860; reprinted Beruit: Librairie du Liban, no date).

Kennicott, Benjamin. *Vetus Testamentum hebraicum cum variis lectionibus* (vols. 1-2; Oxford: Clarendon, 1776-80).

Kimchi, David. *Radicum liber, sive Hebraeum Bibliorum lexicon* (cum animadversionibus Eliae Levitae; ed. J. Biesenthal and F. Lebrecht; Berlin: 1847).

King, Robert D. *Historical Linguistics and Generative Grammar* (Englewood Cliffs, NJ: Prentice-Hall, 1969).

Knierim, Rolf. "Old Testament Form Criticism Reconsidered," *Interpretation* 27 (1973), 435-68.

Knight, Douglas A. *Rediscovering the Traditions of Israel* (revised edition; SBL Dissertation Series, 9; Missoula, MT: Scholars Press, 1975).

Koch, Klaus. *Growth of the Biblical Tradition* (tr. from 2nd German edition by S. M. Cupitt; New York: Scribner, 1969.

Koehler, Ludwig, and W. Baumgartner. *Lexicon in Veteris Testamenti libros* (vols. 1-3; Leiden: Brill, 1953-8).

Könnecke, Clemens. *Die Behandlung der hebräischen Namen in der Septuaginta* (Stargard, 1885).

Kopf, L. "Das arabische Wörterbuch als Hilfsmittel für die hebräische Lexikographie," VT 6 (1956), 286-302.

______. "Arabische Etymologien und Parallelen zum Bibelwörterbuch," VT 8 (1958), 161-215; 9 (1959), 247-87.

Kraemer, Jörg. *Theodor Nöldekes Belegwörterbuch zur klassischen arabischen Sprache* (Berlin: Walter de Gruyter, 1952).

______, et al. *Wörterbuch der klassischen arabischen Sprache* (Wiesbaden: Harrassowitz, 1957-).

Kraus, H.-J. *Psalmen* (vols. 1-2; Biblischer Kommentar, Altes Testament, 15; Neukirchen: Verlag, 1961).

Krauss, Samuel. "Saadya's Tafsir of the Seventy *Hapax Legomena* Explained and Continued," *Saadya Studies* (ed. E. Rosenthal; Manchester: University Press, 1943), 47-77.

Kühne, Cord. "Mit Glossenkeilen markierte fremde Wörter in akkadischen Ugarittexten II," UF 7 (1975), 253-60.

Kuhn, Karl G. *Konkordanz zu den Qumrantexten* (Göttingen: Vandenhoeck & Ruprecht, 1960).

______. "Nachträge zur 'Konkordanz zu den Qumrantexte,'" RQ 4 (1963-4), 163-234.

Kutscher, E. Y. *The Language and Linguistic Background of the Isaiah Scroll (1QIsa[a])* (Studies on the Texts of the Desert of Judah, VI; Leiden: Brill, 1974).

______. *Studies in Galilean Aramaic* (tr. and ed. M. Sokoloff; Bar-Ilan Studies in Near Eastern Languages and Culture; Jerusalem: Bar-Ilan, 1976).

______. "Yemenite Hebrew and Ancient Pronunciation," JSS 11 (1966), 217-25.

______. "Mittelhebräisch und Jüdisch-Aramäisch im neuen Köhler-Baumgartner," *Hebräische Wortforschung* (ed. B. Hartmann, et al.; VTS 16; Leiden: Brill, 1967), 158-75.

Lagarde, Paul de. *Hagiographa chaldaice* (Leipzig: B. G. Teubner, 1873).

Lambert, W. G. *Babylonian Wisdom Literature* (Oxford: Clarendon, 1960).

Lamsa, George M. *The Holy Bible from Ancient Eastern Manuscripts* (tr. of the Peshitta; Philadelphia: A. J. Holman, 1957).

Landberg, Carlo de. *Glossaire datînois* (vols. 1-2; vol. 3 published by K. Zetterstéen; Leiden: Brill, 1920-42).

Lane, E. W. *An Arabic-English Lexicon* (Book I, Parts 1-8; 1863-93; reprinted New York: Frederick Ungar, 1955).

Lane, William R. *A Handbook of Phoenician Inscriptions* (unpublished Ph.D. dissertation; Baltimore: Johns Hopkins, 1962).

LaSor, William S. *Bibliography of the Dead Sea Scrolls 1948-1957* (Fuller Library Bulletin, 31; Pasadena, CA: Fuller Theological Seminary, 1958).

Lehmann, Winfred P. *Historical Linguistics: An Introduction* (revised edition; New York: Holt, Rinehart and Winston, 1973).

Lehrer, Adriene. *Semantic Fields and Lexical Structure* (North-Holland Linguistic Series, 11; London: North-Holland, 1974).

Leibreich, Leon J. "Notes on the Greek Version of Symmachus," JBL 63 (1944), 397-403.

Leiman, Sid Z. (ed.). *The Canon and Masorah of the Hebrew Bible* (New York: Ktav, 1974).

Lesky, Albin. *A History of Greek Literature* (tr. J. Willis and C. de Heer; New York: Crowell, 1966).

Leslau, Wolf. *Lexique Soqoṭri* (Collection Linguistique publiée par la Société de Linguistique de Paris, 41; Paris: C. Klincksieck, 1938).

______. *Gafat Documents, Records of a South-Ethiopic Language* (American Oriental Series, 28; New Haven, CT: American Oriental Society, 1945).

______. *Etude descriptive et comparative du Gafat (Ethiopien méridional)* (Collection Linguistique publiée par la Société de Linguistique de Paris, 57; Paris: C. Klincksieck, 1956).

______. *Ethiopic and South Arabic Contributions to the Hebrew Lexicon* (Berkeley: University of California, 1958).

______. *Etymological Dictionary of Harari* (Near Eastern Studies, 1; Los Angeles: University of California, 1963).

______. *Hebrew Cognates in Amharic* (Wiesbaden: Harrassowitz, 1969).

______. *Concise Amharic Dictionary, Amharic/English--English/Amharic* (Wiesbaden: Harrassowitz, 1976).

______. "Vocabulary Common to Akkadian and South-east Semitic (Ethiopic and South-arabic)," JAOS 64 (1944), 53-8.

______. "Southeast Semitic Cognates to the Akkadian Vocabulary," JAOS 82 (1962), 1-4; 84 (1964), 115-18; 89 (1969), 18-22.

______. "Observations on Semitic Cognates in Ugaritic," Or 37 (1968), 347-66.

Lévi, Israel. *The Hebrew Text of the Book of Ecclesiasticus* (1904; reprinted Leiden: Brill, 1969).

Levy, Jacob. *Chaldäisches Wörterbuch über die Targumim und einen grossen Theil des rabbinischen Schriftthums* (vols. 1-2; reprinted Darmstadt: Joseph Melzer, 1966).

______. *Neuhebräisches und chaldäisches Wörterbuch über die Talmudim und Midraschim* (nebst Beiträgen von H. L. Fleischer und den Nachtragen und Berichtigungen von L. Goldschmidt; vols. 1-4; 1924; reprinted Darmstadt: Wissenschaftliche Buchgesellschaft, 1963).

Lewis, Jack P. "What Do We Mean by Yabneh?" JBR 32 (1964), 125-32.

Lewy, Heinrich. *Die semitischen Fremdwörter im Griechischen* (1895; reprinted Hildesheim: Georg Olms, 1970).

Lisowsky, Gerhard, and Leonhard Rost. *Konkordanz zum hebräischen Alten Testament* (2nd edition; Stuttgart: Württembergische Bibelanstalt, 1958).

Littmann, Enno, and Maria Höfner. *Wörterbuch der Tigrē-Sprache* (Wiesbaden: Franz Steiner, 1962).

Löw, Immanuel. *Die Flora der Juden* (vols. 1-4; Leipzig: R. Löwit, 1928-34).

Loewenstamm, Samuel E. "The Muzzling of the Tannin in Ugaritic Myth," IEJ 9 (1959), 260-1.

______. "The Ugaritic Fertility Myth--the Result of a Mistranslation," IEJ 12 (1962), 87-8.

______. "The Expanded Colon in Ugaritic and Biblical Verse," JSS 14 (1969), 167-96.

______. "Anat's Victory over the Tunnanu," JSS 20 (1975), 22-7.

______. "The Expanded Colon, Reconsidered," UF 7 (1975), 261-4.

Lohse, Eduard. *Die Texte aus Qumran* (2nd edition; Munich: Kösel-Verlag, 1971).

Long, Burke. "Recent Field Studies in Oral Literature and their Bearing on OT Criticism," VT 26 (1976), 187-98.

Loretz, Oswald. "Textologie des Zephanja-Buches," UF 5 (1973), 219-28.

______. "Der Gott *šlḥ*, he. *šlḥ* I und *šlḥ* II," UF 7 (1975), 584-5.

McCarthy, Dennis J. "'Creation' Motifs in Ancient Hebrew Poetry," CBQ 29 (1967), 393-406.

Macintosh, A. A. "The Problems of Psalm II. 11 and 12," JTS 27 (1976), 1-14.

Maclean, Arthur J. *Dictionary of the Dialects of Vernacular Syriac* (1901; reprinted Amsterdam: Philo Press, 1972).

Macuch, Rudolf. *Handbook of Classical and Modern Mandaic* (Berlin: Walter de Gruyter, 1965).

______, and E. Panoussi. *Neusyrische Chrestomathie* (Porta Linguarum Orientalium, Neue Serie, XIII; Wiesbaden: Harrassowitz, 1974).

Mandelkern, Solomon. *Veteris Testamenti concordantiae hebraicae atque chaldaicae* (corrected by F. Margolin and M. Goshen-Gottstein; Jerusalem: Schocken, 1959).

Mansoor, Menahem. "Some Linguistic Aspects of the Qumran Texts," JSS 3 (1958), 40-54.

______. "The Thanksgiving Hymns and the Massoretic Text," RQ 3 (1961-2), 259-66, 387-94.

______. "The Massoretic Text in the Light of Qumran," *Bonn 1962* (VTS 9; Leiden: Brill, 1963), 305-21.

Marcais, W., et A. Guīga. *Textes arabes de Takroûna: 2. Glossaire* (vols. 1-8; Paris: Imprimerie nationale, 1958-61).

Margoliouth, J. (Payne Smith). *A Compendious Syriac Dictionary* (Oxford: Clarendon, 1903).

______. *Supplement to the Thesaurus Syriacus of R. Payne Smith* (Oxford: Clarendon, 1927).

Margolis, Max L. *A Manual of the Aramaic Language of the Babylonian Talmud* (Clavis linguarum semiticarum, III; Munich: C. H. Beck, 1910).

______. "Pronunciation of the שוא according to New Hexaplaric Material," AJSL 26 (1909), 62-70.

Martin, Annie. *Home Life on an Ostrich Farm* (New York: D. Appleton, 1891).

Martinez, E. R. *Hebrew-Ugaritic Index to the Writings of Mitchell J. Dahood* (Rome: Pontifical Biblical Institute, 1967).

Masson, Emilia. *Recherches sur les plus anciens emprunts sémitiques en grec* (Etudes et Commentaires, 67; Paris: C. Klincksieck, 1967).

Meyer, Rudolf. Review of Sperber, *A Grammar of Masoretic Hebrew*, VT 11 (1961), 474-86.

Michel, Walter L. *The Ugaritic Texts and the Mythological Expressions in the Book of Job (including a New Translation of and Philological Notes on the Book of Job)* (Ph.D. dissertation; University of Wisconsin, 1970).

Milik, J. T. *The Books of Enoch, Aramaic Fragments of Qumran Cave 4* (with collaboration of M. Black; Oxford: Clarendon, 1976).

Millard, A. R. "*Scriptio Continua* in Early Hebrew," JSS 15 (1970), 2-15.

Miqra'ot Gedolot (rabbinic Bible with targums and commentaries, reprinted many times).

Montgomery, James A. *Aramaic Incantation Texts from Nippur* (University of Pennsylvania, Museum Publications of the Babylonian Section, 3; Philadelphia: University Museum, 1913).

______. "Notes on the Mythological Epic Texts from Ras Shamra," JAOS 53 (1933), 97-123.

Moor, Johannes C. de. *The Seasonal Pattern in the Ugaritic Myth of Baᶜlu* (AOAT 16; Neukirchen: Verlag, 1971).

______. "Studies in the New Alphabetic Texts from Ras Shamra II," UF 2 (1970), 303-27.

______, and P. van der Lugt. "The Spectre of Pan-Ugaritism," (review of Fisher, *Ras Shamra Parallels*, I), BO 31 (1974), 3-26.

Morag, Shelomo. *The Hebrew Language Tradition of the Yemenite Jews* (Heb with English summary; The Academy of the Hebrew Language Studies, IV; Jerusalem: Magnes, 1963).

______. "The Vocalization of Codex Reuchlinianus: Is the 'Pre-Masoretic' Bible Pre-Masoretic?" JSS 4 (1959), 216-37.

______. "Oral Traditions and Dialects," *Proceedings of the International Conference on Semitic Studies in 1965* (Jerusalem: Israel Academy of Sciences and Humanities, 1969), 180-89.

______. "On the Historical Validity of the Vocalization of the Hebrew Bible," JAOS 94 (1974), 307-15.

Moscati, S. (ed.). *An Introduction to the Comparative Grammar of the Semitic Languages* (Porta Linguarum Orientalium, Neue Serie, 6; Wiesbaden: Harrassowitz, 1964).

Mowinckel, Sigmund. "שחל," *Hebrew and Semitic Studies Presented to Godfrey Rolles Driver* (ed. D. W. Thomas and W. D. McHardy; Oxford: Clarendon, 1963), 95-103.

Müller, Walter W. *Die Wurzeln Mediae und Tertiae Y/W im Altsüdarabischen* (Inaugural-Dissertation; Tübingen: Eberhard-Karls-Universität, 1962).

______. "Altsüdarabische Beiträge zum hebräischen Lexikon," ZAW 75 (1963), 304-16.

Muraoka, Takamitsu. "Did the Septuagint Translators Confuse *Gimel* with ᶜ*Ain*?" VT 21 (1971), 612-18.

Murtonen, A. *An Etymological Vocabulary to the Samaritan Pentateuch* (Materials for a Non-Masoretic Hebrew Grammar, II; Helsinki: Suomalaisen Kirjallisuuden Kirjapaino, 1960).

Muss-Arnolt, William. *Assyrisch-englisch-deutsches Handwörterbuch* (vols. 1-2; Berlin: Reuther u. Reichard, 1894-1905).

Naveh, J. "A Hebrew Letter from the Seventh Century B.C.," IEJ 10 (1960), 129-39.

Nida, Eugene A. *Toward a Science of Translating* (Leiden: Brill, 1964).

______. *Componential Analysis of Meaning* (Approaches to Semiotics, 57; The Hague: Mouton, 1975).

______. "Implications of Contemporary Linguistics for Biblical Scholarship," JBL 91 (1972), 73-89.

______. "Semantic Structure and Translating," BT 26 (1975), 120-32.

Nöldeke, Theodor. *Compendious Syriac Grammar* (tr. J. Crichton, from 2nd German edition; London: Williams & Norgate, 1904).

______. *Mandäische Grammatik* (1875; reprinted Darmstadt: Wissenschaftliche Buchgesellschaft, 1964).

______. Review of Delitzsch, *Prolegomena eines neuen hebräisch-aramäischen Wörterbuchs*, ZDMG 40 (1886), 718-43.

______. "צלמות und צלם," ZAW 17 (1897), 183-7.

Noth, Martin. *Die israelitischen Personennamen im Rahmen der gemeinsemitischen Namengebung* (1928; reprinted Hildesheim: Georg Olms, 1966).

Orlinsky, Harry M. "Problems of Kethib-Qere," JAOS 60 (1940), 30-45.

______. "On the Present State of Proto-Septuagint Studies," JAOS 61 (1941), 81-91.

______. "The Septuagint--Its Use in Textual Criticism," BA 9 (1946), 21-42.

______. "Current Progress and Problems in Septuagint Research," *The Study of the Bible Today and Tomorrow* (ed. H. Willoughby; Chicago: University of Chicago, 1947), 144-61.

______. "Studies in the St. Mark's Isaiah Scroll," JBL 69 (1950), 149-66; JNES 11 (1952), 153-6; JJS 2 (1951), 151-4; JQR 43 (1952-3), 329-40; IEJ 4 (1954), 5-8; HUCA 25 (1954), 85-92; *Tarbiz* 24 (1954-5), 4-8 (English summary I-II).

______. "Notes on the Present State of the Textual Criticism of the Judean Biblical Cave Scrolls," *A Stubborn Faith* (ed. E. C. Hobbs; Dallas: Southern Methodist, 1956), 117-31.

______. "Studies in the Septuagint Text of Job," HUCA 28-30, 32-3, 35-6 (1957-9, 1961-2, 1964-5).

______. "Qumran and the Present State of Old Testament Text Studies: The Septuagint Text," JBL 78 (1959), 26-33.

______. "Prolegomenon: The Masoretic Text: A Critical Evaluation," *Introduction to the Massoretico-Critical Edition of the Hebrew Bible* by C. D. Ginsburg (reissued; New York: Ktav, 1966).

Ornan, Uzzi. "The Tiberian Vocalisation System and the Principles of Linguistics," JJS 15 (1964), 109-23.

Palais royal d'Ugarit, Le (Mission de Ras Shamra; vol. 1- ; Paris: Imprimerie nationale, 1955-).

Pardee, Dennis. "The Preposition in Ugaritic," UF 7- (1975-).

Payne Smith, R. *Thesaurus Syriacus* (vols. 1-2; Oxford: Clarendon, 1879-1901).

Plater, W. E., and H. J. White. *A Grammar of the Vulgate* (Oxford: Clarendon, 1926).

Ploeg, J. van der, and A. van der Woude. *Le targum de Job de la grotte XI de Qumran* (Leiden: Brill, 1971).

Pope, Marvin H. *El in the Ugaritic Texts* (VTS 2; Leiden: Brill, 1955).

______. *Job* (3rd edition; The Anchor Bible 15; Garden City: Doubleday, 1973).

Pritchard, James (ed.). *Ancient Near Eastern Texts Relating to the Old Testament* (3rd edition; Princeton, NJ: Princeton University, 1969).

Rabin, Chaim. *Ancient West-Arabian* (London: Taylor's Foreign Press, 1959).

______. "The Dead Sea Scrolls and the History of the O. T. Text," JTS 6 (1955), 96-104.

______. "The Historical Background of Qumran Hebrew," *Aspects of the Dead Sea Scrolls* (Scripta Hierosolymitana, IV; ed. C. Rabin and Y. Yadin; 2nd edition; Jerusalem: Magnes, 1965), 144-61.

______. "The Translation Process and the Character of the Septuagint," *Textus* 6 (1968), 1-26.

Rad, G. von. "Das Werk Jahwes," *Studia Biblica et Semitica* (ed. W. van Unnik and A. van der Woude; Wageningen, Netherlands: H. Veenman, 1966), 290-8.

Rainey, Anson F. "Observations on Ugaritic Grammar," UF 3 (1971), 151-72.

______. "The Word 'Day' in Ugaritic and Hebrew," *Leshonenu* 36 (1971-2), 186-9 (Heb with English summary).

Reider, Joseph. *Prolegomena to a Greek-Hebrew and Hebrew-Greek Index to Aquila* (Philadelphia: Dropsie College, 1916).

______. *An Index to Aquila* (completed and revised by N. Turner; VTS 12; Leiden: Brill, 1966).

______. "Contributions to the Hebrew Lexicon," ZAW 53 (1935), 270-77.

______. "Etymological Studies in Biblical Hebrew," VT 4 (1954), 276-95.

Revell, E. J. *Hebrew Texts with Palestinian Vocalization* (Near and Middle East Series, 7; Toronto: University Press, 1970).

______. "A New Biblical Fragment with Palestinian Vocalisation," *Textus* 7 (1969), 61-75.

______. "Studies in the Palestinian Vocalization of Hebrew," *Essays on the Ancient Semitic World* (ed. J. W. Wevers and D. B. Redford; Toronto Semitic Texts and Studies; Toronto: University Press, 1970), 51-100.

______. "The Oldest Evidence for the Hebrew Accent System," BJRL 54 (1971-2), 214-22.

______. "The Relation of the Palestinian to the Tiberian Massora," *Masoretic Studies 1* (1972 and 1973 Proceedings of the IOMS; ed. H. M. Orlinsky; Missoula, MT: Scholars Press, 1974), 87-97.

Rignell, L. G. "Notes on the Peshitta of the Book of Job," ASTI 9 (1973), 98-106.

Roberts, Bleddyn J. *The Old Testament Text and Versions* (Cardiff: University of Wales, 1951).

______. "The Dead Sea Scrolls and the Old Testament Scriptures," BJRL 36 (1953-4), 75-96.

______. "The Second Isaiah Scroll from Qumran (1QIs[b])," BJRL 42 (1959-60), 132-44.

______. "The Old Testament: Manuscripts, Text and Versions," *The Cambridge History of the Bible* (vol. 2, ed. G. W. H. Lampe; Cambridge: University Press, 1969), 1-26.

Robertson, David A. *Linguistic Evidence in Dating Early Hebrew Poetry* (SBL Dissertation Series, 3; Missoula, MT: Society of Biblical Literature, 1972).

Robinson, Theodore H. "Basic Principles of Hebrew Poetic Form," *Festschrift Alfred Bertholet* (ed. W. Baumgartner, et al.; Tübingen: J. C. B. Mohr, 1950), 438-50.

______. "Hebrew Poetic Form: The English Tradition," *Congress Volume, Copenhagen* (VTS 1; Leiden: Brill, 1953), 128-49.

Rosenthal, Erwin I. J. "Saadya's Exegesis of the Book of Job," *Saadya Studies* (ed. E. Rosenthal; Manchester: University Press, 1943), 177-205.

Rosenthal, Franz. *Die aramaistische Forschung seit Theodor Nöldekes Veröffentlichungen* (1939; reprinted Leiden: Brill, 1964).

______. *A Grammar of Biblical Aramaic* (Porta Linguarum Orientalium, Neue Serie, V; Wiesbaden: Harrassowitz, 1961).

Rossi, Johannis de. *Variae lectiones Veteris Testamenti librorum* (vols. 1-4; Parma: Ex Regio, 1784-86).

Roth-Laly, Arlette. *Lexique des parlers arabes tchadosoudanais* (vols. 1-4; Paris: Editions du Centre national de la recherche scientifique, 1969-72).

Rowley, H. H. *Job* (The Century Bible; London: Thomas Nelson, 1970).

Ryckmans, Gonzague. *Les noms propres sud-sémitiques* (vols. 1-3; Louvain: Bureaux du *Muséon*, 1934-5).

Sarna, Nahum. "A *Crux Interpretum* in Job 22:30," JNES 15 (1956), 118-9.

Sawyer, John F. A. *Semantics in Biblical Research* (Studies in Biblical Theology, second series, 24; London: SCM, 1972).

______. "Root-Meanings in Hebrew," JSS 12 (1967), 37-50.

______. Review of Holladay, *Concise Hebrew and Aramaic Lexicon*, JSS 17 (1972), 257-9.

______. "Hebrew Words for the Resurrection of the Dead," VT 23 (1973), 218-34.

______. "The 'Original Meaning of the Text' and Other Legitimate Subjects for Semantic Description," *Questions disputées d'Ancien Testament* (Bibliotheca Ephemeridum Theologicarum Lovaniensium, 33; Gembloux: J. Duculot, 1974), 63-70.

Schleusner, J. F. *Novus thesaurus philologico-criticus: sive lexicon in LXX* (vols. 1-3; London: Jacob Duncan, 1829).

Schramm, Gene. *The Graphemes of Tiberian Hebrew* (Near Eastern Studies, 2; Los Angeles: University of California, 1964).

Schulthess, Fridericus. *Lexicon syropalaestinum* (Berlin: Georg Reimer, 1903).

Sebeok, Thomas A. (ed.). *Linguistics in South West Asia and North Africa* (Current Trends in Linguistics, 6; The Hague: Mouton, 1970).

Segal, Moshe H. "The Promulgation of the Authoritative Text of the Hebrew Bible," JBL 72 (1953), 35-47.

Segert, Stanislav. *Altaramäische Grammatik* (Leipzig: VEB Verlag Enzyklopädie, 1975).

______. *A Grammar of Phoenician and Punic* (Munich: C. H. Beck, 1976).

Sekine, Masao. "The Subdivisions of the North-West Semitic Languages," JSS 18 (1973), 205-21.

Semple, W. H. "St. Jerome as a Biblical Translator," BJRL 48 (1965-6), 227-43.

Siegel, Jonathan P. *The Severus Scroll and 1QIs*[a] (Masoretic Studies, 2; Missoula, MT: Scholars Press, 1975).

Siegfried, Carl. "Die Aussprache des Hebräischen bei Hieronymus," ZAW 4 (1884), 34-83.

Skehan, Patrick W. *Studies in Israelite Poetry and Wisdom* (CBQ Monograph Series, 1; Washington, DC: Catholic Biblical Association, 1971).

______. "Qumran and the Present State of Old Testament Text Studies: The Masoretic Text," JBL 78 (1959), 21-5.

______. "The Biblical Scrolls from Qumran and the Text of the Old Testament," BA 28 (1965), 87-100.

______. "The Scrolls and the Old Testament Text," *New Directions in Biblical Archaeology* (ed. D. N. Freedman and J. C. Greenfield; Garden City: Doubleday, 1969), 99-112.

Smith, Morton. "The Present State of Old Testament Studies," JBL 88 (1969), 19-35.

Snaith, Norman H. "Prolegomenon," Jacob ben Chayim's *Introduction to the Rabbinic Bible* (tr. C. D. Ginsburg, 1867; reissued New York: Ktav, 1968).

Soden, Wolfram von. *Akkadisches Handwörterbuch* (Wiesbaden: Harrassowitz, 1959-).

______. *Grundriss der akkadischen Grammatik* (samt Ergänzungsheft; Analecta Orientalia 33/47; Rome: Pontifical Biblical Institute, 1969).

Sokoloff, Michael. *The Targum to Job from Qumran Cave XI* (Bar-Ilan Studies in Near Eastern Languages and Culture; Jerusalem: Bar-Ilan, 1974).

Speiser, Ephraim A. *Genesis* (The Anchor Bible; Garden City: Doubleday, 1964).

______. "The Pronunciation of Hebrew according to the Transliterations in the Hexapla," JQR 16 (1925-6), 343-82; 23 (1932-33), 233-65; 24 (1933-4), 9-46.

______. "'*ED* in the Story of Creation," BASOR 140 (Dec., 1955), 9-11.

Sperber, Alexander. *A Grammar of Masoretic Hebrew* (Corpus Codicum Hebraicorum Medii Aevi, ed. R. Edelmann; Part II, The Pre-Masoretic Bible; Copenhagen: Ejnar Munksgaard, 1959).

______. *The Bible in Aramaic* (4 vols. in 5; Leiden: Brill, 1959-73).

______. *A Historical Grammar of Biblical Hebrew* (Leiden: Brill, 1966).

______. "Hebrew Based upon Greek and Latin Transliterations," HUCA 12-13 (1937-8), 103-274.

Spuler, B. (ed.) *Semitistik* (Handbuch der Orientalistik, l. Abt., Bd. 3; Leiden: Brill, 1953-4).

Staples, W. E. "The Hebrew of the Septuagint," AJSL 44 (1927-8), 6-30.

Stevenson, W. B. *Grammar of Palestinian Jewish Aramaic* (2nd edition with appendix by J. Emerton; Oxford: Clarendon, 1962).

Stummer, Friedrich. *Einführung in die lateinische Bible* (Paderborn: Ferdinand Schöningh, 1928).

______. "Einige Beobachtungen über die Arbeitsweise des Hieronymus bei der Übersetzung des Alten Testaments aus der Hebraica Veritas," *Biblica* 10 (1929), 3-30.

______. "Hauptprobleme der Erforschung der alttestamentlichen Vulgate," *Werden und Wesen des Alten Testaments* (BZAW 66; Berlin: Töpelmann, 1936), 233-9.

______. "Beiträge zur Exegese der Vulgata," ZAW 62 (1949-50), 152-67.

Sutcliffe, Edmund F. "St. Jerome's Pronunciation of Hebrew," *Biblica* 29 (1948), 112-25.

______. "Notes on St. Jerome's Hebrew Text," CBQ 11 (1949), 139-43.

Talmon, Shemaryahu. "Aspects of the Textual Transmission of the Bible in the Light of Qumran Manuscripts," *Textus* 4 (1964), 259-96.

______. "The Old Testament Text," *The Cambridge History of the Bible* (vol. 1, ed. P. R. Ackroyd and C. F. Evans; Cambridge: University Press, 1970), 159-99.

Thomas, D. Winton. "A Consideration of Some Unusual Ways of Expressing the Superlative in Hebrew," VT 3 (1953), 209-24.

______. "צלמות in the Old Testament," JSS 7 (1962), 191-200.

Thompson, Reginald C. *Dictionary of Assyrian Botany* (London: British Academy, 1949).

Tigay, Jeffrey H. "Toward the Recovery of **Poḥar*, 'Company,' in Biblical Hebrew," JBL 94 (1973), 517-22.

Torrey, C. C. "A New Phoenician Grammar," JAOS 57 (1937), 397-410.

Tov, Emanuel. "Some Corrections to Reider-Turner's *Index to Aquila*," *Textus* 8 (1973), 164-74.

Townsend, J. T. "Rabbinic Sources," *The Study of Judaism* (New York: B'nai B'rith, 1972) 35-80.

Tsevat, Matitiahu. "The Canaanite God *Šälaḥ*," VT 4 (1954), 41-9.

______. "A Chapter on Old West Semitic Orthography," *Joshua Bloch Memorial Volume* (New York: Public Library, 1960), 82-91.

Tur-Sinai, N. H. *The Book of Job* (Jerusalem: Kiryath Sepher, 1957).

Ugaritica V (ed. J. Nougayrol, et al.; Mission de Ras Shamra, 16; Paris: Paul Geuthner, 1968).

Ullendorff, Edward. "Ugaritic Marginalia," Or 20 (1951), 270-4; JSS 7 (1962), 339-51; IOS 2 (1972), 463-9.

______. "The Semitic Languages of Ethiopia and their Contribution to General Semitic Studies," *Africa* 25 (1955), 154-60.

______. "The Contribution of South Semitics to Hebrew Lexicography," VT 6 (1956), 190-98.

______. "Comparative Semitics," *Linguistica semitica: presente e futuro* (Studi Semitici, 4; ed. G. della Vida; Rome: Centro di Studi Semitici, 1961), 13-32.

Vawter, Bruce. "Intimations of Immortality and the Old Testament," JBL 91 (1972), 158-71.

Version arabe du Livre de Job (Oeuvres complètes de R. Saadia ben Iosef al-Fayyoûmî 15, ed. J. Derenbourg; Paris: Ernest Leroux, 1899).

Vida, Giorgio Levi della (ed.). *Linguistica semitica: presente e futuro* (Studi Semitici, 4; Rome: Universita di Roma, 1961).

Vogt, Ernestus. *Lexicon linguae aramaicae Veteris Testamenti* (Rome: Pontifical Biblical Institute, 1971).

Wagner, Max. *Die lexikalischen und grammatikalischen Aramaismen im alttestamentlichen Hebräisch* (BZAW 96; Berlin: Töpelmann, 1966).

______. "Beiträge zur Aramaismenfrage im alttestamentlichen Hebräisch," *Hebräische Wortforschung* (ed. B. Hartmann, et al.; VTS 16; Leiden: Brill, 1967), 355-71.

Walton, Brian (ed.). *Biblia Sacra polyglotta* (vols. I-VI; London: 1663; reprinted Graz, Austria: Akademische Druck u. Verlagsanstalt, 1963).

Wehr, Hans. *A Dictionary of Modern Written Arabic* (English edition ed. J. M. Cowan; Wiesbaden: Harrassowitz, 1961).

Weiser, Arthur. *The Psalms* (tr. H. Hartwell; Old Testament Library; Philadelphia: Westminster, 1962).

Wernberg-Møller, P. "The Contribution of the *Hodayot* to Biblical Textual Criticism," *Textus* 4 (1964), 133-75.

Westermann, Claus. *Der Aufbau des Buches Hiob* (Beiträge zur Historischen Theologie, 23; Tübingen: J. C. B. Mohr, 1956).

Whedbee, J. William. "The Comedy of Job," forthcoming in *Semeia* (paper read before the seminar on Biblical and Literary Criticism; Society of Biblical Literature annual meeting; Washington, DC, 1974).

Wheeler, Samuel B. "The Infixed -*t*- in Biblical Hebrew," JANESCU 3 (1970-1), 20-31.

Whitaker, Richard E. *A Concordance of the Ugaritic Literature* (Cambridge, MA: Harvard, 1972).

Wild, Stefan. *Das Kitāb al-ᶜAin und die arabische Lexicographie* (Wiesbaden: Harrassowitz, 1965).

______. "Neues zur ältesten arabischen Lexikographie," ZDMG 112 (1962), 291-8.

Williams, Edna R. *The Conflict of Homonyms in English* (Yale Studies in English, 100; New Haven, CT: Yale, 1944).

Wolff, H. W. *Hosea* (tr. G. Stansell; Hermeneia--A Critical and Historical Commentary on the Bible; Philadelphia: Fortress, 1974).

Woodhead, D. R., and Wayne Beene (ed.). *A Dictionary of Iraqi Arabic: Arabic-English* (Washington, DC.: Georgetown University Press, 1967).

Wright, W. *A Grammar of the Arabic Language* (vols. 1-2; 3rd edition ed. R. Smith and M. de Goeje; Cambridge: University Press, 1898).

Yadin, Yigael. *Masada* (tr. M. Pearlman; New York: Random House, 1966).

______. *Bar-Kokhba* (London: Weidenfeld and Nicolson, 1971).

______. "New Discoveries in the Judean Desert," BA 24 (1961), 34-50.

______. "More on the Letters of Bar Kokhba," BA 24 (1961), 86-95.

______. "Expedition D," IEJ 11 (1961), 36-52; 12 (1962), 227-57.

______. "The Excavation of Masada--1963/1964, Preliminary Report," IEJ 15 (1965), 1-120.

Yeivin, Israel. *The Babylonian Vocalization and the Linguistic Tradition it Reflects* (in Hebrew with English summary; unpublished dissertation; Jerusalem: The Hebrew University, 1968).

Yellin, David. "Forgotten Meanings of Hebrew Roots in the Bible," *Jewish Studies in Memory of Israel Abrahams* (The Alexander Kohut Memorial Foundation; New York: Jewish Institute of Religion, 1927), 441-58.

York, Anthony D. "The Dating of Targumic Literature," JSJ 5 1974-5), 49-62.

Young, G. Douglas. "The Significance of the Karatepe Inscriptions for Near Eastern Textual Criticism," OTS 8 (1950), 291-9.

Zevit, Ziony. "The So-Called Interchangeability of the Prepositions *b*, *l*, and *m(n)* in Northwest Semitic," JANESCU 7 (1975), 103-12.

______. "The Linguistic and Contextual Arguments in Support of a Hebrew 3 m.s. Suffix *-Y*," forthcoming in UF 9 (1977).

Zgusta, Ladislav. *Manual of Lexicography* (Janua Linguarum, Series Maior, 39; The Hague: Mouton, 1971).

Zimmern, Heinrich. *Akkadische Fremdwörter als Beweis für babylonischen Kultureinfluss* (2nd edition; Leipzig: J. C. Hinrichs, 1917).

Zorell, Franciscus, et al. *Lexicon hebraicum et aramaicum Veteris Testamenti* (reprinted Rome: Pontifical Biblical Institute, 1968).